PRAISE FOR

UPRISING

A REVOLUTION OF THE SOUL

BY

ERWIN RAPHAEL MCMANUS

"*Uprising* is a thoughtful and restless look at what the church needs to do and be if it is to touch the soul. I hope it produces restless and thoughtful readers."

—JOHN ORTBERG | AUTHOR OF *EVERYBODY'S NORMAL TILL YOU GET TO KNOW THEM*

"Erwin McManus is one of the most creative young leaders I know. Every time I have the opportunity to hear him speak or read his words, he brings fresh perspective on basic truths. *Uprising* will take you on the most important quest of your life—the quest for character."

—JOHN C. MAXWELL | FOUNDER, THE INJOY GROUP

"If you feel as if you have been sleepwalking through life and you want to change, *Uprising* is for you. If you gave your life to Christ believing the journey would be the adventure of a lifetime but you have lost your compass, *Uprising* is for you. If you want to live life with passion, purpose, and no regrets, pick up this book and start reading today."

—SHEILA WALSH | FEATURED SPEAKER AT WOMEN OF FAITH™ CONFERENCES

OTHER BOOKS BY
ERWIN RAPHAEL MCMANUS

The Barbarian Way

An Unstoppable Force

Chasing Daylight

UPRISING

A Revolution of the Soul

Erwin Raphael McManus

NELSON BOOKS
A Division of Thomas Nelson Publishers
Since 1798

www.thomasnelson.com

Published in Nashville, Tennessee, by Thomas Nelson, Inc.

Nelson Book titles may be purchased in bulk for educational, business, fund-raising, or sales promotional use. For information, please e-mail SpecialMarkets@Thomas Nelson.com.

Published in association with Yates & Yates, LLP, Attorneys and Counselors, Orange, California.

Scripture quotations are taken from the HOLY BIBLE: NEW INTERNATIONAL VERSION®. Copyright © 1973, 1978, 1984 by International Bible Society. Used by permission of Zondervan Publishing House. All rights reserved.

Library of Congress Cataloging-in-Publication Data

McManus, Erwin Raphael.
    Uprising : a revolution of the soul / Erwin Raphael McManus.
        p. cm.
    ISBN 0-7852-6431-0
    ISBN 10 0-7852-8803-1 (Trade paper)
    ISBN 13 978-0-7852-8803-9
    1. Christian life. I. Title.
BV4501.3.M376 2003
248.4—dc22   2003015490
Printed in the United States of America

07 08 09 10 RRD 9 8 7 6 5 4 3

TO AARON—

My son, my son.

From first breath you have been a marvel to me.

His image, your destiny.

His heart, your passion.

His mark, your legacy.

Your life inspires me to this great quest.

With strength of character you have

chosen this dangerous adventure.

His courage will not fail you.

My son,

My friend,

My fellow sojourner,

May we always be warrior poets!

—YOUR WINGMAN

THE QUEST

POINT OF ORIGIN

1 - Running Free

2 - The Drowning Pool

A QUEST FOR ENLIGHTENMENT

11 - Unlocking Divine Mysteries

10 - Waiting Game

9 - The Weight of Small Things

A QUEST FOR NOBILITY

8 - Incurable Romantics

7 - Escaping From a Black Hole

6 - Endless Wellsprings

A QUEST FOR HONOR

5 - Brave Hearts

4 - Turned Inside Out

3 - Rising Downward

DESTINATION

12 - The Greatness of Servanthood

TABLE OF CONTENTS

*If you would like a different reading experience,
see this alternative table of contents:*

ABOUT THE AUTHOR

ACKNOWLEDGMENTS

POINT OF ORIGIN

1

Running Free

The roar was a combination of fury and hunger. Its sound rumbled through us like an ominous warning of the danger to come. In spite of all our efforts, our momentum kept us moving toward its mouth. Our struggle seemed futile as we found it impossible to reverse our course. This particular summer the American River was more unforgiving than usual. The heavy rains had turned the rapids into more than an adventurous joyride. Already the summer had been filled with reports of the tragic end for some of those who had braved its waters. Now it was our turn to either pass or fail the river's test.

It seemed like such a good idea when we said yes. Though Kim and I had never been rafting, the team who spearheaded this annual adventure assured us it was nothing but great fun. Most of the forty or so who were with us were also novices, so there seemed to be no reason for concern. The water at the point of entry was so calm and peaceful that it didn't even bother me when our particular guide confessed this was his first solo run. Certainly for the first hour or so it seemed like this journey was anything but a challenge. In fact, beyond soothing, it was at times even a bit mundane. The lifejackets seemed about as important as wearing a seat belt when you're parked. Funny how a sleepy little river can lull you into virtual unconsciousness.

But the roar woke us all up. It's not that we were asleep, but we were not alert. The rumblings literally shook us. We looked ahead and saw a giant boulder protruding out of the river's center. Coming out of a blind turn, there was enough distance for us to see two of the rafts in front of us crash head-on into the boulder, flipping them like toys and throwing our companions into the white water. We had enough time to adjust. I am certain that skilled navigators would have found a way around the crisis, but that would have been someone other than us. All I remember is "Row!"

Looking back, I realized we were all rowing, frantically, desperately, with all the strength we could muster. The left side was rowing; the right side was rowing. We were all neutralizing each other's efforts. In the end, all we accomplished was to increase the velocity at which we hit the very boulder we were working so desperately to avoid. We flipped. Our raft was pointing straight up to the sky. I held on to the side handles, fighting to stay in. One of the men fell directly on top of me, using me to stay above the water and on the raft. I imagine in that moment he considered my head an answer to prayer for his foot. This was working out great for him. It was dramatically less advantageous for me. I knew he was not a strong swimmer, so I was apprehensive to let go and have us both go under. But when I was coming down to my last breath, I decided he could learn to swim if he really wanted to. And so I let go, and we both went plummeting into the river.

Once I fought my way to the top, I immediately began swimming upstream looking for my wife, Kim. Our raft had stabilized and two of our crew had somehow avoided falling out. Even while fighting the waters, I noticed that all the men fell out, but the two women somehow remained in the raft. Once I saw that Kim was fine, I stopped wasting my energy working against the currents and allowed myself to begin the trek down the rapids.

It was at this point that our prerafting instructions became far more critical. We were reminded to keep our lifejackets tight against our chests. It was so uncomfortable. The river seemed so peaceful. At the time I didn't see any reason to really pull it that tight. Only now, as my life vest kept working its way up to my chin, did I fully understand the importance of a snugly fitting lifejacket. But this wasn't the right time to punish myself for not paying attention to the instructions. So I moved on down the list of important things to remember. Our instructor's voice was so clear in my head: "If you fall into the rapids, keep your legs up. At the bottom of the river there are all kinds of rocks forming nooks and crannies. If you don't keep your legs up, they could get easily caught in between the rocks and snap against the weight of the river."

The idea of bouncing down the river with a broken leg was more than unattractive to me and highly motivating, so I kept my feet up. I wanted to see my feet above the water, but every time I got my feet up, my head would slip under. It was impossible to breathe, and I would then have to risk lowering my legs to get my head back up, which in turn caused me great concern. So I would immediately pull my legs back up, trying with all my being to follow the instructions given us. There was just one problem—I don't breathe with my feet. This system just didn't seem to work.

Before I knew it I had exhausted myself as I fought the rapids, and I felt it overtake me—not just the water, but surrender. I wondered if my efforts were only a symphony of futility. Was it simply better to calmly accept my fate and give myself over to the river? It was a surreal moment. I watched the water swirling around me. I could see the sounds but could not hear them. I don't remember any fear. Just regret—regret of things undone. Flooding into my mind were thoughts like, Would I leave my wife when we still had so much love to share? Would my son and daughter grow up without their father? Would I give up on them so easily? That's when I knew. There would be a day when the end would come, but if I had anything to do with it, this would not be it. I knew there was more life in me than there was water in that river. It was as if I could hear a voice inside of me both crying out and confessing without shame, "I want to live!"

I fought my way back to the surface and noticed that there were branches ahead with vines hanging down to the water's surface. As my body came under an extended branch, I reached and grabbed one of the vines. As I held it with my right hand, I was able to pull myself back against the water and grab it with my left hand also. As I began to pull myself toward the branch, the vine gave under my weight and I found myself plunging backwards down the river. As quickly as I could turn, I saw another branch low enough to grab, waiting there for me. I pulled myself to the shore, exhausted and grateful for being on land. I looked up, after catching my breath, and there was my wife, Kim, waiting for me. I still don't understand how she got so far down so fast and happened to be exactly where I pulled out.

A TRANSFORMING JOURNEY

The journey I am inviting you on is not unlike my trek down the American River. There will be moments of great calm, but they must not fool us or lull us into a slumber. This journey is filled with rapids and laced with white waters. There will be times you will find yourself drowning, overwhelmed by the circumstances that surround you. At every turn there is the invitation to journey ahead on an adventure that will not leave you unchanged.

And it is important to note that in reality there is no way back. One moment I will never forget is when we all finally found ourselves at the other side of the rapids and how many had no desire to continue. There were some who made earnest requests to be taken back to the beginning point. There was no meanness in the instructor's voice, no attempt at insensitivity. He was simply stating the facts. "There are still hours ahead, and there is no way out except forward." We had been told about a place on the river known as Satan's Cesspool. We began to ask for affirmation that it was now behind us.

Our guide gave us the unwanted news: this challenge remained ahead, and the most dangerous was yet to come.

The same people who fell out of the rafts got back into the rafts, but we were not the same. We were so attentive, so focused. No instructions were seen as too trite or meaningless. What was really important became very clear to us, and it was the important things that really mattered. It was such a great trip, so much fun, the kind of adventure you live for. You know, the kind of experience you avoid at all costs, but when it's unavoidable, it changes you when you've made it through.

This is how life is supposed to work. It's an adventure, a journey, a trek filled with uncertainty, excitement, and risk. One bad or painful experience can cause you to remain on the banks. But when you do, you neither move forward nor backwards; there you sit, just watching life go by. Yet I am convinced in all of us there is a voice crying out, a confession waiting to be declared without shame, "I want to live!" This journey requires many confessions and declarations, but this is a good place to begin. Sometimes this yearning has been neglected or even rejected. The longing to be alive is drowned by lesser ambitions. We just want to make it through the day, survive, make ends meet, go through the routine, and then exist rather than live. If you have conceded to this lesser form of humanity, let me invite you to hear the roar inside your own soul. You may be apprehensive at first but let the trembling turn into rumbling. If you would dare risk it, stop right now, stand up wherever you are, and declare without shame, "I want to live!"

The theme of life and death has been with us from the very beginning of the human journey. God's warning to man was that if he ate of the forbidden fruit, he would surely die. Adam and Eve did eat of the tree, but there was no apparent death at the moment. I think we often assume God was speaking metaphorically. Yet what we find throughout the Scriptures is that in the most important way we truly did die. We are now dead in our trespasses and sins. We are in a sense even dead to life. We merely exist and think we are alive. We have traded the authentic for the imitation. Human history can be summarized as a desperate search for life. We look for it everywhere and in everything. We pursue wealth, power, success, pleasure, and endless experiences just to feel alive. Yet with all that we gain, there is always the inescapable stench of death all around us. Even if we gain the whole world, we die with our souls empty and hollow.

Ironically, what we are so often willing to sacrifice is the very thing most essential for life—God. God formed us in His image and then breathed life into us. His life in us is sustained by His character. When we lose the character of God, we lose the life of God in us. But to have His character, we must first die to ourselves, because to become like Him is what it means to really live. Because this book is a quest for life, it is also a quest for character, a quest to regain what was lost in the Fall. It is a journey to unleash what is promised in the future and to discover and live out a God-given destiny.

A PASSION TO LIVE

We were created with a passion to live. When a person loses his will to live, he has essentially begun the first stage of dying. This is why some people live until their final breaths and others die long before their bodies are laid to rest. This is also why suicide is both tragic and traumatic. To take one's own life is to first give up on living. What a horrible place to stand, to look at your life and conclude there is no hope of ever being alive, to be so overwhelmed by despair that you lose all desire to live. Suicide is the strange intersection between hopelessness and a refusal to live in the status quo. It is an emphatic declaration, "I am empty, and I will never be full." There is a consciousness of a present condition without an awareness of the future possibilities. Suicide is antipathy toward existence; antagonism against the myth of aliveness. The conclusion: there is nothing worth living for, so why live? Passion is turned to anger and then hatred, and our final act of violence is against ourselves.

Yet most of us are not consumed with antipathy toward life. We have not become overwhelmed with the awareness of our existence.

We simply accept that this is just the way it is. We surrender ourselves to the mundane. It is not antipathy that defines us, but apathy. The first leads to the violent and abrupt ends of our lives; the second, to a torturously slow decay. To be apathetic is literally to be without passion. Perhaps you're familiar with the construction: Atheist—no God; agnostic—no knowledge; apathetic—no passion.

Several years ago I was invited to present an idea I had to a CEO who managed millions of dollars that were funneled into various projects. I was given about an hour of his time, and it was a one-shot deal. When I finished my presentation, he said something I have never forgotten. Just before he declined to give me any money, he said, "It's rare to meet anyone with a passion for anything." I think he genuinely appreciated the intensity of my commitment, even while concluding he would not invest in my idea. But what he gave me was priceless. I walked away remembering that passion was a rare commodity.

The fifteen years since that conversation have only confirmed this conclusion. So many of us have abdicated our passions for obligations, as if passion is a luxury for the young, and we must all grow up one day. We, even if reluctantly, fall into place to live a life of conformity that we describe as "maturity." We've made acting like an adult synonymous with living apathetic lives. Maybe this is why when senior adults finally leave the assembly line of their careers and begin to do what they have always really wanted, they are described as being in a "second childhood." If apathy is adulthood and passion is childish, then I understand all the more the words of Jesus when He said that to enter His kingdom we must come as little children.

The Christian faith hasn't been very helpful in this arena over the past few hundred years. Our incessant focus on the elimination of sin has more than contributed to the problem of passionless living. To an overwhelming degree, human passions are seen as both adversarial to God and corrupting in their nature. We've been taught that God's solution to restraining our passions is His commands. The result has been a Christian religion focused on rules, rituals, and obligations. In this regard Christianity as a religion is essentially no different or better than the other major world religions. Whether it is Buddhism, Islam, Hinduism, or Christianity, we are instructed to follow certain practices that will restrain our passions and make us better people. In large part world religions seem predominantly focused on the restraint, sublimation, or even elimination of human desires.

Ironically, the Scriptures place human desires and passions at the epicenter of human action. This is true in both the arena of sin and the arena of holiness. Nothing explains why we sin more poignantly and clearly than human passion.

In Romans 7:5 Paul writes, "For when we were controlled by the sinful nature, the sinful passions aroused by the law were at work in our bodies, so that we bore fruit for death." Paul is just stating the obvious. We do what we do because we love it. We desire it. When we sin, it is for no more profound reason than we enjoy it. Of course there is also the added dynamic that the very nature of those things that are counted as sin have a corrosive, corrupting, and addictive nature to them. That's why they're called sins. Their very essence will destroy you and most likely damage or hurt those closest to you. Nevertheless, the fuel of these destructive patterns is passion, and the process of transformation requires a revolution of your passions.

Paul illuminates this passion transformation in Galatians 5:24: "Those who belong to Christ Jesus have crucified the sinful nature with its passions and desires." Whatever else must happen within us, there must be a death to the passions and desires fueled by a heart absent of God. Yet so much of the Christian faith has stopped here. We have been so vigilant to assure the death of passions, and as Paul said, all who belong to Christ Jesus must have their passions crucified—put to death—eradicated—end of story.

But what we have failed to recognize is that when our Christian teaching concerning passions ends here, we are far more Buddhist than we are Christian. It is Buddhism that teaches that our ultimate end is the elimination of all desire. Buddhism builds its practice around this lifelong goal with the promised outcome that in the end you will become nothing more than a part of the cosmic energy. This is the essence of the Buddha—to exist without desire. This perfectly aligns with a view of an impersonal God. Or perhaps more accurately, of no God at all. All that makes us human must be lost to all that would allow us to merge into this cosmic energy. I have always been amazed that in Western culture, where desire is the fuel of so much corruption, Buddhism has become so attractive. We've managed to literally materialize Buddhism's spirituality, to meditate away our desires so that we can go pursue our lusts and cravings while never losing our center.

The Scriptures have an entirely different view of human desire and passion. The goal of the Christian journey cannot be the elimination of desire and passion since the Scriptures teach that God created us in His image and likeness, and a part of this reflection of God is a heart designed for passionate living. It has never been God's intention to move us toward apathetic living. He desires that we live passionate lives in Him. Rather than eliminate our passions, He intends to overwhelm them with new passions. The furnace of our passions is our character, and while evil character burns hot for destructive passions that consume and destroy, the character of God ignites passion for what is good and true. Our quest is to have God's character formed in us so that His passions might burn in us.

CRY "FREEDOM!"

Human passion inflames within us desire. Our hearts crave the freedom of pleasure and the pleasure of freedom. What often eludes us is the fact that these two are not the same. As much as we are driven to live, a significant part of our odyssey is to find this elusive experience called freedom. It is a driving force within every major transition in our life. From our first independent steps as infants to our striving for financial independence for our retirement years, we are constantly fighting for and redefining what it means to be free. Deeper than our instinct to live is our longing to be alive. Aliveness is different from existence. The latter is a struggle to survive; the former, a thirst for life. All of us have an intuitive connection between being alive and living free. We all long for freedom.

There is something strangely elusive about freedom. No matter what state we are in, it seems that freedom is to be found somewhere else, in a place or experience that we do not have. The child can't wait to be a teenager; the teenager can't wait to have a driver's license. When you're in high school, you can't wait until you're in college. So many of our developmental years are spent longing for the years to come. We see in them a freedom that is being withheld from us at the present. Then, even though we are absolutely free to choose our career paths, we often find ourselves in prisons of our own choosing. We hate our jobs. We dream of other opportunities. We become certain that we have missed our true life callings or personal destinies.

There has been perhaps no time in human history when individuals have had as much opportunity as most Americans do now to not only choose their own lives, but to personally design their own careers. But an overwhelming number of us feel trapped in the lives we've created. We find ourselves slaves to our jobs, the clock, and our debt. The irony is that *we* are the cruel tyrants who hold ourselves captive. But our self-imposed slavery goes far deeper than simply the ruts we have trapped ourselves in. The tragedy of our imprisonment reaches into the deepest caverns of our soul. Our passion to be free both ignites us and betrays us, and more often than not leads us to be consumed by an unforgiving fire. The very fire that burns within us can destroy us.

How many of us didn't wait eagerly for the freedom to do whatever we wanted? How many did not rebel against the rules and regulations imposed upon us by our parents or others seemingly committed to limiting our freedoms? When we were at last free, what actions defined our freedom? We were now free to drink ourselves into a mindless stupor every Friday night and to use one another through meaningless sex without being required to make any meaningful or lifelong commitment. We were free to pursue our own success, pleasure, and ambition without regard to the well-being of those around us. These cravings have become the symbols of our freedom. In turn, the

Ten Commandments become symbols of religious oppression, and so as free people we can now, without apprehension, live beyond these archaic restraints. We are now at liberty to be untrue to each other and to kill our enemies, to take what we want, whether material or marital, and to forsake God in the process. After all, we are free.

Yet the things we choose in our freedom soon hold us as their prisoners. So much so that we choose freely what we later find ourselves trapped within. Your passions can create the exhilaration of freedom while leading you straight into a dark and merciless dungeon. Not all free acts lead to freedom. In fact if you're not careful, the choices you freely make may cost you a life of genuine freedom. This is why the Bible talks about human experience in terms of being slaves to sin. One of the odd characteristics of sin is that it is a free act that enslaves you. Sin creates the illusion of freedom. In the end it fools us into seeking freedom *from* God rather than finding freedom *in* God.

In Galatians 5:1 Paul reminds us, "It is for freedom that Christ has set us free." He is obviously building on Jesus' own words, "So if the Son sets you free, you will be free indeed" (John 8:36). Jesus also promised, "Then you will know the truth, and the truth will set you free" (John 8:32).

Whatever else Jesus came to do, one thing is clear—He came to set you free. It's important that we don't miss this point. God has been so misrepresented. He's been cast as the divine legalist, the eternal killjoy. It's as if God spends His time in eternity designing straitjackets and molding shackles just for you. No wonder so many people start running for their lives whenever the name *God* is mentioned. God is not a warden; He is a deliverer. And so earnest is He about your freedom that He was willing to be taken captive and crucified on your behalf just so you could run free. It is for this very reason that Paul warns us that we were "called to be free. But do not use your freedom to indulge the sinful nature; rather, serve one another in love" (Gal. 5:13).

Is it only coincidence that the entire journey of the nation of Israel was from slavery to freedom? And not just once, but over and over again—slaves to Egypt, slaves to Babylon, slaves to Rome. So much of Israel's expedition through the wilderness was working out their freedom. They seemed to know neither how to cope with all their opportunities nor how to live up to all their responsibilities. God, who was their deliverer, was often treated as their oppressor. Given unlimited possibilities, they constantly found themselves paralyzed by their own fear and doubt. Beyond the borders of Egypt, a mind-set born of slavery kept them from living free.

While this could be immensely discouraging, God seems determined to convince us that there is no condition that can stop us from living free. The church of Jesus Christ was not born among a free people, but among the slaves to Rome. Yet not even the Roman Empire had power enough to stop the unleashing of a movement of dreamers and visionaries. How many of us read the book of Acts as the work of slaves under the dominion of the pagan empire? The church was born within this very context. Yet their political slavery could not diminish the freedom they found in Jesus Christ.

You were created to be free. If you are a follower of Jesus Christ, you're also called to be free. Yet to experience this freedom there must first be an uprising—a revolution of the soul. This is exactly what Jesus Christ calls you to. Your liberation will require you to see beyond the illusion of freedom—free acts that lead to bondage. Our freedom must never be about us and us alone. Freedom is the gift of serving others out of love. This is the freedom that only God can give, where we once again become like Him. It is here and only here that freedom exists without boundaries. You are free to love without limit, to forgive, to be merciful, to be generous, to be compassionate, to risk, to sacrifice, to enjoy, and to live.

WIDE-OPEN SPACES

There are indulgences that are good without limit. Every genuinely free act only liberates and never oppresses. When you are living a life of freedom, there are no chains to hold you down or weights to keep you back. And when you are free, you know it. Freedom is no longer an elusive experience outside of your present parameters. Yet so many of us have been fooled by false freedoms. We freely followed our passions and found that our passions robbed us of our freedom. And after we have done all that we wanted to do, there is still a voice crying out from within our souls, "I long to be free."

In the closing moments of the Academy Award–winning movie *Braveheart,* William Wallace was being slowly tortured. But then he was offered a quick death if only he would confess his crime of treason. He gathered himself, took in one final, deep breath, and cried out for the entire crowd to hear, "FREEDOM!" His final breath, his final declaration, his final choice—to live and die free. In the midst of his story, we are reminded that all men die, but not all men live. There is an inseparable relationship between living, passion, freedom, and death.

While a common definition for passion is "a compelling emotion or desire," the most unusual definition of passion is the sufferings of Christ on the cross. This second definition was for many years the primary definition in *Webster's Dictionary.* It is not incidental that the death of Jesus has come to be known as the Passion. The cross of Jesus Christ points to everything that God is passionate about. God the Son so passionately hates the destructive force of sin that He was willing to die to overcome it. And He so passionately loves humanity that He was willing to give even His own life on our behalf. You know what you are really passionate about when you are willing to lay your life down for it.

By this definition I wonder how many of us are really passionate about anything. When our passions are transformed by the presence of God, they always lead to freedom. As with all true passions, the life that is born out of them must come through death. This is why only when we die to ourselves do we finally begin to live. Then, like William Wallace, we will understand that freedom comes not by avoiding pain and suffering, nor by prolonging our existence, but through the freedom from fear and the confidence that not even death can rob us of life.

Living is no low-risk proposition. If life is an adventure, then danger is inherent to the journey. In the same way freedom and fear are great adversaries. How often have we surrendered our freedoms under the weight of our fears? This is one of the main reasons we abdicate living for existing. As mundane and routine as it is, existing does provide for us a level of certainty, predictability, and safety. Freedom is wild and wide-open. It is filled with uncharted territory and unmapped terrain.

In Psalm 119:32, David declares, "I run in the path of your commands, for you have set my heart free." What a different perspective he has on the relationship of God's truth to our personal freedom. It is because God set his heart free that he's able to run in and pursue a life of truth. David unlocks for us the real essence of freedom. It is only when God sets our hearts free from the passions that imprison us that we are finally free to be fully alive. In Psalm 37:4, he gives us the secret to living a life of unrestrained passion: "Delight yourself in the LORD and He will give you the desires of your heart."

When you make God your primary passion, He transforms all the passions of your heart. The result of this transformation is that it will be God's pleasure to fulfill those passions. Beyond this wonderful promise is the realization that when this transformation occurs, your passions become your best compass for your spiritual journey. When God is your desire, you can trust the passions of your heart. It is in this state that you can most fully live a uniquely passionate life.

When you begin to live like this, you find yourself running free, which brings me back to Adam and Eve. What were they doing just hanging around that tree? Given a garden of delight, of endless indulgence, why did they choose to hang around the one tree that was forbidden? Now, I know that the Tree of Knowledge of Good and Evil was planted in the middle of the garden. But the Lord did tell them, "You are free to eat from any tree in the garden." How big was that garden? How much of our earth did the garden actually cover?

LIFE WITHOUT LIMIT

I have wondered if God established boundaries to the garden. The Genesis description does give us enough detail to know that there was a river watering the garden, which flowed from Eden and then separated into four headwaters. It even gives us the names of those rivers. It tells us of the lands into which the rivers flowed and goes on to describe in detail the richness of the land filled with gold, aromatic resin, and onyx (Gen. 2:10–14). Yet it never mentions any borders.

Is it possible that Eden had no boundaries? Certainly there was no command to just hang around the tree. Why didn't Adam take some wood, build a raft, sweep Eve off her feet, and say, "Baby, this is the love boat and we're going on a cruise"? Is it possible that Adam and Eve fell into the same trap that we have—a view that freedom is to go and experience that which God has forbidden rather than to fully experience all that God created for our pleasure? Remember, Eden was no dump. This was not God forcing man to slum it. Eden was not a cruel experience in sensory depravation. No monastic life here. Adam and Eve were naked and were not ashamed. This was a nudist colony. Eden itself means "pleasure" or "delight." It was an all-you-can-eat buffet without any potential for becoming overweight. It was endless pleasure without gluttony. God's first command in the Garden of Eden was "Eat freely . . ." (Gen. 2:16). Adam and Eve's birthright was a life of freedom and pleasure. Yet with so much to discover, so much to experience, and so much opportunity, they chose to hang around the one tree bearing the one fruit that was forbidden them.

And then they bought into the lie, "God doesn't want you to be free. Look at the terrible prison He has created for you. Quick, break out while you can! Run free before He sees you! And oops! I forgot to mention, this path of freedom leads only to your enslavement." This would be the equivalent of the grizzly thinking to itself, "If I could just get my paw right in the middle of that trap, I would be free."

If you have had about all you can take of this kind of freedom, then join me in leaving the middle of the garden and the shadow of the tree and venture out to explore the true essence of freedom. Freedom is filled with opportunity, and with that comes responsibility. We are magnetized to a world filled with opportunities and often paralyzed by the inherent responsibilities. When we abdicate our responsibilities, we eliminate our opportunities. We begin to look more like an assembly line than living beings created with divine uniqueness. It is not enough to simply exercise our power to choose; we must also accept the consequence or benefit of our actions. This is why behind real freedom there lies discipline.

Several years ago I was mesmerized by the amazing talent of a classical pianist named Chris Crossan. After playing a wide spectrum of music, spanning from Beethoven to Bach to the Beatles, he invited an admiring student to come up and play. The student seemed a bit off balance by the invitation. It wasn't that he was timid before audiences; it was that he didn't know how to play the piano. But Chris insisted, almost as if missing the most important part of the information. Chris kept emphasizing he was free to play anything he wanted. Again the student, in a somewhat embarrassed manner, explained that he didn't know how to play the piano. And then Chris pressed his point.

Although the student had the opportunity, he really didn't have the freedom. Opportunity and freedom are not the same thing. Chris's freedom to play the full spectrum of music, to passionately express the music within his soul, was only available to him as a result of years and years of discipline. Discipline can be confused with conformity. Many times we run from discipline or at least resist it because we feel we are being forced to conform in the most negative sense of the word. No one wants to be a clone. No one's life ambition is to be a carbon copy of someone else (except, of course, all those Elvis impersonators). Yet the irony is that when we forsake discipline in our attempt to avoid conformity, we lose our potential to be truly free. The course set before us offers the freedom that comes from a discipline of the soul. There is a gauntlet you must be willing to pass through. At first the pursuit of character has the feel of learning scales, but soon what is formed becomes music to your ears. Without character all you're doing is playing the radio. When the character of Christ is formed within, you are no longer simply an echo but a voice.

While modern science has raised new possibilities and great concerns in the area of human cloning, human history is not new to the cloning process. We have historically allowed ourselves to be mass-produced. We have relinquished our uniqueness by becoming far less than we were intended to be. We have confused negligence with freedom. And while neglecting discipline, we have destined ourselves to become just like everyone else. The journey to freedom is paved by the substance of our character. Character is literally "the aggregate of features and traits that form the individual nature of a person." Or simply put, character is a defining mark. Our capacity to run free is related to our commitment to stand firm. There is a discipline of the heart that marks the free spirit. All of us long to play the song within our soul, and I imagine we would all do so if it didn't require the endless hours of studying the notes.

When we forsake discipline in our attempt to avoid conformity, we lose our potential to be free.

THE GREAT ESCAPE

There is a human side to divine change. In Romans 12:2, Paul exhorts us, "Do not conform any longer to the pattern of this world, but be transformed by the renewing of your mind. Then you will be able to test and approve what God's will is—his good, pleasing and perfect will." For all the promise laced within this text, there is a command that is often neglected. It is clear enough that we are responsible to not become conformists no matter how much pressure the world puts on us. Still we often miss the subtle yet significant command that follows: "Be transformed." The Scriptures are clear that there is an undeniably divine activity that changes the human heart forever through Jesus Christ.

Second Corinthians 5:17 reminds us, "Therefore, if anyone is in Christ, he is a new creation; the old has gone, the new has come!" This is nothing less than a divine metamorphosis of our very essence. At the same time there is a significant role we play in the journey of transformation. It is this part of the journey that will be the focus of our run for freedom. No one can force this on you, nor can it be anyone else's ambition for your life. It has to come from within you. Sometimes it takes a menagerie of different experiences to bring us to it. Some of us will insist on going through tremendous pain, disappointment, and failure before we come to it. Eventually we have to be able to look at ourselves in the mirror and decide there's someone else that we want to see there. But everyone who's going to make this particular trek has to pass through the same gauntlet that has brought me and so many others to that place where in the deafening silence we hear the cry of our own soul screaming, "I want to change!"

The journey to freedom is paved by the substance of our character.

You wake up in the morning, you look in the mirror, and you see the person you despise the most. You've done everything you can think of to get away from yourself, but you're still right there, staring *you* in the face. It isn't a nightmare; you're wide-awake. But then again, those are the worst kinds of nightmares, the kinds you can only escape when you finally fall asleep. Of all the disorders you could have ever imagined falling prey to, this one tops them all. After all, everyone has a phobia. But now the fear of heights or the fear of spiders doesn't seem that strange. You have a rare or at least rarely talked about form of claustrophobia. It's not that you're afraid of being trapped in close or enclosed spaces. You can deal with that. All you'd have to do is just avoid elevators, closets, and Korean-made automobiles.

This particular form of claustrophobia is epidermal in nature. You can't stand being trapped inside your own skin. You've met people you like or at least read about them; you're just not one of them. You compensate with cockiness, but that's nothing more than a mask. If only you could fool yourself as easily as you seem to fool everyone else. But at the end of the day, while everyone else gets to go home, you can't escape the one place you can't stand. You're desperate to escape, but there's no way out, nowhere to run, nowhere to hide. You're stuck—with yourself. You would give everything to be anyone else but you. But not even Houdini could figure out how to get out of this straitjacket. What do you do when the very thing that's suffocating you is the person you've become? What do you do when you can't stand the sight of yourself?

And then it hits you. There is a way out. There is an escape hatch that you've overlooked. No, not suicide. You're not ready to give up, but you are ready to surrender. You can't escape who you are. You will be forever stuck inside of your skin. But you can *become* someone else. You can leave behind the person you've grown to despise and become a person that even you can admire. Penn and Teller can't pull this one off. The last thing you need is an illusion. This requires no one less than Jesus Christ. No illusion, no magic, no sleight of hand. He sets you free through the power of change. His is the gift of transformation. You know there's a human side to divine change, but first you need to access the divine side of human change. One thing is certain—you need to change.

Change: (1) To make different in form; (2) to transform; (3) to exchange for another, e.g., *The witch will change the prince into a toad*; (4) to become transformed, e.g., *The toad will change back into a prince.*

Change into what? From who you are to who you can become only with Christ. Your character will reflect the very character of God. What will you look like? Only God really knows, but it will be like no one else, unique in the person God created you to be. Are you sick of being a conformist, looking like everyone else? Is the rut and routine of your life nothing less than the hollow pattern of this world? Will you refuse to be nothing more than an echo in a world full of meaningless noise? If you've lived in the echo chamber far too long, then join me on this quest that will lead us to where the echoes stop. This is not a location but a condition of the soul—a place for those who would move from imitation to authenticity. Not the kind of authenticity that simply wants to be real, but the kind that is determined to be the real thing. Not a copy, not a clone—an original. A unique and authentic expression of what God created you to become.

If you are to run free, you must first see the counterfeit that holds and molds you to the pattern of this world. Second, you must know the way through the character matrix. To want godly character is one thing; to know how to acquire it is quite another. This journey's course is set by none other than Jesus Christ. The path is unveiled by His footprints. To choose his way is to engage three quests that will not leave us unchanged—a quest for honor, a quest for nobility, and a quest for enlightenment. With each we will cast away the false and find true liberation. He calls us to leave a life of self and to choose a path of servanthood. It is a difficult thing to move ourselves out of the center. It seems unlikely we would find what our soul longs for if we are willing to lose ourselves for others. Yet even the Wachowski brothers preach this gospel in their blockbuster film, *The Matrix*, starring Keanu Reeves. With Morpheus and Trinity calling him out of the delusion of the Matrix, Neo must chose to leave an intoxicating dream for a dangerous reality. Like Neo's journey out of his own Matrix, we must first see the lie and then leave it for a life of freedom. There is an uprising—a revolution of the soul that awaits you. If you choose to break free, you will stand apart from the masses. At times it will be a lonely place, and you will be required to stand alone. But if you are willing to risk everything, you will find two things that will change your life forever—God and yourself!

2

The Drowning Pool

He was handsome beyond description. No, maybe for him it would be right to call him beautiful. Just past sixteen years old and a magnet for affection and desire, if he had lived in our time, he would have certainly graced the screens of theaters across the world. He wasn't just beautiful in the eyes of the beholder; he was a picture of perfection. His list of suitors was countless and his offers of love seemed endless, yet he rejected them all. He had never seen his own image, but the praise and descriptions of others secured his own sense of uniqueness. His name was Narcissus, and he is perhaps the best candidate to serve as humanity's patron saint.

The Greek myth from which we gain his story explains that he rejected the love of all others, concluding he had never found a suitor worthy of him. Then one day while passing through a forest, Narcissus bent down to drink from a clear, shaded pool. There he saw an image so beautiful that for the first time he found himself wrapped in love. He reached out to embrace this vision of beauty, to place his lips upon the lips of his newfound love, but in his effort, upon his first touch, the image shattered into a thousand ripples.

He, of course, had fallen in love with his own reflection. His own likeness he had never known, yet only himself would he ever love. Each time his object of affection would be lost in the troubled waters, he would weep in anguish. Then when the image would return, he would once again be captured and held by its beauty. One part of the legend tells us that eventually Narcissus realized he was in love with his own reflection, and knowing he could never hold himself, lost his will to live and passed away on the banks of the water. While never leaving the shore, he pined away, longing for nothing more than his own reflection. His self-love paralyzed him, leaving him at the drowning pool and costing him a life of divine quality.

Oddly enough, Narcissus' greatest admirer was a nymph called Echo. They were, after all, a perfect match. He only spoke about himself, and she in turn could only repeat his self-indulgent praise.

When we are in love with ourselves, we are prone to only listening to what we want to hear. We become more than willing to trade insight for affirmation. We want to feel good about ourselves more than we want ourselves to become good.

WHAT KIND OF FOOL AM I?

Echo loved Narcissus, but we must spurn them both. This is not to say that you and I are not important. You are uniquely created in the image and likeness of God. Even Jesus said, when asked what is the greatest of all the commandments, that we are not only to love the Lord our God with all of our hearts, souls, minds, and strength, but we are also to love our neighbor as ourselves.

There is an aspect of self-love commended and even commanded by Jesus himself, yet there is a difference between loving ourselves and being *in* love with ourselves. The first rests in our value before God; the second demands a value above all others. When we value ourselves properly, we do not devalue others. When we devalue ourselves, we deny our divine value. When we treat others as immeasurably valuable, we ourselves become invaluable.

Jesus describes an inseparable relationship between loving God, loving ourselves, and loving others. While loving others comes from the overflow of loving ourselves, loving ourselves is the natural result of yielding ourselves to the love of God. The Scriptures explain that loving God is a response to His first loving us. It is here that love ignites and burns away self-love for selfless love. It is in selfless love that we find ourselves full and fulfilled. Self-love voraciously feeds itself and destines us to live in the vacuum of an empty center. It's easy to make the shift from "It's all about me" to "I'm all I need." Yet when we conclude that we don't need anyone but ourselves, we have made a foolish, if not tragic, mistake. When we choose to live a life of "self," we become the contemporary version of what the ancients called a fool.

Now, I realize that I'm treading in dangerous waters here. Solomon warned us that, "Though you grind a fool in a mortar, grinding him like a grain with a pestle, you will not remove his folly from him" (Prov. 27:22). In other words if you want to live and die a fool, no one can stop you. Somehow foolishness seeps deep within our bones and works all the way to the core of our being. I imagine a lot of beautiful goddesses desperately tried to pull Narcissus away from the pond before he drowned in his own reflection. But if you insist on indulging in self-love, nothing and no one is going to pull you away.

Solomon even paints this unsightly picture: "As a dog returns to its vomit, so a fool repeats his folly" (Prov. 26:11). I find this to be indescribably unappetizing, yet I am certain I have sat at that trough more than once. And just so that we don't get too cocky looking over at the fool, Solomon cautions us, "Do you see a man wise in his own eyes? There is more hope for a fool than for him" (Prov. 26:12).

Whatever else there is to take away from these truths, we should take seriously the need to start with ourselves. Each of us needs to break free of the reflection in the pool, or perhaps more appropriately, we need to stop and take a good look at ourselves in the mirror. We need to accept the fact that the world does not begin and end with us. We need to recognize that our need to be loved and valued is placed within us by God and can ultimately only be fulfilled by Him. Our insecurities and, yes, even our sinfulness has led us to take this assignment on for ourselves.

Ironically, when we fill our lives with loving ourselves, we make no room to experience God's love for us. When our lives are defined by self-love, we not only make ourselves unlovely, but at the same time diminish our capacity to experience and give love. Certainly this life could only be described as that of a fool. But if you're like me, there comes a time when you're tired of your own foolishness. Like a glutton sitting at an all-you-can-eat buffet, even self-indulgence will eventually become sickening. I've come to the abrupt realization that a life that is all about me is not even important enough for me to give my life to. I don't need my life to be all about me. I don't even want my life to be all about me. But I desperately desire something important enough for which to give all my life.

A SELF-MADE PRISON

So how do we break ourselves free of the drowning pool and begin this journey of transformation? How can we move from loving our own reflections to reflecting the God who created us? If our ultimate destination is to once again be untainted expressions of the Creator, where do we begin?

In Philippians 2:3–11 we find that Jesus shows us the way.

Do nothing out of selfish ambition or vain conceit, but in humility consider others better than yourselves. Each of you should look not only to your own interests, but also to the interests of others.

Your attitude should be the same as that of Christ Jesus: Who, being in the very nature God, did not consider equality with God something to be grasped, but made himself nothing, taking the very nature of a servant, being made in human likeness. And being found in appearance as a man, he humbled himself and became obedient to death—even death on a cross! Therefore God exalted him to the highest place and gave him the name that is above every name, that at the name of Jesus every knee should bow, in heaven and on earth and under the earth, and every tongue confess that Jesus Christ is Lord, to the glory of God the Father.

While the journey is filled with promise of all that is to come and all that we are to become, our quest begins first with what we must relinquish and leave behind. We are instructed to do nothing out of selfish ambition or vain conceit. The journey to become the person that God dreams of requires that we move away from lives filled with pride and greed. When we live life fueled by these motives, we resign ourselves to the life of a fool. How many times have we given ourselves to our baser motivation of selfish ambition?

It's important to note that ambition itself is not wrong. In fact the Bible never speaks of ambition itself as a negative. Ambition is a God-given motivation. One of the great tragedies among many followers of Christ is the loss of ambition after coming to faith. They have become convinced that any personal ambition is dishonoring to God. I have met some who have gone so far as to only do the opposite of what they desired because they were so persuaded that any passion to achieve had to be rejected and overcome. Their simple reasoning is "It can't be God's will if I want to do it."

Somehow we have missed the most important aspect of the warning against selfishness. Ambition is not the problem; it's *selfish* ambition from which we need to be freed—and there is plenty of that going around. Ironically, we've been better at destroying ambition than we have been at eliminating selfishness. It shouldn't surprise us that the root meaning of the phrase *selfish ambition* is the word *strife*.

Selfish ambition manifests itself in greed. It is about taking for ourselves at the expense of others. All of us live with the danger of being lost in the wanting. Half of the Ten Commandments focus on our propensity to want what other people have for ourselves. The *fuel* of ambition is not the problem; it is the *focus* of ambition that frees or betrays us. Pursuing medicine to heal is as noble as pursuing medicine to steal is ignoble. Most every profession or human enterprise can be fueled by honorable or equally dishonorable motivation.

Selfish ambition makes us emotional, relational, and material black holes, consuming everything around us. All that has the potential for light is swallowed up by the darkness of our hearts. Our inclination toward wanting, getting, and taking is one thing when we are children, but quite another when we move to adulthood. As a parent coming home from a long trip, I would just naturally translate, "What did you bring me?" to mean, "I missed you so much and couldn't wait to squeeze you again, Daddy."

While selfish ambition could be described as proactive selfishness, vain conceit, on the other hand, is fueled and motivated by self-centeredness. If selfish ambition aspires to take everything for ourselves, vain conceit longs to make everything a tribute to our own greatness. At its worst, pride moves us beyond self-adulation to self-worship. Yet laced within the meaning of vain conceit is its more precise translation: empty glory.

While there is a healthy sense of pride that should describe all of us—a pride in our work, our families, our children, a rich sense of accomplishment—there is a corrupting nature described in our pridefulness. Though the same language is used to describe both a person who can be proud of his accomplishments and that person who *is* prideful, the differences between them is profound. One lives a life worthy of attention and the other spends life seeking to gain attention.

When we are driven by vain conceit, we become slaves to performance. In our desperate quest to gain the praise of others, we end up living our lives as inauthentic performers. The tragedy of self-centeredness is that our center is essentially hollow. We become who we think other people want us to be. We surrender the person known only in the dreams of God to become a persona shaped by the whims of others. The arrogant man is less himself and more the sum total of everyone else's opinion. The woman lost in vain conceit spends more time on the cosmetic and neglects the spirit.

Vain glory is all that clothes our nakedness. No matter how many bright lights we might manage to turn our way, there is the haunting absence of the glory that God longs to have illuminate our lives. Only the life that resists selfish ambition and vain conceit and rejects a life defined by pride and greed can break free from the drowning pool.

DROWNING IN PRIDE AND GREED

We should not underestimate the difficulty of this undertaking. You would think it would be easy to move away from a life filled with greed and pride once we chose to. Yet as soon as we begin to live lives that move us out of the center, we find that the magnetic appeal of lives that are all about us is very difficult to break free from, even when we recognize that a life of self-indulgence, motivated by self-ishness and self-centeredness, is nothing more than the life of a fool. Sometimes only when we find ourselves entangled and even exposed by our greed or pride do we become painfully aware of our own fool-ishness. Like a drunk university student who thinks he was being so smooth with the ladies while everyone around him knows he was acting like an idiot even before he lost his lunch, so the fool sees him-self (or herself) as infinitely wise until forced to see his folly.

This may be why it is so difficult for us to change until we see our own foolishness. Until that moment comes, we are essentially unteachable. In the end no one can make you live a life that is not about you. No one can drag you down this particular path or make you something you do not want to become. In regard to your char-acter, you don't have to change alone. In fact you cannot change alone, but you alone have to desire to change. All my informal sur-veys confirm that every one of us struggles with some aspect of pride.

We all need to break free from its gravitational pull on our lives. The challenge to do nothing from the motivation of vain conceit is genuinely one of epic proportions. And so it is with this dark twin that we know as greed.

We were probably no more than fourteen years old when my brother, Alex, our next-door neighbor, and I began our first company, the Roadrunner Lawn Mowing Company. While other kids were getting two, three, or maybe five dollars a lawn, we were a high-end landscaping enterprise. We would hardly even consider a job if it wasn't in double figures. Some of our jobs ranged from sixteen bucks to three times that. Those were big dollars for a junior-high kid back in the '70s. We had held all of our profit to be divided at the end of the summer. Even while buying some equipment of our own, we were left with several hundred dollars to divide among the three of us.

Everything was working out smoothly until the last penny. There was one copper cent left to be divided among the three of us. It wasn't that big of a deal until our third partner demanded the penny. He insisted that the last penny was rightfully his. Honestly that penny didn't matter at all to Alex or me—until that moment. Then that penny took on immeasurable value. With almost a psychic communication, Alex and I looked at each other and then immediately explained to our disgruntled partner that since we owned two-thirds of the company, that penny would remain in our possession. Our former partner left angrily for his home next door.

When my mom heard about this—and I suppose she would be the equivalent of the board of directors—she was not particularly happy with Alex or me. She expressed her disappointment and even her shame that we would fight over a penny. We, of course, defended ourselves and insisted it wasn't about the penny; it was a matter of principle. She didn't buy it and was invoking a higher law—the law "You will do what I tell you or else." Alex and I begrudgingly returned the penny and made peace with our long-time friend.

It shouldn't amaze us that greed and strife are made inseparable in the Scriptures. So much of what motivates us in our longings is what others have and we do not. In fact some things only have value because someone else wants them. And the more people who want the same thing, the more valuable it becomes. Even when we grow up we are still like children in preschool, where everyone wants the one toy that the first child grabbed.

OUT OF CONTROL

Against the backdrop that we are told to do nothing out of selfish ambition or vain conceit, how much of our lives are in fact defined by no more fundamental motives than these? In a solar system where self is the sun around which everything revolves, pride, greed, and foolishness are our largest planets. And in this scenario, the gravitational force that works in the dark spaces in between is our need for control. As long as we're living for ourselves, and our lives are about us, we will strive to control everything around us. The more self-oriented we are, the more controlling we are. Everything in our universe is required to work the way we determine it should.

Unfortunately, the more we try to control the world around us, the more out of control our world becomes. There are some things that are simply out of our hands. When God is not a part of our lives, we tend to begin to act as if *we* were God. This is one significant reason why those who live life without God attempt to bring everything under their control.

In a meeting with former president Bill Clinton, I was struck when he made this intriguing observation: "I do not think people wish to live chaotic, lost lives." All of us seek some way to manage the chaos in the world around us. When we are in proper relationship with God, we entrust Him with all that is in His control, and are able to focus our lives on that for which we are given responsibility. When we do this, we can stop worrying about things over which we have no control.

But our incessant need for control is so obvious and sometimes even funny.

In our home the best metaphor for this spiritual dysfunction is the remote control. I'm pretty sure we have more remote controls than we have technology that could possibly be controlled by them. We actually have baskets where we place the remotes to prevent our endless searching for the right one. We have the TV remote and the VCR remote and the DVD remote and the Dolby sound remote— and, of course, the universal cable remote. We even have a few other remotes, and have no idea what they control. We just can't bring ourselves to throw them away because we might need them someday to turn something on or off.

Many of us are willing to settle for the feeling of being in control rather than making the choices that will genuinely give us freedom.

There have been a few times when we've desperately wanted to change channels. We were missing the start of one of our favorite shows, and we would all be frantically searching for the TV remote. Tempers would even begin to flare, and accusations would begin to fly about who was the last one to use it. We'd look under the sofas, behind tables—I've gone as far as looking in the kitchen, in the bedrooms, and yes, I confess, I have in desperate searches opened the refrigerator. What's so funny about all this is that in the midst of the frenzy, it wouldn't occur to anyone to just walk up to the TV and change the channel manually.

And then there are more than a hundred options for our viewing pleasure. I don't know if it's like this in your home, but in our house, channel surfing is an addiction. It's no longer enough just to watch one show; you have to watch at least two at the same time. After years of training and the refinement of critical skills, you might be able to watch three, four, or maybe even five shows at once. But in the end, it's all about control. All power resides in the one who holds the remote. There are times when it requires nothing less than brute force to pry individuals' fingers from this instrument of endless possibilities.

Our teenage son, Aaron, has grown intimately connected to the remote. Even when he's not allowed to choose the show, he just likes to hold it, just in case. There have been many times I have felt like an ATF agent on a highly dangerous weapons raid when I've given Aaron the instructions, "Put it down, Son. I said, just put it down."

Not too long ago I decided to do a control experiment, and I told Aaron that he was not allowed to touch the channel changer. Not only that, but his ten-year-old sister would now be completely in charge of this dangerous technology. I know what you're thinking; this is too much power in the hands of a child. But our situation demanded radical intervention. The results were conclusive. It wasn't at all about having a TV on the channel they wanted; it was all about the power to control that choice.

Isn't this pretty much the bottom line for much of our lives? Many of us are willing to settle for the feeling of being in control rather than making the choices that will genuinely give us freedom. One of the most perplexing things about a life of greed and pride is that we become slaves to shame and guilt. And while we live our lives for no greater purpose than ourselves, we end up being controlled by the fears of failure and rejection. This is why the path Jesus offers leads us on a journey diametrically opposed to a life of self.

THE DIVINE QUEST

While we strive to fill ourselves and remain empty, Jesus emptied Himself and lived fully. While we exhaust our energies protecting our personal rights and looking out for ourselves, Jesus, in contrast, who was in His very nature God, did not consider equality with God something He had to hold on to. He made Himself nothing. The journey we are invited to take looks nothing like Narcissus and everything like Jesus. And we will have to decide at a critical juncture which reflection we will choose to worship.

The mysterious author of the book of Hebrews challenges us to "throw off everything that hinders and the sin that so easily entangles, and let us run with perseverance the race marked out for us. Let us fix our eyes on Jesus, the author and perfecter of our faith, who for the joy set before him endured the cross, scorning its shame, and sat down at the right hand of the throne of God" (12:1–2).

While we strive to fill ourselves and remain empty, Jesus emptied Himself and lived fully.

This pilgrimage begins when we take our eyes off ourselves and fix them on the One who suffered on our behalf. The way is not easy, but it is right. To choose another path may lighten the load at first, but will make even life itself a burden in the end. The writer continues with this encouragement: "Consider him who endured such opposition from sinful men, so that you will not grow weary and lose heart" (v. 3).

The road Jesus walked was not an easy one. There was no yellow brick road for Him, nor any solutions given Him by the great and mighty Oz. So what Jesus offers us on this journey of transformation is not a free pass. There is no detour from which we can escape the real challenges and even painful realities of life. What Jesus does offer is a way to true greatness. He promises that if you and I follow Him, we will become like Him at journey's end. Rather than safety and comfort, He promises adventure and risk. More important than any earthly benefits, like wealth and success, He assures us that our greatest treasure will be the undeniable reality of Christ in us, the hope of glory. He asks, "What good will it be for a man if he gains the whole world, yet forfeits his soul?" (Matt. 16:26).

On this voyage our progress is not measured by the standards of this world, but by the quality of our character. This one is an inward trek that has undeniable outward effect. You cannot follow Jesus and remain the same. The journey itself will change you forever—not only your priorities, but your passions. It alters not only your direction, but your desires. It transforms not only your actions, but your values. It makes you just like Christ and unlike anyone else. It is nothing less than leaving the fake for the real. There is great risk in abandoning the artificial in pursuit of the authentic. Yet if we've never known the real thing, it is easy to understand why we are mesmerized with the best versions of the imitation.

Over the years we've developed a wonderful friendship with a family in New Zealand. Some of the Crawford clan recently crossed the ocean to enjoy our place here in Los Angeles. I remember when I took them to Downtown Disney. I eagerly brought them to one of my favorite spots, where a miniature waterfall produces a soothing sound as it works its way over rocks into a small pool. I have to admit I was a bit thrown back when Phillip's response was a somewhat nonresponsive, "Come to New Zealand, and we'll show you the real thing." What did I expect from residents of Middle Earth?

I realized my appreciation was shaped by the context in which I live. In comparison to a city filled with endless concrete, even a facade of the natural gained my admiration. From their vantage point, even the most beautiful expression possible from the skilled hands of men was inadequate in comparison to the majesty of the awe-inspiring work of God.

As strange as it may seem, to discover what it really means to be truly human, the only one we can turn to is God. In all of our efforts, rather than confess that we have lost our way, we have set the course of our lives on a misdirected view of greatness. We have chosen to build facades and to build them on foundations of sand, which leads us back to where we began.

Jesus summarizes the options for us:

Therefore everyone who hears these words of mine and puts them into practice is like a wise man who built his house on the rock. The rain came down, the streams rose, and the winds blew and beat against that house; yet it did not fall, because it had its foundation on the rock. But everyone who hears these words of mine and does not put them into practice is like a foolish man who built his house on sand. The rain came down, the streams rose, and the winds blew and beat against that house, and it fell with a great crash. (Matt. 7:24–27)

It's not that the fool doesn't know what to do; he just chooses to ignore the voice of God. A person God Himself deems as wise is one who not only hears His voice, but immediately begins to act on what he or she has heard. In the pages ahead we will walk a path marked by the footprints of Jesus. The disciple John summarized it like this: "This is how we know we are in him: Whoever claims to live in him must walk as Jesus did" (1 John 2:5–6).

A person God Himself deems as wise is one who not only hears His voice, but immediately begins to act on what he or she has heard.

This path will be experienced in three quests born out of the Scriptural triad of faith, love, and hope. They are the path of freedom from pride, greed, and foolishness. In each quest the ultimate result is to not only walk as Jesus did, but to become as Jesus is. And if life is found in abandoning ourselves to Jesus, then let us begin with these words that summarize His invitation to each of us:

"Come, follow Me!"

DEVELOPING LEADERS WHO SERVE

3 - HUMILITY

4 - INTEGRITY

5 - COURAGE

MAKING WHOLE DISCIPLES OUT OF BROKEN PEOPLE

6 - GRATITUDE

7 - WHOLENESS

8 - GENEROSITY

BUILDING GREAT LIVES FROM SMALL BEGINNINGS

9 - FAITHFULNESS

10 - PERSEVERANCE

11 - WISDOM

You now stand before a gauntlet. The destination you seek requires that you pass through treacherous terrain. This journey guides you down one path that brings you to three quests: a quest for honor, a quest for nobility, and a quest for enlightenment. No one can tell you where to begin. You must choose your course. Begin where your heart longs for freedom most. The shape of your character is the shape of your future. These soul places cannot simply be passed through; they must be conquered and liberated. Go first where there is the greatest captivity and instigate an uprising—a revolution of the soul.

Your fellow sojourner,

—ERM

A QUEST FOR HONOR
UNEARTHING THE WARRIOR'S HEART

An uprising against a self-centered life.

A revolution of the soul overthrowing pride and fear.

This gauntlet leads us through humility to

integrity and ultimately to courage.

Rising out of the ashes through the power of faith!

3

Rising Downward

There was once a large port city that was invaded by pirates and marauders. Everywhere these raiders went, bedlam and mayhem followed. Their presence was like a magnet to those who loved violence and revelry. The city's only hope was that they were known to pillage and then move on. Fortunately for those of us who live in Los Angeles, the Raiders finally moved back to Oakland and took their infamy with them. While fighting a reputation of being thugs and criminals, Raider fans did their cause no favor by setting the streets on fire after their team's loss to the Tampa Bay Buccaneers in Super Bowl XXXVII. The arrest ratio was somewhere close to 50 to 1. Nearly a hundred of the Raider Nation were arrested while only two underachieving Buck fans found their way to jail.

On this particular Super Bowl Sunday, the Raiders were humiliated by the Buccaneers. It was like watching one group of pirates pillage and destroy all the stolen goods of another class of pirates. It just seems so appropriate that a team called the Buccaneers would steal a championship from a group called the Raiders. Though the Raider loss did not make everything right in the world, it certainly helped.

Actually I like the Raiders. I've been tempted to even pull for them. I am not unmoved by those heartwarming human-interest stories, especially the ones around the lives of Rich Gannon, Jerry Rice, and Tim Brown. It's just that all that is admirable seems to continually be overshadowed by all that's not. But like Gandhi's determination that he would become a Christian if it were not for Christians, I find it difficult to align myself with the darker side of the Raider Nation. Some fans are just cockier than others. There's a kind of cultural arrogance that permeates the entire environment. While all true fans are intensely loyal and at least mildly delusional, some fans take it to the point of nauseam, which I think explains why the response is more violent with some than with others. The higher on the pedestal you climb, the farther and harder you fall when your legs are cut out from under you.

Violence is arrogance when it doesn't get its way. Losing isn't humbling if you aren't humble already; losing is humiliating. Arrogance always wants its way. When we can't earn it or win it, we then either try to take it or destroy it so no one else can enjoy it. Defeat is a great teacher, just as is failure. It is not so much what we learn about the activity, but what we learn about ourselves. Nothing positions us better to act in dishonor than pride.

Ironically, when we are most full of ourselves, we are most likely to make fools of ourselves. And when we are full of ourselves, we leave no room for God to place in us the very things we need the most. Pride fills up the space where integrity needs to reside. When we are arrogant, we may lash out in violence, but we will not live genuinely courageous lives.

THE COURAGE OF HUMILITY

On this quest we will discover that courage is the strength of heart born out of integrity. Without integrity we will never live a truly courageous life. The question then becomes, how do we grow in integrity? A person of integrity is a person of truth. We cannot grow in integrity if we do not grow in truth. Yet truth itself is not what forms integrity, but what *informs* integrity. For truth to serve as the fuel in our quest for honor, our hearts must be properly positioned.

Only the teachable heart will embrace whatever truth is needed for the moment. If we are not teachable, there will be no transformation. If we are unwilling to listen, we are incapable of learning. This is why Jesus calls us to be disciples and to make disciples. It is the student of life who will learn how to live. And while intelligence, discipline, focus, and determination are all critical to the learning process, there is one characteristic that is essential: humility.

Integrity is formed in the heart of the humble. Without humility we will not even begin this particular quest. The quest for honor leads us to courage through integrity and to integrity through humility. There is no other path. If we refuse to humble ourselves, we will find ourselves, no matter how far we travel, falling once again back to the starting point. Pride not only comes before a fall, but its magnitude also affects how far we fall.

We can become very successful while being very prideful. In fact some of the world's most successful individuals would be easily defined as self-absorbed by those close to them. If anything, it would seem that arrogance facilitates success rather than hinders it. This of course is the dilemma. If your personal ambitions are focused on wealth, power, prestige, and pleasure, it's very possible that pride will not get in your way, but in fact guide your way. If all your personal aspirations are vacant of divine virtues, then you're more than on your way. But if you aspire for greatness as defined by God, it is an entirely different story. If you aspire for the kind of greatness that not only inspires admiration of others, but leads to a life where genuine friendships and true intimacy result, then only the way of humility will do.

Yet even in a world without God, unrestrained self-adulation often has, at best, short-term benefit. And even when we gain great success in this life, the accomplishments that are fueled by pride are both short-lived and shortsighted. If all you care about is yourself, that's all you're going to have. Be prepared to live and die alone. Humility, on the other hand, is one of humanity's most elusive and attractive characteristics. While we ourselves may not pursue humility, we are drawn to it in others. Humility not only draws others to us, but draws God to us.

THE HUMILITY TO LEAD

Speaking on spiritual leadership, Peter instructs:

> Be shepherds of God's flock that is under your care, serving as overseers—not because you must, but because you are willing, as God wants you to be; not greedy for money, but eager to serve; not lording it over those entrusted to you, but being examples to the flock. And when the Chief Shepherd appears, you will receive the crown of glory that will never fade away.
>
> Young men, in the same way be submissive to those who are older. All of you, clothe yourselves with humility toward one another, because,
>
> *"God opposes the proud, but gives grace to the humble."*
>
> Humble yourselves, therefore, under God's mighty hand, that he may lift you up in due time. Cast all your anxiety on him because he cares for you. (1 Pet. 5:2–7, italics added)

As spiritual leaders, we are called to serve those that have been entrusted to us. Leadership in God's kingdom is always about a downward rising. We are also called to clothe ourselves with humility. We are to relate to one another in such a way that the other is always valued above ourselves. Imagine a world where everyone competed to outserve the other.

At Mosaic we are continuously being asked by those who are new to our community, "If my focus is to be on serving others, how am I going to get my own needs met?" In the midst of this call to humble ourselves and serve each other, we are to "cast [our] cares on the LORD" (Ps. 55:22). It is He who gives careful attention to meeting our needs. It doesn't make sense that if you spend your life giving yourself away you will not find yourself empty in the end, but it's true.

Not only are we called to relate to one another out of humility, but we are reminded that there is no more sure or expedient way to put ourselves in opposition with God than to become proud. God does not oppose the weak, the broken, the poor, the hurting, or even the sinful, but he does oppose the proud. In fact He is the advocate of all who are the most unlikely recipients of His grace. He gives grace to the humble.

Humility's closest attribute is honesty. Humility doesn't require us to be self-deprecating. Humility is not about having a low self-image or poor self-esteem. Humility is about self-awareness. It is important to be self-aware in relationship to our gifts, talents, skills, and intellect, but in regard to our spiritual health, it is far more essential that we are self-aware in the arena of personal character. If you see yourself for who you are and embrace it honestly, humility is the natural result. God isn't asking you to say something about yourself that isn't true. God is asking that we take a good, long look in the mirror and see ourselves for who we truly are, and then after that, to have the courage to ask for help.

Our humility allows God's intervention. The word *humble* comes from *humus*, which is simply translated "earth" or "dirt." Humility is about coming to grips with our humanity. The Scriptures describe a proud person as one who is "puffed up." Pride is a determination to be seen as bigger than we are. When we are humble, we are down to earth. No energy is wasted on pretension. A humble man can be taken at face value. It is ironic that the imagery of being humble is one where we lower ourselves. Humility sees nothing as beneath it in terms of servanthood. It is in this position that God finds delight in reversing the order. When we lower ourselves, God is eager to lift us up. Only for the humble is there a promise from God of being exalted. Only to the lowly will God leave a legacy of greatness.

When Israel was in captivity to the Egyptians, God heard their cries and chose Moses to deliver them. While we know from Stephen that Moses was powerful in speech and action and educated in all the wisdom of the Egyptians (Acts 7:22), it was not for these reasons that God selected Moses. Sometimes we speak of God as if His only use for people is to *use* them. But God created us for relationship, not only with each other, but with Him. God enjoys us. While he calls us to serve Him, He also calls us to receive His friendship. Jesus was not only the Savior of sinners but also the Friend of sinners. And Moses conversed with God face to face, as a man speaks with his friend (Exod. 33:11).

It would make sense that if God's ultimate intent is not a utilitarian use of humanity, but an intimate communion with His children, He would desire and destine us to express the virtues that He most admires. In Numbers 12:3, written by Moses himself, God interjects a parenthetical thought about Moses: "Now Moses was a very humble man, more humble than anyone else on the face of the earth."

It is here that we find God's criteron for selecting Moses. Not that all the rest didn't matter. Certainly Moses was a composite of many things needed to fulfill his extraordinary task. But the defining characteristic of Moses was his humility. Only God would know that no one on the entire earth walked with greater humility.

FALLING FROM HIGH PLACES

It seems hard for us to believe, but God is not impressed with talent nearly as much as He is with character. Perhaps no characteristic is more central to the heart of God than humility. Humility, gratitude, and faithfulness are the critical triad if we are to walk in the steps of Jesus. Like David, Moses exhibited unimaginable courage in the face of tremendous opposition. To Moses' nemesis, the Pharaoh of Egypt, God asked a very simple question: "How long will you refuse to humble yourself before me?" (Exod. 10:3).

Pharaoh was exactly what Moses was not—arrogant before God.

And in refusing to relinquish his pride, he became God's enemy. Moses was exactly what Pharaoh was not. By choosing the path of humility, Moses began a divine odyssey that would forever mark human history. When God called Moses, all Moses could see was his inadequacy. When God called Moses close, he was all too aware of his unworthiness. When God commanded him to go and accomplish great things, Moses was overwhelmed with fear and wondered how even God could accomplish so much through him. Moses so lacked the necessary courage that he asked God to give the task to someone else. But God knew that the humility Moses had on this day would nurture the integrity for the days ahead and would unleash a courage that Moses could not even imagine.

There was a time earlier in his life when Moses struck and killed a man. For forty years after this tragic mistake, he hid in the desert, marked by his failure. His action wasn't a failure of timing or strategy but a failure of character. It took four more decades for Moses to become a different man. Where once he was defined by the wisdom of Egypt, he was now marked by the wisdom of God. He learned the hard lesson that God's purpose must always be fulfilled in line with God's character.

When Kim and I were first dating, our relationship was rather turbulent. Some couples never fight while they're going out. They live in premarital bliss. It is more of a sedative than anything else. It leads them foolishly down the aisle with the assumption that it will always be like this. The world almost turns upside down when they have their first real conflict.

Kim and I were exactly the opposite. We fought all the time. Any decent relational prognosticator would have predicted that we would have never made it to our wedding day. I imagine a good counselor might have discouraged us from actually getting married, wondering if we'd really make it. Actually, I think all the fighting before marriage served as a tremendous help to us. We hardly had a fight for eighteen months after our wedding day. And the fact that we stayed together when we didn't have to makes it so much easier to stay together now that we live in covenant. We understand that everyone has conflict and that it, too, will pass.

I remember one of our first disagreements. I don't actually remember the subject; I just remember the feeling. For some reason we just couldn't get past whatever we were fighting over. A couple of days went by, and I was about to leave for New Orleans to go to the Mardi Gras. Every year I would go to share the life of Christ with anyone who would listen. While everything else is blurry, the one conversation Kim and I had before I left has stayed with me. As she was staring me down, fueled by fury, she unleashed a series of words that cut me open mercilessly. "You are so full of pride."

I couldn't believe she had the audacity to say that. It really ticked me off. Why was I even wasting my time with this woman? I should be dating someone who really appreciates me. It was just about then I knew I had to marry her. It's a rare thing to have someone in your life who will tell you the truth. She was absolutely right about who I was, and I didn't want to be like I was, but like a saber-toothed tiger stuck in a tar pit, I couldn't seem to work my way out. The more I struggled, the more I seemed to sink. If you are afraid of drowning, sometimes all you think to do is stick your neck up as high as you can. I didn't want to lose my life in insignificance, but at the same time, I didn't want my life to be defined by arrogance.

A HUMBLE PURSUIT

How do you move toward humility without losing it in the pursuit? Once you see yourself as you really are, you will know how much you need to change. Humility begins with self-awareness that must be followed with selflessness. Remember the old adage, "As soon as you think you're humble, you're not"? Isn't it prideful to pursue humility? Is this just a vicious circle with no real beginning or end? If God gives grace to the humble, that's where I want to be. Yet this path was not well paved or well-worn. What has become clear to me is that even in the religious institutions that are expressions of the Christian faith, talent supersedes character.

Certainly a great deal of the conflict that exists in churches is a result of individuals being moved to prominence for reasons irrelevant to character. Instead of raising up leaders, churches hire by résumé. We prostitute ourselves in the name of Christ. Isn't that exactly what we're doing when we receive payment for our skills regardless of our character? How many people have been used for their talents and later discarded for their infidelity? We should not be astonished when leaders fall when our criteria fall short of the standards of Christ. Fallen leaders reflect flawed communities. It is easy to point at the public offender and castigate him in shame and judgment. It is far more difficult to look at ourselves and acknowledge that our systems and organizational values may be even more corrupt than the persons we exalted. Simply because something is religious does not mean that it's spiritually admirable. There's way too much evidence out there to the contrary.

Yet for all who genuinely desire to walk the path of humility, while it may be a rarely traveled path, it is not one that remains unwalked. In fact, if no other feet have ever touched the ground that marks the way of humility, the path is clearly marked by the footprints of God. This is the most astonishing insight I have ever come to know. That God is more powerful than all of us wasn't surprising to discover. That God in His infinite wisdom knows more than all of us, again, is a no-brainer. But the realization that God, in all of His power and knowledge and wonder, is more humble than any of us is virtually beyond comprehension. The humility of God is perhaps one of His most overlooked and underappreciated virtues. It should not astound us that God calls us to a life of humility, nor should we be caught off guard in discovering that this is the path that Jesus chose for Himself. In Philippians 2 we find the template for this quest that engages us. Paul maps our course when he calls us to "do nothing out of selfish ambition or vain conceit, but in humility consider others better than yourselves. He calls us to humility, reminding us that Jesus, being found in appearance as a man, he humbled himself and became obedient to death—even death on a cross!" (v. 8)

The posture that Paul calls us to embrace is that which is reflected in the life and person of Jesus Christ. If we are genuine in our search for humility, but have yet to find the way, we need only to follow closely behind Jesus of Nazareth, and we will find ourselves clothed in the same humility He wore. While humility is rarely a highly pursued virtue among men, it is essential if we are going to be restored to the image and likeness of God.

The humility of Christ should not be seen as a new experience for God. This wasn't God's first effort at humility. God in His nature is humble. He relates to Himself in humility. The Father glorifies the Son, the Son glorifies the Father, and the Spirit never seeks glory for Himself but always gives it to the others. Even within God's triune nature, He is a model of humility. Though infinite in power, He does not use His power to showboat. When Jesus was called upon to perform miracles to prove His divinity, He refused. When He did perform a miracle, it was only to glorify God and bring genuine help and healing, not to impress the skeptics.

THE HUMILITY OF GOD

Without humility a God of infinite power would use His resources to impress rather than to transform. Without humility God would find no value in us, nor would He be concerned for our well-being. It is a frightening thought to imagine being the creation of an arrogant and self-absorbed God. The place Jesus chose for Himself as He was born into human history was perfectly in line with His character. He came in anonymity to a family of humble means and low position. He was comfortable living for thirty years in obscurity earning His wages as the son of a carpenter. Hard work was not beneath God. Calluses on His hands were not unseemly. The sweat of physical labor and the life of a commoner did not make Him less like God; they showed us more of God.

Yet even in His humility, His participation with humanity set new standards. Though He was in very nature God, He was more than willing to disrobe Himself of His royalty and wear the garment of humanity. He held nothing back in His generosity and sacrifice. He made Himself nothing.

Were God not humble, surely a different way would have been chosen. Good arguments could be made that it would be far more effective to come as royalty. For God to walk among us as king would certainly hold our attention longer than for Him to come as a servant. Wouldn't His claims be taken seriously if He held all the treasures of the earth or wielded all the world's power and held every prince and lord under His authority? Wasn't He risking being over-looked by choosing such an understated expression of His divinity? How could He expect anyone to recognize Him as God when He chose to look so common?

Yet if He had come in any other way, He would have affirmed all our wrong assumptions about who God is. Had He come with power and royalty, wealth and prestige, it would have only approved all the things we lust after. Had He chosen the path that pointed to the highest treasures of men, it would have led us away from the way of God. Jesus had to come in humility or He would have led us astray. We would have been convinced that the dark longings of our hearts were rightly aligned with the heart of God.

God came in humility because God *is* humble. He calls us to hum-bleness to be reflections of divinity. What God loves and treasures is that which is meek and loves to serve. God would not have even con-sidered becoming a man were it not for His humility. If He was con-cerned with His reputation, why would He demean Himself in such a way? He was able to strip Himself of everything, not for His sake, but for ours. His humility was expressed not only through integrity, but through courage. He humbled Himself and became obedient to death—even death on a cross. Through His turmoil in the Garden of

Gethsemane, where he cried out to his Father asking if there was any other way, his posture remained, "Not my will, but yours."

Proverbs 11:2 reminds us that wisdom comes only with humility. Humility brings obedience to the voice of God not only when it brings blessing and prosperity, but also when it brings hardship and suffering. The humility of Christ drove Him to the cross. His death was an emptying of Himself so that we might become full.

The book of Proverbs also tells us that humility comes before honor (15:33). And so it was for Jesus. Paul tells us, "Therefore God exalted him to the highest place and gave him the name that is above every name, that at the name of Jesus every knee should bow, in heaven and on earth and under the earth, and every tongue confess that Jesus Christ is Lord, to the glory of God the Father" (Phil. 2:9–11).

Jesus was most honored because He was most humble. He has been exalted to the highest place for He alone was willing to go to the lowest place. Jesus lights the way to a hidden path long forgotten. It is not an easy thing to see honor hidden behind humility. This journey is violently counterintuitive. When we strive to climb up, we become entirely unaware of how low we may actually be going. Is it possible that the way down leads to the highest pinnacles? Like a journey through an ancient portal, we must go against our natural instincts and trust the path that leaves us rising downwards.

One of my favorite musicians is my friend Joby Harris, who writes worship songs specifically for our community at Mosaic. In a song called "I Live for You," he writes:

> *Father, hear my praise,*
> *There is no known place*
> *Low enough for me*
> *To bow down properly.*

These are the sentiments of humility. Humility brings us to God not out of obligation, but out of gratitude. Humility demands nothing of God nor in any way would ever consider claiming any rights or position. When we humble ourselves, we choose the place of least honor and allow God to call us to any role of servanthood He might desire.

Humility begins with an emptying of ourselves so that we can receive from God all that we need for the journey. While Jesus had to empty Himself of His divine attributes while keeping His divine virtues, we on the other hand have to empty ourselves of our selfish ambition and vain conceit. We are called to unload and leave behind everything that is motivated by self-centeredness.

An Empty Pursuit

It was Thanksgiving Day, 1976. I was trying my hand at being a lumberjack. We were working the foothills of Virginia bringing down large trees that were made available for those who would come and clear the land. I was a novice surrounded by veterans. For me it was just another job that would provide some good money and allow me to work outdoors. The plan was to work all morning and be home in time to enjoy Thanksgiving dinner with our families.

It was a cold, wet day. The temperatures were just above freezing, so what would have been snow had mostly been rain. Everything was going well, and we were making great progress. As the day began to come to a close and nightfall was inviting us to make our way home, we boarded our trucks and prepared to return to North Carolina from where we had come.

It didn't take long to realize we weren't going anywhere. The immense weight of the trees had pressed the trucks deep into the muddy soil. Our wheels just kept spinning and spinning. No matter how hard we tried, our efforts were to no avail. After applying various theories from rocking the trucks to placing wood under the tires to anything else we could think of, we realized we were stuck. There was only one way we were going to leave these mountains: We would have to unload every tree we had cut and loaded and leave them behind. Even then we were uncertain whether the trucks would dislodge.

We spent the rest of the evening taking the trees off. They were heavy when we put them on, but they were heavier now. There's an adrenaline that flows when your work is productive. There is no such adrenaline when all your efforts are counterproductive. We had hoped to salvage at least part of our product, but this, too, was hopeless. We had to leave everything behind. In the end we were just glad to get out of there. Thanksgiving was pizza that night. I also retired from my career as a lumberjack.

It just didn't make sense to me to work all day to gain something and then have to work twice as hard to get rid of it, yet this is the same insanity by which most of us live our lives. We give our whole lives to gain the world, and then when we discover that we're stuck in the mud and cannot make our way home, we ascertain far too late in the process that the only way that we can get unstuck is to empty ourselves and begin afresh.

Humility begins by emptying ourselves *of* ourselves. It is about coming to God without agenda and without reservation. If you are still relating to God through negotiations, you have not yet found the path of humility. If your question is still "How much can I keep?" or "How much do I have to give up?" you're still at the pool of Narcissus. The quest for honor begins with a humility that leaves us empty. This is not an emptiness that makes us hollow, but a humility that makes us teachable. There is much to discard if we are to engage in this particular quest. We must make ourselves nothing in order to receive everything that God longs to give us. Humility not only calls us to empty ourselves, but also to submit our lives to the One who is most humble.

STRENGTH DOWN LOW

On one of our trips to Japan, we took time to visit the ancient castle of Shogun. One of the unusual features of this highly guarded home was how the doors were shaped on the outer wall. The doors were at least a foot off the ground, and for a man of average height, about two feet too low. To enter the house of the Shogun, you have to lower your head and pass through the door headfirst. In other words, to gain admission to the home of this warrior master, you would have to expose your head to his sword. This was both a physical and visceral expression of submission. You would place your life in the hands of him whose home you entered. No enemy would position himself in such a way or allow himself to be so vulnerable.

Submission came before admission and admission was necessary for communion. This is equally true in our relationship with God. We cannot enter into a genuine relationship with God without coming to Him in humility. Every follower of Jesus Christ has at least once walked in humility. You may have recovered quickly but repentance requires humility. We are to not only come to God in humility, but to live in humility throughout our lives. Humility is most practically expressed in submission. The proud will not submit themselves to anyone. The humble will always submit themselves to what is right, good, and true.

Jesus submitted Himself to His Father, even when it led Him to the cross. We are called to do the same. We are to submit our lives to the person of Jesus Christ, to place them in His hands. If we are to live where God lives, we must become as God is. God is holy and in His holiness chooses to dwell among the humble. This is both the destination and the journey, and, perhaps most poignantly, it is also the point of entry.

Isaiah writes in regard to this very issue, "Build up, build up, prepare the road! Remove the obstacles out of the way of my people. For this is what the high and lofty One says—he who lives forever, whose name is holy: 'I live in a high and holy place, but also with him who is contrite and lowly in spirit, to revive the spirit of the lowly and to revive the heart of the contrite'" (57:14–15).

When we submit ourselves to God, we are placing our lives under His mission. Of course this is always easier when we agree with God and far more difficult when we do not. We cannot assume that we are living a life of genuine submission to God simply because we do what God says when we are in agreement. The real test of submission is when we disagree, when we don't like what God has said because it goes contrary to our personal interests or desires. If we find ourselves unwilling to submit to truth in those cases, then we are living by truth not because we agree with God, but because God agrees with us.

RAISING THE STANDARD

When I first came to Mosaic, we were only attenders. I had no intention of ever becoming the pastor of this community of faith. We had been there about a year when we accepted the church's invitation to replace the former pastor of twenty-four years.

The church had an annual leadership retreat where those who had accepted a certain level of responsibility would meet and plan for the future. Attendance was mandatory, and from all that I heard and read was not negotiable. The leadership guidelines clearly stated that any leader who did not attend would be released from his position. I have never been a big fan of policies and rules and always try to keep them to a minimum, but if they exist, I am pretty committed to fleshing them out. My view is that you shouldn't have any policies that you are not willing to implement or back up. That's why the fewer the better. But since I was entirely new to the process, I was trying to be careful to respect all the procedures that were in place.

As the meeting began and I stepped into my new role, I casually announced that it was good to see all of our leaders present and reminded them that any leaders who were not there would, of course, be removed and could pick up again the next year. It wasn't really that big of a deal. I just assumed everyone was there. I didn't know the history, so I was certain this was an annual leadership realignment.

Almost immediately after I stepped down, one of our staff members ran to me in a state of panic and asked me what in the world did I think I was doing. Confused, I asked him what he meant. He explained that they never remove leaders who do not attend. I reminded him that it was a written policy. He quickly corrected me with the unnerving clarification that it's only said, never upheld.

Fortunately, it seemed I had caused no major damage until early Sunday morning when I received an unexpected phone call. It was one of the elders of the church. He had been newly elected and had been serving only as long as I had been lead pastor, but he was a long-standing member of the church. He had come in the '70s, and for nearly a decade had been personally mentored by the former pastor, who was still on the board of elders.

The phone call began with, "Pastor, we have a problem." He quickly began to explain that he was not at the leadership retreat. His wife had been at the meeting and had called him to inform him he was no longer an elder.

My heart was in my throat, and my stomach was in knots. I couldn't believe what I had done. I would have never knowingly dismissed an elder in such a public and trivial manner. Not only is it insensitive to the individual, but it's really bad leadership.

I quickly moved toward damage control. I said, "Rick, I'm sure you had a good reason for not being there."

He responded, "No, I just chose not to come."

I countered, "No, Rick, I'm certain there was a good reason. Was there a family issue? A work-related issue?"

He said, "No, I went to a ball game instead."

I wanted to scream at him and tell him, "Work with me, man!" but it was no use. I accepted his resignation over the phone.

Rick Yamamoto is genuinely one of the most humble men I've ever had the privilege of knowing. I didn't know him well, but this experience fast-forwarded our relationship by years. After he resigned he asked what he could do to make amends for his error in judgment. He would be willing to watch all the tapes and insisted on going before the congregation and asking for forgiveness. From his perspective, he had dishonored my leadership as the new pastor and had not lived up to his commitments.

It was the next Wednesday night service when I invited Rick to step up to the podium and share with the congregation. He began with such contrition that it brought a deafening silence throughout the whole building. He spoke in terms of failure, sin, and repentance. His language carried the heaviness of a tragic moral failure. As he began to speak, I realized what was happening. Everyone was rushing to judgment. The natural conclusion was that Rick had resigned his eldership as a result of a significant violation. I imagine either adultery or embezzlement came to mind.

After expressing the depth of his sorrow, he went on to explain that he had carelessly neglected his responsibility to be at the leadership retreat. You could almost feel the shock and relief in the air. At the same time, the genuineness of Rick's humility and the determination of this man to live under authority established a level of respect for spiritual leadership like we had never known. Rick was not only one of our elders, but also a successful businessman who managed a two-billion-dollar investment firm. In his lack of pridefulness, the texture of his humility made him not only value but comfortable with spiritual submission. He became living proof that individuals of great power can live under submission.

Immediately after offering his resignation, Rick stepped down as the congregation watched in silence. I stepped to the podium and thanked Rick for his humility and his willingness to be a person under authority. I then asked the congregation if this wasn't exactly the kind of person we wanted as an elder. I moved to immediately reinstate Rick as an elder. Through acclamation, we instantly recalled Rick to his position of spiritual leadership. Rick serves as an elder at Mosaic to this day and is one of my closest friends and partners in ministry.

Submission is not about powerlessness; it is about meekness. To be meek is to have controlled strength. Like the Roman centurion (Matt. 8:5–13), he was a man of authority and under authority. It requires strength of character to be both under authority and entrusted with authority. Both are equally challenging and both are tests of character. We cannot be entrusted with authority over others if we cannot be trusted to live under the authority of others. That's one reason why children who are never taught to honor and submit to their parents make such poor adults. Humility gives us the mobility to adapt to whatever context we are placed within. When we are prideful, we become hard-hearted and stiff-necked.

In South America the llama serves as a cultural metaphor for pride. To keep a herd of llamas corralled, you don't even need a fence. All you need is one rope circling around the herd to keep them enclosed. Just by placing it at a height beneath the head and base of the neck, the llamas are secured in this makeshift pen. Rather than stooping beneath the rope, the llamas stand tall, but remain captive. They either refuse or are physically incapable of bending their necks, and thus are seen as a symbol of arrogance.

The proud will not bow their heads or bend a knee. They hold their heads up and remain prisoners when they are just inches away from freedom. How tragic it will be if we have never bowed our hearts to Jesus Christ in this life when we recognize how very close freedom and life were to us. God's promise to us is, "Humility and the fear of the LORD bring wealth and honor and life" (Prov. 22:4).

A HUMBLE QUEST

It is here where the quest for honor begins. We are never called in the Bible to pray for humility; instead we are commanded to be humble. There are some things God does and some things God requires. While humility is a divine attribute, it is placed squarely on our shoulders to choose this path. If we refuse to humble ourselves and God is required to act in our place, it is more than humbling; it is humiliating. The Scriptures warn us, "A man's pride brings him low, but a man of lowly spirit gains honor" (Prov. 29:23).

When we choose the lowly path, there is nowhere to fall and the only way is up. If we find ourselves overwhelmed with the feeling that we are too good or above this calling, we should remember that anywhere God walks is not beneath us. To keep perspective, we are invited to take on the attitude of Christ. The word *attitude* addresses our position. In biblical language it encompasses our disposition, feelings, and even our physical posture.

The emotions we feel and our physicality are interrelated. We cross our arms when we're closed; we slump when we're discouraged; we're told to keep our heads up when we lack inspiration. It is no surprise that spiritual expressions such as prayer and worship are both emotive and physical experiences. Our attitude toward God is often expressed in postures such as kneeling, the raising of hands, and even falling prostrate.

When we choose the attitude of Christ, our lives become firmly grounded. The attitude of Christ both humbles and inspires us. No circumstance, regardless of its difficulty, is overwhelming. No failure, however devastating, is pervasive or permanent. In the same way that perspective is shaped in the context of gratitude, expressing where we fall on a continuum of greed to gratefulness, attitude is shaped in the context of humility.

Neither perspective nor attitude is formed in a vacuum. They are expressions of deeper realities within us. When a person has an attitude problem, what he or she really has is an arrogance problem. A bad attitude is evidence of a lack of humility. Attitude is an accurate monitor of where we fall on the spectrum of pride and humility. This is why two people can step into the same experience and respond to it so differently. It's why sometimes we need an attitude adjustment. Humility is the chiropractic remedy when our necks are stiff and incapable of bending.

In Jesus we see that the power of God is unleashed to accomplish His greatest good when we are willing to walk in humility. The quest for honor is not where we pursue humility for greatness, but where we pursue the greatness of humility. The goal is not to know if you're humble, but to live as a servant, to give your life away for the good of others regardless of personal benefit or consequence.

Would you be willing to give your life to save the world if no one ever knew your name? If anonymity was the price you would have to pay for significance, would it be too great a price? To live a life of courage is not a guarantee of prestige or adulation, but there is a freedom in humility. It doesn't matter anymore what anyone else thinks or what others say. It only matters if you live and die fulfilling the mission you were born for.

Solomon once observed the paradox of a man who accomplished great things and remained unknown. "There was once a small city with only a few people in it. And a powerful king came against it, surrounded it and built huge siegeworks against it. Now there lived in that city a man poor but wise, and he saved the city by his wisdom. But nobody remembered that poor man" (Eccl. 9:14–15).

Obscurity has never stopped God from accomplishing great things. Our poverty has never been His limitation, our position not important for His advantage. Our reputation seems nothing more than incidental. Only our pride can leave us empty, and only when we empty ourselves can we begin the journey. This is the quest for honor.

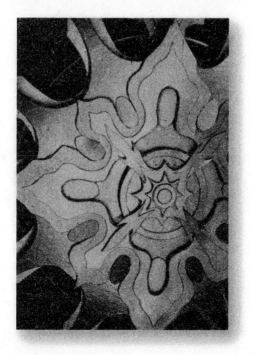

品
格

i n t e g r i t y

4

Turned Inside Out

We were not five minutes into our flight from Dubai to New Delhi when we received the news that we would be turning back. The United Arab Emirates was only a stopover on our journey through Pakistan, India, and then on to Asia. The flight attendant was preparing us for what would be an abrupt turnaround, while at the same time assuring us that we were perfectly safe. It was somewhat disconcerting that as the attendant confidently explained the reason for our need to return, the pilot interrupted over the intercom and gave us a different reason. Was it weather patterns or technical problems or something else? We would never know. We just knew that on this particular flight it would take two takeoffs just to get out of Dubai.

In that moment I knew someone wasn't telling me something—but I wasn't sure I really wanted to know. Since I had no other choice, I quietly reaffirmed my trust in the flight crew, but the fact that they were saying two different things put a real strain on that confidence. It's easier to trust someone when he or she demonstrates continuity. While I'm sure the crew's motives were to comfort us, what they did instead was jeopardize their integrity.

Whether in flight or on ground, this principle remains true: You can't say two things at the same time and expect to be trusted. Perhaps more to the point, you can't say one thing and do another and consider yourself a person of integrity.

Integrity is the context from which courage is formed. Integrity, like wholeness, is a by-product of our spiritual integration. *Integrity* comes from the root word *integer*, which means to be complete, indivisible—in other words, to be a whole. If a plane lacks integrity, it disintegrates. If its engine lacks integrity, you cannot finish the flight. If its captain and crew lack integrity, you cannot fully expect to reach the intended destination.

Each one of these applies well to us as we find ourselves in flight on our quest for honor. When it comes to our success or failure on this venture, in the end it will have nothing to do with the outside turbulence. While some will find their particular journeys smooth sailing, others will find theirs nauseatingly turbulent. In either case the outside pressure and wind conditions can make the journey more challenging but cannot stop us from arriving at our ultimate destination. This journey is entirely dependent on the integrity of the vessel and its pilot—meaning, of course, you and me.

THE GENUINE ARTICLE

In recent times in our culture we have put an increasing value on authenticity and a decreasing focus on integrity. This is strongly influenced by a disdain for the pretentious and a longing for anything that is real. In principle I wholeheartedly embrace the shift, except where authenticity is romanticized. When calling for authenticity, we need to take seriously the brokenness and sinfulness of the human heart. If to be authentic means to be who we really are or to express what we really feel, then in most cases I'm going to vote for hypocrisy. Our prisons are filled with men and women who acted on their feelings and impulses. If authenticity is about being true to yourself, these individuals should be our models of inspiration.

We don't want to think about it, and we certainly don't want to acknowledge it as true, but sometimes what's really inside of us is darker and uglier than what people see. If someone's honest feeling toward me is hatred, and he would like nothing more in the world than to bring my life to an end, *I* hope he will choose the way of hypocrisy. I want the person who is a thief at heart not to steal, even if he really wants to. I want the individual who's convinced he's in love with someone other than his wife to go against what his heart is telling him and to refuse to have an affair.

Authenticity can establish a self-righteousness that justifies abuse.

Our claim that we are committed to being authentic can actually be a facade for self-indulgence. If we're not careful, *authentic* can be the new word for *arrogance*. As long as you're true to yourself—say what you mean—just get it out—how can anyone fault you in any way? This perspective frees us from any concern for the feelings of others. I've seen more situations than I care to where a person, just committed to being honest and real, lambasted everyone around him, leaving team members wounded and hurting. His only ethical compass was if it felt right to him to do it. Authenticity can establish a self-righteousness that justifies abuse. Is it really OK to do something because you want to, to say something because you feel it?

If we are committed to being the genuine article, we'd first better look closely at what we're made of. Authenticity without integrity is lethal. To be authentic when our hearts are dark and corrosive is equivalent to opening Pandora's box. As much as we may disdain the external constraints of society, we need to recognize that humanity's best solution without God is to establish laws that limit or at least attempt to restrain the evil that lurks within us.

Beyond this there is another obstacle to being truly authentic. To be authentic means literally that we are not false or copied, that we reflect the original, that we are genuine in regard to the intent of the creator. When something is authenticated, you are able to establish it as a genuine production of the originator. The beauty of the work is a reflection of the artist's imagination. While a copy can duplicate the image, it lacks the value of an original. Only a work created by the hand of the artist qualifies as the real thing. No replica will do.

Our separation from God has not only made us echoes, but imitations, no longer reflections of the Creator, but replicas of a poor copy. Though we are born of a template designed in the image of the Creator God, that template is broken, and the reproduction flawed. We are classic counterfeits. To the untrained eye, we pass as the real thing. We might even fool ourselves. Yet the evidence of our inauthenticity can be seen in our departure from the character of God. We have become carbon copies of each other in the worst of ways. Rather than the themes of humanity being love, forgiveness, and compassion, our common themes are the very things we would say we despise. We don't have to teach each other to take; it comes naturally. Our history is filled with violence and betrayal, poverty and gluttony, war and apathy. The human heart is skewed toward the self. We need to teach our children values that are admirable. They do not embrace them naturally.

The first and most important step in the process of becoming genuinely authentic is to be once again authenticated by the original designer. This is a part of the divine side of human change. God desires to place within each of us a new heart, a heart that reflects him not only in action, but in desire. The Scriptures speak of this transformation as a metamorphosis. We are literally transformed into new creations; not a different kind of creature, but a different kind of humanity.

AUTHENTICATED

The divine transformation that God seeks to bring is nothing less and nothing more than making us truly human. What it means to be human has become so foreign to us, and God's original intent so lost to us, that we experience it as a new way to be human. It is an actuality, a return to the authentic. God literally turns us inside out. When the box is opened, we find that God has transformed the contents. There is a resonance between our actions and desires. How we live becomes a genuine expression of what we care about. We are no longer guided by laws, but by values.

While religion works to restrain our actions from the outside in, God always works from the inside out. Only this kind of change lasts. Its sustaining power comes not only from the Spirit of God, but from your desire to become the person God dreams of. Your motivation is not what others think of you, nor even the consequence of your actions if you choose another way, but your longing to have the image of God revealed in you. You simply want to be a different person.

It is in this state that we become people of integrity. It's more than "what you see is what you get." Integrity is not just about who you are, but who you seek to become. When we have integrity, we don't need to pretend. We are well aware of our weaknesses and shortcomings. Integrity is not about being flawless, but being "false-less." When you watch a person of integrity, you can know exactly what's inside him or her. That individual is transparent. You can see inside the heart and witness the light emanating from within.

Everything God creates has integrity. The entire cosmos is a work of integrity. Our solar system would not hold together without integrity. Everything God creates is in proper relationship with itself and its environment. In fact, the Scriptures tell us that today the cosmos lacks integrity and groans for its redemption. Nevertheless, the elegant organization of the universe still marvelously reflects the integrity of God.

When God creates something, there is an essence of truth within it. We take this for granted in our everyday lives. We just expect that when we inhale, the air we breathe will be properly balanced for our respiratory needs. We never think twice about the phenomenon of a liquid flowing down mountains and forming rivers, strangely carrying the composition to not only quench our thirst, but also keep us alive.

Fruits are also a subtle reminder of the integrity of God. Have you ever gone to the store to buy bananas? If you have, what you really did was buy banana *peels*. You never actually saw the meat of the banana; you just knew it was there. All you ever saw was the peel. Yet every time you skinned one, there was a banana inside. Is your response each time surprise? Is there a process of anticipation and delight as you choose a banana and slowly open it to see what you might find? No, you just take it for granted. You know exactly what's going to be there.

If you've ever bought a watermelon, there again you have an interesting scenario. You spend your hard-earned money buying a watermelon rind. Have you ever checked to see if your melon is going to be ripe and juicy? What do you do? You thump it. And what do you listen for? For a hollow sound. If the watermelon rind sounds empty, you buy it. Are these the actions of educated and rational beings? Shouldn't you instead peel all the bananas before you dish out your cash to make sure you're getting your money's worth? Can you imagine buying a watermelon and getting home and finding it empty? How are you going to get your money back? What are you going to tell the manager? "I thumped it, it sounded empty, and when I got home, it was. I want my money back."

I can say with confidence that this is never going to happen for one simple reason: Everything God creates has integrity. If we had made the watermelon, it might turn out empty. After all, we're the people who claim we're selling cars when actually we're passing off lemons. We really need to stay out of the fruit business. How about you? If someone cut you open or peeled off the outer layer, what would he find? Would he or she be shocked?

AN INTEGRATED LIFE

With integrity comes integration. We align what others see with who we really are becoming. And more important, we align who we really are with who God is. When Jesus prayed for His disciples that they would be one as He and the Father are one (John 17), the focus of His prayer was unity. While unity among ourselves was obviously a direct result of the oneness Jesus prayed for, I am convinced that it was His secondary, not primary, meaning. The oneness He spoke of first and foremost dealt with our communion *with God.* This is critical because only in oneness with God do we find wholeness and integration.

God created everything to be in proper relationship with Himself. He is the source of all that is good. It is good for everything and everyone to be in relationship with Him. For God to seek our good, He must seek our reconciliation to Himself. We were created and designed to be one with Him. When we are one with God, we find both wholeness and integrity. Integrity is born out of relationship with God and flows into our relationships with others. Integrity is the personification of truth. When we build our lives on truth, and live by that which we know to be true, we begin to live from the inside out. Even Jesus' enemies were able to identify this characteristic in the person they so despised.

Mark describes an encounter with the Pharisees and Herodians as they tried to trap Jesus in His words and find some way to accuse Him. "They came to him and said, 'Teacher, we know you are a man of integrity. You aren't swayed by men, because you pay no attention to who they are; but you teach the way of God in accordance with the truth'" (Mark 12:14).

Even though their words were filled with hypocrisy, their observation was accurate. As a person of integrity, Jesus did not compromise His values. Whether you were rich or poor, oppressed or powerful, famous or anonymous, Jesus would relate to you in the same way. He didn't change His convictions either on the basis of your position or His feelings toward you. Even those who hated Him knew He was the same person with everyone He met, regardless of context. His actions were informed by truth, and as such, He always acted with integrity.

When we lack integrity, we might alter our decisions based on who others are or even how we feel about them. If we admire someone or aspire to be valued by that individual, a lack of integrity will cause us to conform to what we believe that person wants us to be.

Jesus had only one face. When we show different sides of ourselves to different people, we become two-faced at the very least. When we lack integrity, we find ourselves being several people, depending on the circumstance. We subdivide our lives and justify our differing value systems based on the context. Our character becomes a product to be sold. We become personality salesmen rather than people of substance.

Once Kim was considering buying a red car. It was amazing how quickly the salesman began to share with us his story of how his wife was at first apprehensive when he bought her a red car, but overnight she came to love it. Kim, in her unflappable way, looked at him and said, "If I was considering a blue car, would it have been a blue car your wife had come to love?"

Jesus was always the same person, and this is exactly what God both desires and requires of us. This same kind of integrity is to be formed in us and to shape our lives. As with Jesus, integrity is best showcased in the context of opposition or even persecution. We can appear to have integrity when in fact all we are doing is conforming. If the decision of least resistance is one of integrity, we might convince ourselves that we are actually defined by this characteristic. It's when we face a moment of truth that our integrity is tested and proven genuine or not.

In Jesus' three years of ministry, His environment grew in hostility and every decision of integrity increased its volatility. That Jesus walked in integrity at all times, even when it cost Him His life, was the ultimate proof of who He was. When we are defined by integrity, we respond with moral courage. Courage is the ultimate expression of integrity. Integrity gives us the courage to walk in truth even when it means walking straight into the mouth of the dragon.

Solomon tells us that the wicked flee when no one pursues; but the righteous are as bold as a lion (Prov. 28:1). When we lack integrity, we live in fear. While that fear may manifest itself in many ways, it is fundamentally the fear of getting caught, of someone knowing who we really are. When we walk in righteousness and love what is right, when we live lives of integrity, we have nothing to fear at all.

Solomon also tells us, "The man of integrity walks securely, but he who takes crooked paths will be found out" (Prov. 10:9). Mark Twain pointed out that "if you tell the truth you don't have to remember anything." But then again, if you're a liar, you'd better have a great memory. When we tell the truth, that's all we have to remember. When we live in deceit, we have too many faces and lies to keep track of.

THE COURAGE OF INTEGRITY

As we grow in integrity, we grow in the courage to live lives of conviction. Integrity also reduces the number of options we have to consider. Only those actions that would reflect the character of God are open for consideration. Integrity gives us the strength to hold on and hold out for the good. And while it limits our actions to those things that are true and good, it also increases our capacity to live and act in a genuinely heroic way.

One of the individuals in biblical history that best personifies courage is David, son of Jesse. David comes on the scene in two distinct scenarios. The first was when Samuel was looking for an heir to the throne of Saul and went to the family of Jesse in Bethlehem to anoint one of his sons to become king. As Jesse's son Eliab stood before Samuel, God said, "Do not consider his appearance or his height, for I have rejected him. The LORD does not look at the things man looks at. Man looks at the outward appearance, but the LORD looks at the heart" (1 Sam. 16:7). One by one, the seven oldest sons of Jesse passed before Samuel. God rejected each. In the end, God chose the youngest of them all, David, the young shepherd who was overlooked even by his own father. The criterion was the texture of David's heart, not the strength of his personality or even the quality of his physical stature or abilities.

The second scenario for which David is perhaps best known is when he stood against Goliath. David wasn't supposed to be there. He was far too young to be a warrior. While his brothers were at war, he was left tending sheep. It certainly wasn't because he didn't want to be there. He is described as going back and forth between the front lines, where Saul stood with his army, and his father's sheep in Bethlehem.

On one particular occasion David came to deliver food to the soldiers and cheese to their commander. While he was there, he heard the champion warrior known as Goliath taunting the armies of Israel. Goliath was a giant, and even the bravest of the army of God trembled with fear when they heard his voice. Each time he came in defiance to mock both them and the name of the Lord, the men of Israel would run, overwhelmed with fear.

It was here that David rose to the occasion and established his legacy. In one moment he went from shepherd to warrior—or so it would seem. When he offered his services to Saul, Saul questioned whether David was up to the challenge. David's response was a summary of his résumé as a shepherd:

> Your servant has been keeping his father's sheep. When a lion or a bear came and carried off a sheep from the flock, I went after it, struck it, and rescued the sheep from its mouth. When it turned on me, I seized it by its hair, struck it and killed it. Your servant has killed both the lion and the bear; this uncircumcised Philistine will be like one of them, because he has defied the armies of the living God. The LORD who delivered me from the paw of the lion and the paw of the bear will deliver me from the hand of this Philistine. (1 Sam. 17:34–37)

We find in David not a moment of inspiration, but a pattern of integrity. What he was willing to attempt was nothing more than the overflow of what he was already living. Who would have faulted him if he had allowed a sheep to be lost to a bear or lion? No one would have expected him to pursue his foe and literally knock the sheep out of its clutches. But David was willing to fulfill his responsibilities even to the point of attacking a lion and risking his life for the lambs under his care.

Asaph, a contemporary of David, writes these words about the shepherd-warrior king: "[God] chose David his servant and took him from the sheep pens; from tending the sheep he brought him to be the shepherd of his people Jacob, of Israel his inheritance. And David shepherded them with integrity of heart; with skillful hands he led them" (Ps. 78:70–72).

The courage to face lions, bears, and giants was the outflow of the integrity of his heart. Courage is what integrity looks like when facing the forces of darkness and evil. Without integrity we will lack the courage necessary to face our greatest challenges and to stay the course and pursue the quest for honor. It was because of his integrity that David could be trusted to lead the people of God. Yes, he led them with "skillful hands," but it was not his skill that qualified him for spiritual leadership. How often do we place more emphasis on the development of our skills than the development of our character?

Often when we hear the word *pastor* or *shepherd,* we think of someone whose primary characteristic is as a caretaker or nurturer. For David to be a shepherd meant something dramatically different. A shepherd was an individual of courage who was willing to risk even his own life. David, even when he was alone caring for the sheep, responded with the courage born out of integrity. The integrity of heart to shepherd God's people was demonstrated in his warrior spirit. David passed the test of whether he would protect himself or provide protection. He could have easily justified a selfish action when comparing his own life to the life of a sheep. Yet it wasn't about the value of the sheep at all, but the value of his word. To do anything less would make David a lesser man. He had been entrusted with the responsibility, and he would see it through. The seriousness with which he took his responsibility as a shepherd was the best indicator for how he would respond if entrusted with responsibility over God's people.

A GOD-SHAPED HEART

Integrity moves us to intervene on behalf of the powerless. A heart of integrity cannot remain unmoved when we have the power to help. Integrity not only unleashes a heart of courage, but delivers us from apathy and passivity. Integrity is not just about keeping our hands clean. At times it is about getting our hands dirty. Integrity does not simply move us away from the path of evil, but moves us aggressively toward the path of good.

Perhaps the best summary of integrity is that the heart of God is joined with the heart of man. The heartbeat of God pounds within our chests; His blood flows through our veins. What brings God pleasure brings us pleasure. What angers God brings our blood to a boil. Integrity will not stand by and watch the wicked oppress the weak. Like David, we make ourselves strong, not for the purpose of judging those who are afraid, but for delivering them from their fear.

When Nehemiah was rebuilding the walls of Jerusalem, he had the difficult task of choosing trustworthy leaders to direct the project. In his journal he gives us tremendous insight concerning leadership: "I put in charge of Jerusalem my brother Hanani, along with Hananiah the commander of the citadel, because he was a man of integrity and feared God more than most men do" (Neh. 7:2).

Nehemiah makes the correlation between having integrity and fearing God. Again, this is in line with the whole development of courage. When you fear God, you fear nothing else. When we fear God, that fear is absorbed in His infinite compassion and unconditional love. We are free from all the fears that haunt our hearts apart from God. This proper fear and reverence understands that there is nothing to be afraid of when our hearts are aligned with the God who created us to live in all that is good.

The fear of God aligns us with all that is true and good and transforms the core motivation of our heart to become love. As we grow in integrity, we will grow in trustworthiness. Integrity not only makes us more trustworthy, but makes us easier to trust. When we live from the inside out, others know who we are and can put their confidence in our influence and leadership.

Years ago I owned a car with over 100,000 miles on it. It had always run perfectly and never had one mechanical problem. It was starting to look pretty worn out so I thought I should put some money into it. I paid for a brand-new paint job, and it looked as good as new. But about a year later, it died, never to run again. I had made the outside beautiful while ignoring the problems on the inside.

Integrity fixes the engine even if the paint is peeling. When the engine is taken care of, you can have confidence that the car will take you where you're going. A beautiful paint job only promises you will look great while you're broken down on the side of the road.

There is a reason why we place our trust in people who have integrity. Integrity, or the lack of it, has everything to do with how we use power. When we perceive someone as having integrity and later find ourselves victims of the abuse of power, we become disillusioned and perhaps even embittered. The perception of integrity led us to place more confidence in an individual than he or she deserved.

This kind of character reversal has led us to a false conclusion of the relationship between power, authority, and character. There's an adage that says, "Absolute power corrupts absolutely." While this may seem absolutely true, it's absolutely false. There is only one who has ever known absolute power, and that is God. Yet He is the only one who has never abused His power. This is exactly what separates God from the rest of us. He really is different from who we are without Him. In fact we find that God does exactly the opposite of what we would expect with unlimited power.

In John 13 it says that "Jesus knew that the Father had put all things under his power" (v. 3a). While Jesus relinquished His omnipotence to walk among us, at this point all the power that He had put on reserve was returned to Him. He could do whatever He wanted. Nothing could stop Him. Yet what we find is that the motivation that directed His power determined how that power was used. Two verses before, John tells us, "Having loved his own who were in the world, he now showed them the full extent of his love" (John 13:1).

The end result of absolute power motivated by undiluted love was servanthood, not tyranny. Jesus' first act after knowing that all power had been placed under His authority was to wrap a towel around His waist and wash His disciples' feet.

Absolute power

does not

corrupt;

it reveals.

With Jesus absolute power did not corrupt absolutely because it never does. Absolute power does not corrupt; it reveals. Jesus is our proof of this. Our hostility toward Him would be more than enough to justify His retaliation, yet even while suffering on the cross, He refused to use His power to do anything but good. In contrast, how many of us have been restrained from harming someone simply because we felt powerless? If absolute power corrupts absolutely, then wouldn't absolute powerlessness be the key to all virtue? Corruption is not an issue of power; it is an issue of passion. Power simply allows us to unleash our passions. What is hidden when we are powerless is exposed when we are empowered. With absolute power what you see is what you get. The power and authority that Jesus held did not change Him but allowed us to see Him in His purest form. The reason it appears that power corrupts is that power magnifies what is hidden within us. We can appear to have integrity when in fact all we are is powerless. It is not an act of integrity to treat someone well or justly when we are afraid of him or feel powerless to do otherwise. You cannot call someone "moral" simply because he is restrained from acting on his deepest desires.

Otherwise Hannibal Lecter would be considered the ultimate expression of morality simply because he was strapped into a strait-jacket. He's not moral just because he can't eat you. True morality in this case would be that he no longer *wants* to have you for dinner.

Our Defining Mark

Character is neither conformity nor uniformity. Character is the mark that defines who we really are when you get to the core. When our character is defined by integrity, we can be trusted with power. Power does not become a corrosive agent, but a creative energy. When we lack integrity, we use power to control. When we lead with integrity, we use power to bless. Power minus integrity equals the will to power. Power plus integrity equals the will to empower. The condition and depth of your integrity determines how you will use authority when entrusted with it.

In Matthew 28:18, Jesus tells his disciples, "All authority in heaven and on earth has been given to me." I don't know what kind of promotion you have received recently or how much authority has been entrusted to you, but I know it pales in comparison to this. How Jesus used His authority was an extension of His use of power. With His power He served; with His authority He authorized; with His place of authority He chose not to hold power but to release it. After declaring that His was all the authority in heaven and on earth, He then commissioned them, "Therefore go and make disciples of all nations, baptizing them in the name of the Father and of the Son and of the Holy Spirit, and teaching them to obey everything that I have commanded you. And surely I am with you always, to the very end of the age" (Matt. 28:19–20).

When we lack integrity, we use power to control. When we lead with integrity, we use power to bless.

Instead of hoarding His power, Jesus unleashes His power. For Him, neither love nor power is a limited commodity. There is no scarcity of either and no need to keep them under lock and key. Just like love, the nature of power expands when it is given away. When we are afraid to lose power, it has already begun to diminish. When we see power as a gift we have received for the benefit of others, we have learned the true secret—power can either control you or be controlled by you.

When you lust for power, you are its slave. When you live for others, you are a powerful servant of God. Only those who would live to serve can be trusted with the power of God. We seem to reverse this. We pray for God's power while we contemplate whether we will choose to serve God with our lives. But the power of God without the heart of God would result in unimaginable godlessness. God finds pleasure in entrusting His power to those who are serving Him in their weakness.

We have enough examples in our history of the level of violence we can perpetrate when we are unrestrained in our power. Yet never, not once, did power corrupt. Power is a tool. It allows us the freedom to be who we truly are. This is why it is critical to pursue integrity rather than power. If you lack integrity, thank God that you are not more powerful. Only God knows the damage you might cause given the opportunity. Resist being promoted to higher authority on the basis of your talent. Though David led with "skillful hands," his compass was the integrity of his heart. When you are promoted based on your abilities, without regard to the content of your character, it is a disservice both to your subordinates and to you.

Authority and position without the substance to undergird them leaves you vulnerable not only to causing great harm, but to facing great humiliation. How many spiritual leaders have been exposed in the most public formats because their positions were gained through the strength of their talent and not the strength of their character? We do no one a favor when we put abilities over integrity.

Integrity cannot be gained by power and authority. Integrity must be gained long before these have been placed in our hands. Jesus lived an obscure life for thirty years preparing for a public ministry that lasted only for three. We need to resist the fast track to public recognition and take instead the long road that leads us on a quest for honor.

When you pursue power and prestige, you cease to pursue character. If your ambition is to be great in the sight of men, you are not pursuing greatness in the sight of God. If you want to be first before God, you cannot push yourself to be first before men. You cannot live for yourself and live for God. Some things, when pulled in combination, will stop you in your tracks.

A NOBLE AMBITION

Integrity requires that you decide what kind of person you want to become. This journey goes against the natural flow of human history. There is a dramatic difference between seeking honor and being honorable. The quest for honor is not the end of ambition. It does not call us to relinquish our pursuit for greatness, but to redefine the meaning of greatness. Arrogance is not to be replaced by apathy any more than self-centeredness is to be replaced with indifference.

The quest for honor is a passionate pursuit of a different kind of greatness. Though its path runs counter to selfish ambition, it is no less ambitious. It inspires those who long to live heroic lives. It calls us to a new kind of courage. It demands much of us. Integrity not only harnesses our passions, but focuses our intentions. There are some paths, some options, some directions that we simply will not choose. We will not merely be true to ourselves, but will bind ourselves to truth. We are not free from the emotion of fear, but we are free from its control and paralyzing effect. Our course is guided by an internal compass of convictions fueled by passions.

While we are aware of our circumstances and understand clearly the full weight of the potential consequences, we make decisions based neither on circumstances or consequences. When we choose this journey, we choose to relate to power and authority in a way that goes against that which is self-serving. Whatever we gain in power and authority, we receive as a gift to be given away.

We understand that it is not necessary for others to lose power for us to be more powerful. The real measure of our power is the freedom and opportunity we create for others. Men and women who are marked by integrity point the way to freedom. Leaders of integrity don't simply lead by example; they lead by essence. These leaders call others only to choose the life they have already chosen. They don't point the way down a certain path; they pave the way where no path exists. They inspire others not only by their words and actions, but by the promise of the kind of people we can become. A person of integrity never lies about the journey. He acknowledges in humility where he came from, who he is, and where he hopes to go. His accomplishments, as great as they may be, never overshadow his character.

When King David was preparing the people of Israel to build the temple, he called them together and asked them to give freely of their wealth, possessions, and skills. He led the way by giving generously of his own possessions. He would not ask the people under his care to do something he was not willing to do. And in his prayer, we discover why.

> But who am I, and who are my people, that we should be able to give as generously as this? Everything comes from you, and we have given you only what comes from your hand. We are aliens and strangers in your sight, as were all our forefathers. Our days on earth are like a shadow, without hope. O Lord our God, as for all this abundance that we have provided for building you a temple for your Holy Name, it comes from your hand, and all of it belongs to you. I know, my God, that you test the heart and are pleased with integrity. All these things have I given willingly and with honest intent. And now I have seen with joy how willingly your people who are here have given to you. (1 Chron. 29:14–17)

David wasn't just modeling the right thing; the right thing was the longing of his heart. He understood that God could see beyond actions and look straight into the soul. Among all of Israel, David had been entrusted with ultimate power and authority. His response was to give first and above the rest. Nothing he did was out of constraint or obligation. There was a joy and exhilaration in doing something that would bring pleasure to God.

Perhaps the most amazing thing about integrity is when you still choose to do what's right when you're all alone, no one sees you, and no one will know what you do. It's a wonderful thing when you look inside your own heart and like what you see.

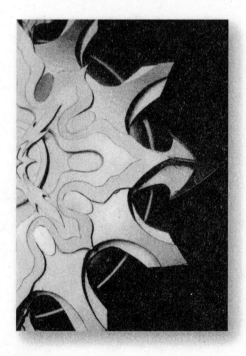

勇氣

5

Brave Hearts

After my family left San Salvador, Miami became my childhood home. Every couple of years we would relocate to a new neighborhood somewhere in Dade County. I was in the fifth grade, and we were about to break in a new school. The first day of school for the new kid in the neighborhood is always challenging. The added textures of our cosmopolitan community at times made it even turbulent.

I was sitting in the back of the room where all the overachievers tend to hang together. Just before the class began I realized I needed to sharpen my pencil to prepare for the day's work. I picked the shortest route to the sharpener at the front but found the way barricaded by a rather large fifth grader named Robby. Being a rather polite kid I looked at him and said, "Excuse me."

He looked a bit irritated. As he slowly and reluctantly leaned his chair back down, he recommended that I find another way back to my seat. "Don't come back this way" was how he put it.

I took longer than I needed to sharpen the pencil. I knew my time was limited, or I would whittle the instrument down to the eraser. I knew I had to make my first really important decision. Oh, the heavy responsibility of being in the fifth grade. Would I go back the same way? Would I dare challenge this oversize adolescent bully, or would I choose the path of least resistance and go around? Perhaps if I had been a Buddhist monk I would have chosen differently, but I was a ten-year-old kid trying to establish a reputation and find my place in the pecking order of the rough-and-tumble society otherwise known as elementary school. I really didn't have a choice. If I avoided the confrontation, everyone would know that I was a coward. (I *was* a coward. I just didn't want everyone to know I was a coward on the very first day. Reputation, after all, can save your hide.)

So I went back the way I came and faced my newfound nemesis. I was polite, as my mom had always taught me to be. I just said, "Excuse me." You could almost feel the heat coming off his head. I thought he was going to explode, which would have been a good thing. It would have saved me so much pain and suffering. This time he warned me more passionately to not choose this path again. I was in total agreement with him. I was so careful with my pencil that day. The last thing I wanted was to hear that lead point break. If I could just hang in the back and stay out of everyone's way, I could survive the first day. But with every story whose central character is a geek, it just couldn't work that way. For whatever reason the teacher picked me to come to the board and answer some question I am sure I didn't know. It's amazing how unaware teachers can be of what is actually happening in the classroom. They think it's an educational environment; we know it's a jungle.

Given little choice, I was forced to repeat the scenario, but this time he added a new line to his response. It was short and succinct, yet clear and without ambiguity. All he said was "Three o'clock."

I was new to the neighborhood, but I knew this was not a term of endearment, nor was he looking for an opportunity to get to know me better. It was a declaration of war. Three o'clock, when school ends, life ends. When the bell rang, it was for me that the bells would toll.

I didn't run. I waited in the playground, a battleground by any other name. He was running late. I could only hope he wasn't going to show. Maybe he was all talk. Maybe seeing me standing out there in the field alone brought fear and horror to his heart. Was it possible that this solitary figure caused him to run away with regret that he had ever challenged me?

No, it wasn't possible. As he approached me, I noticed he had two large bouncers walking behind him. Twin brothers, obviously related to Goliath. Just a few hours earlier Robby had been the biggest kid I had ever seen. Now he was in third place, and I faced a triad—Robby, Bobby, and Billy.

My brother, Alex, sat on a log a few feet away cheering me on. I was not encouraged. And as they approached I kept searching for something meaningful to say, something witty, something that might get me out of this situation. Instead I said something stupid: "I see you brought help." It was clear to me he didn't need help. It just sounded like something Paul Newman would say when playing Cool Hand Luke. I guess it escaped me how many times Luke got beaten up by the warden and prison guards.

Not missing a stride, Robby quickly responded, "No, they're just here to watch." A bully, but an honest man.

And then God intervened. At least now I know it was God.

We had a nanny from El Salvador who lived with us. For some reason Mom had instructed her to make sure we got home safely that day. It's a little embarrassing to have your nanny show up when you are about to rumble, but this was a good thing. My adversaries were a little confused. They didn't speak Spanish. They couldn't understand what was going on. I explained that she worked for my mom and was insisting that I leave. I told him to give me a minute and I'd take care of it.

I looked at her and shouted something like "Go home. I have business to take care of." And then I explained to them that she didn't understand English well enough and I would need to translate into Spanish. So I shouted in her direction, "No me dejas aquí. Me van a matar!" Which of course translates, "Don't leave me here. They're going to kill me!" I made several more attempts (in English, of course) to get her to leave, but she stepped in and made me leave by force.

Thank God I was bilingual. I figured I would have to face him again tomorrow, but at least for today I was alive and injury free. I'm not really sure what happened after that. Robby just dropped it. I think he was just astonished that I showed up at all. In any case it was over.

NATURAL-BORN HEROES

As you might have already gathered, I am not a natural-born hero. I suppose there are some people who are just naturally courageous, chiseled out of heroic rock with an infrastructure of nerves of steel. I'm just not one of them. I've always been well acquainted with fear, a rather natural sensation for me. Now, I have been creative with my fear, never stopping with just one. Fear of pain, fear of rejection, fear of failure, fear of humiliation, fear of death—you name it; I've been there. It's not that I'm always afraid. There have been times that I've even surprised myself with an act of bravery. But in order to remove any wiggle room as we begin this third quest, I want to remove any doubt: "Hi, my name is Erwin McManus, and I'm a coward."

We are about to begin a quest for honor. Our final destination is a life defined for courage. From beginning to end, we will be called to make courageous decisions even while we find ourselves gripped with fear. There are no exemptions. Any claims that you should be exempt from having to walk this path are rejected. Any attempt to create an elitist category for those who live heroic lives while placing yourself outside of it is unacceptable. If your argument is that you just aren't cut out for this kind of adventure, you can rest in the comfort that you are absolutely right, which is exactly why Jesus is calling you out. He calls you to begin a quest for honor. Courage is not an issue of birth. It is an expression of the heart. To be courageous is literally to be strong of heart. Both fear and courage are heart conditions. If you are weak of heart, fear not. Everyone who chooses to follow Jesus Christ receives a heart transplant. This new heart comes fully equipped with the spirit and courage of God ready to be pumped right into your timid soul.

To follow Jesus Christ is to choose to live in His adventure. How in the world could you ever imagine a life of faith that does not require risk? Faith and risk are inseparable. It should not come as a surprise to us then that a life of faith is a life of courage. While faith as a noun may be about belief, having faith is all about action. You cannot walk by faith and live in fear. You cannot walk with God and not face your fears. God calls you to dream great dreams and to have the courage to live them. Great dreams require great courage.

We are seldom afraid when our opposition is smaller than us. When we keep our challenges manageable, we not only manage our fear, but squelch our faith. One way to deal with our fears is to surround ourselves with security and predictability. We may look courageous when in fact all we've done is minimize our risk. Whenever God calls us to something, it inspires not only faith, but also fear. God always summons us to something bigger than ourselves. When he calls us to battle, the opposition will always be greater than the strength we have.

When we begin this quest for honor we always find ourselves starting as cowards and then growing in courage. A cursory study of the Bible could easily lead us to conclude that the Scriptures are full of heroic men and women who laughed in the face of danger and were strangers to fear. After all, just the names of those ancient men and women evoke inspiration and awe. Yet the reality is much different. The history of God's people is not a record of God searching for courageous men and women who could handle the task, but God transforming the hearts of cowards and calling them to live courageous lives. Adam and Eve hid; Abraham lied; Moses ran; David deceived; Esther was uncertain; Elijah contemplated suicide; John the Baptist doubted; Peter denied; Judas betrayed. And those are just some of the leading characters.

Every time an angel shows up, he begins the conversation with

"Fear not." The only apostolic prayer in the book of Acts concludes with, "Lord, consider their threats and give your servants courage to speak Your name with boldness" (4:29, author's translation).

Why does one pray for boldness? For one reason only: He's afraid. The same people who had crucified Jesus were now looking in the believers' direction. They feared for their lives, and they asked God for help. But notice what kind of help—not that God would remove their enemies, not even that God would change the circumstance, but that God would give them courage to do what they knew they had to do. The Scriptures are full of cowards who met God and began to live courageous lives.

The Hebrew word *ruach*, which is normally translated "spirit," "wind," or "breath," can also be translated "courage." When God breathes His Spirit into us, He not only gives us His power but, more importantly, His courage. When we read Paul's admonition to "be filled with the Spirit" (Eph. 5:18), we often translate it to mean "be filled with God's power." It would be far more accurate to understand it as "be filled with God's courage." What is the point of having God's power if you lack the courage to actually use it? Only when you embrace God's calling on your life will you need God-inspired courage. We often ask for God's power to accomplish our small dreams. We should instead cry out for God's courage to step out on His bold adventure. Maybe this is why Paul calls us to not be drunk with wine in this same Scripture. When we lack the courage to live the lives we have, when we are overwhelmed by the challenges we face, when we no longer have the strength just to make it through the day, we turn to outside sources just to help us survive. We try to sedate, medicate, and intoxicate our fears—anything for a little relief. What God offers when He invites us to be filled with the Spirit is not simply some elusive or magical power, but the character to live courageously and face our fears. Without courage we cannot live the life we choose—instead we choose to relinquish life. We conform to the path of least resistance and abdicate our freedom. So in the end a life without courage is a life without virtue!

CALLED TO COURAGE

One of my favorite Bible personalities is Joshua. He has become an inspiration and model to many followers of Christ. Fathers name their sons Joshua out of admiration for the qualities he personifies. When it mattered, Joshua always seemed to come through. When twelve warriors spied out the land of Canaan, ten came back gripped with fear. But Joshua and Caleb were ready to rumble. The other ten described their circumstance as a contrast between giants and grasshoppers. The enemies of course were the giants. God's people were like grasshoppers in their sight. They affirmed that the land was great, but their recommendation was to let it go. They would allow the dream of a better life to fall by the wayside to ensure their future existence. They literally would rather exist than live.

Joshua and Caleb saw the same things they saw. They didn't argue with any of the information, but their conclusion was exactly the opposite: "Let's go and take the land" (Num. 13:16–33).

How can you not like a guy like Joshua? The problem, of course, is just that he's Joshua—I'm Erwin. You can hear the difference just by saying the name. When you hear Erwin, you call your accountant. As of yet, there's been no rush to name firstborns Erwin, but thousands of years later, Joshua is still among the favorites. It's just too easy to put Joshua in another category, to draw a fast conclusion that he is so different from us that we could never be like him. Can an Erwin ever really be a Joshua? The answer is not only yes, but the truth is even more astonishing. Joshua was actually once an Erwin. Let's look together in the first chapter of his journal.

> After the death of Moses the servant of the LORD, the LORD said to Joshua son of Nun, Moses' aide: "Moses my servant is dead. Now then, you and all these people, get ready to cross the Jordan River into the land I am about to give to them—to the Israelites. I will give you every place where you set your foot, as I promised Moses. Your territory will extend from the desert to Lebanon, and from the

great river, the Euphrates—all the Hittite country—to the Great Sea on the west. No one will be able to stand up against you all the days of your life. As I was with Moses, so I will be with you; I will never leave you nor forsake you.

"Be strong and courageous, because you will lead these people to inherit the land I swore to their forefathers to give them. Be strong and very courageous. Be careful to obey all the law my servant Moses gave you; do not turn from it to the right or to the left, that you may be successful wherever you go. Do not let this Book of the Law depart from your mouth; meditate on it day and night, so that you may be careful to do everything written in it. Then you will be prosperous and successful. Have I not commanded you? Be strong and courageous. Do not be terrified; do not be discouraged, for the LORD your God will be with you wherever you go." (Josh. 1:1–9)

Joshua's opening entry establishes the vantage point from which he saw God's call to lead the people of Israel. Moses was dead. It was only after his death that God spoke to Joshua.

It is important that we understand Joshua's disposition as he began this new adventure with God. His only self-description was not that he was Moses' right-hand man or trusted warrior, but simply that he was Moses' aide. Yet his first assignment was not only to take over where Moses left off, but to accomplish what Moses didn't. After forty years in the wilderness, Moses failed to get God's people into the promised land. Now God was telling Joshua that he would do what Moses couldn't. The promise is bold and all-encompassing: "I will give you every place where you set your foot."

The second promise Joshua received was as revealing as it may have been inspiring: "No one will be able to stand up against you all the days of your life." A promise of conquest, yes, but not a promise of tranquillity. Joshua's enemies would not be able to stand against him, but they would try. The promised land would be a place of peace through conquest, not of peace through comfort. There would be two sides to the fulfillment of this challenge: God's part, "I will never leave you nor forsake you," and Joshua's part, "Be strong and courageous." This command was given to Joshua three times in the same discourse, much like the angelic "Holy, holy, holy." This is God's way of making something emphatic. It's like when we say "Yes!" "Yes!" and "Yes!" Joshua's success would be equally contingent on both sides of this equation.

GOD IS CALLING YOU OUT

We find here a perfect example of the intersection between the divine side and the human side of divine change. The magnitude of the responsibility that Joshua was entrusted with cannot be overstated. But God was specific in how He would accomplish His purpose in human history. He said, "You will lead these people to inherit the land I swore to their forefathers to give to them." It was God's promise, but it was Joshua's responsibility to bring it to pass.

This was not presumption on Joshua's part. To do anything less than take full responsibility for this enterprise would be negligence and disobedience. In the same way that God was with Moses, he would be with Joshua. It was Moses who faced down Pharaoh. It was Moses who called out the ten plagues and raised the staff to ignite the parting of the Red Sea. No one was confused about God's role in all of this. Neither was anyone confused about Moses' place in history. The people of Israel saw no dichotomy between the sacred work of God and the significant role of men and women to do that work. It was both God and Moses. It would be both God and Joshua. God would lead Joshua, but Joshua would lead Israel.

We seem uncomfortable with this reality in our contemporary understanding of how God works in human history. We feign humility, and without intention, affirm a false belief system. When something bad happens, it was obviously you or me, not God. But when something good happens, it's obviously not you or me, but God. It goes something like this: "It wasn't me; it was the Lord."

Sometimes when we say it, I am certain God didn't want the credit. I've heard some awful singing that the performer explained wasn't him or her, but the Lord. While everyone was applauding, I was wondering to myself, *Does God really sing this bad?* At the same time I've seen and experienced some amazing human kindness. Even when well intended, to say, "It wasn't me, only the Lord," demeans the marvelous work of God in the life of an individual.

There is something that God wants you to do—not to sit back and watch *Him* do or passively *wait* for Him to do, but a calling that God waits for *you* to embrace, pursue, and fulfill. God chooses to entrust His most sacred work to people just like you and me. This is exactly why Joshua was afraid. He understood what was happening. He felt the weight of responsibility falling on his shoulders. He knew it wasn't just a God thing; it was also a human thing.

It would have been great if God had commanded Joshua to set up camp along the Jordan and enjoy a season of fishing and basking in the sun. I imagine Joshua would have been thrilled if God had said, "There are giants in the land. I need a little time to get Canaan ready for you. Just wait and be patient, enjoy your stay, and when everything is prepared I'll send for you." Joshua could have then feigned a warrior's heart. He could have said something like, "No, Lord, I insist. Let me help You. You shouldn't go at this alone." Then God would have said, "No, Joshua, this one's too dangerous for you. I'll have to go it alone, but I'll be back. I would never think of putting you through this."

Wouldn't that be nice? Actually, it would be terribly boring. God expected more from Joshua and His people. God would give them the land, but they would have to take it. God would go *with* them, but He would not go *for* them. The future that God promised was now in Joshua's hands. It would require him to be both a desperate follower of God and an extraordinary leader of men. Joshua did not spare himself the embarrassment of exposing his own fear. He shared his struggle with us and allowed us through his transparency to join him in his journey. "Be strong and courageous . . . Be strong and very courageous . . . Be strong and courageous. Do not be terrified; do not be discouraged, for the LORD your God will be with you wherever you go."

This was essentially the only conversation God had held with Joshua to prepare him to lead. This was Joshua's Achilles' heel. It was where Joshua needed reinforcement. He was afraid to lead, but he would have to face his fear if he was to step into his future. It is not incidental that God exhorted him each time to be both strong *and* courageous. God was calling Joshua to more than just a single act of courage; he was to live a courageous life. His quest for honor would require him to both have a pioneering spirit and to become a spiritual pioneer, shaping a life he would use as the moral compass for his people. He would have to lead the way both in conquest and in character. God always chose people to lead the way.

THE STRENGTH OF COURAGE

There is a difference between momentary courage and moral courage. The first energizes you to rush into a burning building and save a child trapped in a fire. The second empowers you to live a life worthy of being emulated. Both kinds of courage are important. The first can be had without the second. The second is far more profound, and affects every decision and everything in a person's life. The Hebrew words for "be strong" mean to fasten yourself to something. It is a picture of someone grabbing hold of that which is right and true and refusing to let go. This is the pit bull part of character. It is the tenacious part of courage.

One of the less glamorous and most significant aspects in the quest for honor is simply doing what we know is right. It is all about submitting our lives to truth. Whether leading multitudes or just living life, we will find ourselves challenged to sacrifice what is right for what is expedient. To be strong is to be rooted and defined by what is true.

God was calling Joshua to build his life on what He had already said. He instructed him, "Be careful to obey all the law my servant Moses gave you; do not turn from it to the right or to the left, that you may be successful wherever you go. Do not let this Book of the Law depart from your mouth; meditate on it day and night, so that you may be careful to do everything written in it. Then you will be prosperous and successful" (Josh. 1:7–9).

While the future held many uncertainties and there were many lessons yet unlearned for this new leader, his success rested on none of this. The prosperity of his endeavor first and foremost depended on the trueness of his moral compass. He could not deviate to the left or to the right regardless of circumstance but could only move to the moral due north. He would establish his compass and strengthen the magnetic pull of his life course if he would allow nothing to separate him from the words of God. The path to courage would be paved through a life of meditating, day and night, on what God had spoken. His care to do all that God had commanded would be the rise or fall of his leadership.

The problem is not that we don't know what to do, but that we don't do what we know.

How many times have we pointed to not knowing God's will for our lives as the reason we are paralyzed from doing it? Yet, as with Joshua, there is enough truth in the Scriptures to fill our entire lives. The problem is not that we don't know what to do, but that we don't do what we know. Joshua knew what God had already said; now he was commanded to do it.

The key to the future is not revelation, but obedience. When we submit our lives to what God has made known, the future becomes clearer to us. When we neglect to do what we know, we begin to live as if we were walking through a fog. If we are not careful, we will find ourselves condemning God for being silent, when in fact we have condemned ourselves for refusing to listen. You may not know how God is going to solve your financial crisis, but you can know that the solution is never to steal. You may not know when God is going to bring that special person into your life, but the solution is not to compromise. You may fear the consequence of telling the truth, but God's solution is not to lie.

One of the greatest mistakes we make in our spiritual journeys is circumventing the process of accomplishing our God-given dreams by trying to achieve those dreams in a manner that violates God's character. Joshua was about to lead God's people into war, yet God's emphasis was on the quality of his character. Be strong. Have the courage to do what is right regardless of circumstance or consequence. Live a life of conviction.

God was calling Joshua—and He calls us—to live from the inside out. When we live by truth, we establish our integrity. Each "be strong" was followed by a call to be courageous, even *very* courageous. This particular phrase is unique. It implies speed and urgency. It literally means to be alert, to be quick minded. God was ordering Joshua not only to hold on to the good, but to pursue it with passion. He was to move with urgency and purpose.

Our courage directly affects the speed at which the future unfolds. Israel's fear and disobedience set their entry into the promised land back an entire generation. Joshua was to accelerate the process by moving courageously forward. He was to be both quick of mind and quick of foot. Remember, every place that Joshua set his foot would be his. God was waiting to give him the land, but the soles of his feet had to touch the ground before he would gain possession. Canaan would be his literally one step at a time. This imagery reminds me of the words of Paul in Romans 16:20 where he tells us that "the God of peace will soon crush Satan under your feet."

Talk about an interesting clash of metaphors. The God of peace, in all the images that conjures, will in fact crush Satan. As stark as the picture is, it is a good reminder that God is not passive or pacifistic, but He is a peacemaker. He is at war against all the forces of evil. Though we may be His enemies, He is not ours. He fights for us even when we fight against Him. But the last part of that verse is what most specifically relates to Joshua. Satan will be crushed not under the feet of God, which would make far more sense, but under our feet.

God loves to do His work through ordinary people like you and me. Even cosmic battles will be won through dust and breath. Strangely enough, the eternal work of God is done largely on a human timetable. God would wait for Joshua to step out.

Joshua's responsibility was to unleash God's purpose in human history one step at a time. I can imagine there have been many times when God has passionately called us to step up the pace. And one of the things that helps us move faster in a world filled with chaos and uncertainty is acting on what we know. Even if you're only certain about a few things, if you will live by them without wavering, you will find yourself moving forward with increasing velocity.

THE SPEED OF COURAGE

When we walk in truth, we accelerate the process and literally fast-forward the future. When we remove hesitation and disobedience from our lives, we not only begin to live more fulfilling lives, but actually seem to live more life than others. When we are slow to live in God's truth, we begin to experience life as a slow drip. But when we passionately obey God's word, life is unleashed like a wide-open fire hydrant. At the same time, when we are defined by truth, when our lives are shaped by the heart of God, we are able to respond without hesitation when the moment calls for courage. Crisis rarely affords us the luxury of contemplation. If you have to weigh all your options, you may be too late.

Some recent studies of the thinking process of firemen raised some startling conclusions. The researchers were trying to determine how these individuals were able to make such critical decisions in the heat of crisis and at blinding speed. A bad decision would cost them or others their lives. Yet time and time again the best of these just seemed to know what to do. What is being discovered is that these lifesavers are not weighing multiple options at one time. They're not evaluating multiple scenarios and then choosing the best among them. They act on their first thoughts. They have absolute confidence in their instincts. There are no two options from which to choose. They don't wait long enough for the second option to even emerge. They have developed an intuition that allows them to move without hesitation and with the greatest effectiveness. In their line of work, the harsh reality is that he who hesitates is lost.

Yet without this instinct, this unique quality of intuition, another person could make an equally quick decision and fall to his death. Most of us would find ourselves confused and paralyzed as the situation continued to heat up. Though we may have great instincts in other areas and be considered highly intuitive in our fields of specialization, we may lack the essential components to be effective at this particular task. Those firemen upon whom we so desperately depend have instincts that draw on the right information and experience.

I am convinced this is exactly what Joshua had. God built in him the spiritual reservoir from which he would be able to draw in the future. If he absorbed through meditation the truth of God, he would be able to trust his intuition to fulfill God's purpose. If he allowed himself to be shaped by God's voice, he would resonate with the voice of God when he spoke. If he would live to know God, he would know how God wanted him to live. To do the will of God is to know the will of God. When we make the hard choice to be strong—to fasten ourselves—we will then be able to live courageously and to move fast.

The four of us were together at the home of Don Richardson, author of *Peace Child* and *Eternity in Their Hearts*. Paul (Don's son) and Cyndi Richardson and Kim and I were sitting outside in deck chairs enjoying the California sun. All of a sudden Paul and Cyndi's nephew fell into the pool. Within seconds the water was over his head and a look of panic was on his face. I remember thinking to

myself, *Get up! Jump in! Pull him!* From my perspective I was pushing myself out of my chair at meteoric speed.

Then I saw this blur flash right by me. I'm not sure if I actually
saw or heard the splash, but before everything came back into focus,
Cyndi was lifting the small child out of the water. It was nothing less
than superhuman. I felt like a sumo wrestler running the hundred
meters next to an Olympic sprinter. To say I was stunned was an
understatement. Remember the characters from *The Matrix* who
moved at Lava-Lamp speed while Neo dodged bullets? That's exactly
what it felt like.

While I was thinking, she was acting. I can't really remember
what was going through my mind. I can say with all honesty, I was
going to jump into the water, clothes and all, and pull him out, but
there was a difference between us. Her courage resulted in quick
thinking and immediate action. It was passionate urgency. The
strength of her values and the intensity of her passion cut through
every hesitation and got the job done. When courage is fueled by
integrity and formed out of humility, it allows us to act without hesitation when the moment requires it. There is a direct relationship
between courage and our ability to respond quickly.

When courage is fully expressed, it works in this tandem: We
become strong and courageous. We will not relinquish what we
know is right, and we will not hesitate to do the right thing. The
more tenaciously we hold on to the truth, the more we become trustworthy. We can never use the excuse that God has not given us
enough information, nor can we hide behind a claim that God has
not provided enough lead-time.

PASSING THROUGH THE GAUNTLET

The moment you know what God wants of you is the moment to do
it. He doesn't expose sin in our lives so we can take care of it later.
When God speaks, it requires immediate attention. We might be

tempted to put things off until it's easier to deal with them. We might hesitate in an attempt to minimize the consequences. Yet courage does what's right regardless of situation or consequence.

We have to ask ourselves, Am I really trying to discern God's will, or to determine whether I want to do it? Am I really working through all the options to find what God wants, or trying to find the option that has no risk or downside? If God showed you His desired way for you and it was fraught with peril and filled with suffering, would you choose another way?

You cannot live this quest for honor without courage. If you respond to God's call, it will require great things of you. You will be tested to the very core of your being. God will not save you from the fire, but in fact throw you into it. The promise that He will be with you and never leave or forsake you is both promise and warning. A divine journey cannot be completed without divine intervention. It will be like an odyssey without maps to guide your way. Your character will be your only compass on many long and dark nights.

It is here that we often find ourselves paralyzed and incapable of continuing the journey. But we must come to the place where God's calling becomes more important to us than even our own lives.

As we have discovered on this journey, courage is not the absence of fear; it is the absence of self. Courage is the highest expression of humility. Courage moves us to risk ourselves for the sake of others or a higher cause. Courage allows us to live free from self-preservation and to live generously creative lives. Courage frees us from the fears that would rob us of life itself. It is here that courage and creativity come together. Without courage we become conformists. With courage we once again become the creative beings God designed us to become. The fear of God is not only the beginning of all wisdom, but

Courage frees us from the fears that would rob us of life itself.

the place of freedom from all fear. When we are free from fear, we are finally free to live.

For me it was the corner of Ervay and Grand where my heart pounded and my hands were balmy from sweat because I was overwhelmed with fear. The intense streets of South Dallas were an unlikely place for me to choose to pastor, but it was clearly the place God was choosing for me. Driving too fast out of panic, I abruptly stopped my car near that troubled intersection of the dark side of humanity.

When we are free from fear, we are finally free to live.

I waited for a verse to comfort me, some words from God to bring me peace. I had enough of them memorized. "I can do all things through Christ who strengthens me." "Greater is he that is in me than he that is in the world." Even God's words to Joshua, "Be strong and courageous. Do not be afraid; do not be discouraged, for the Lord your God will be with you wherever you go." But none of those came to mind.

The verse I had never committed to memory somehow came crashing through my skull. "To live is Christ and to die is gain" (Phil. 1:21). Those words came uninvited and echoed through every chamber of my soul. It was God's invitation to join Him on the quest for honor, to live a life of genuine courage. The way was clear; if I would just die, I could begin to live. The adventure God was calling me to was only for those who would relinquish their lives and let God raise them from the dead. This path was one where only dead men can go. Cowards are more than welcome, but you should know up front that how you begin the journey is not how you will finish it. Who you will become will surprise even you.

If we choose this way, we'll find our hearts resonating with the words of Paul:

> I eagerly expect and hope that I will in no way be ashamed, but will have sufficient courage so that now as always Christ will be exalted in my body, whether by life or by death. For to me, to live is Christ

and to die is gain. If I am to go on living in the body, this will mean fruitful labor for me. Yet what shall I choose? I do not know! I am torn between the two: I desire to depart and be with Christ, which is better by far; but it is more necessary for you that I remain in the body. Convinced of this, I know that I will remain, and I will continue with all of you for your progress and joy in the faith, so that through my being with you again your joy in Christ Jesus will overflow on account of me. Whatever happens, conduct yourselves in a manner worthy of the gospel of Christ. (Phil. 1:20–27)

A QUEST FOR NOBILITY

UNLEASHING THE GENERATIVE SPIRIT

An uprising against a self-indulgent life.

A revolution of the soul overthrowing greed and hate.

This gauntlet leads us through gratitude

to wholeness and ultimately to generosity!

Creating out of the pieces through the power of love.

信實

6

Endless Wellsprings

"It's a need."

"It's a want."

That pretty much summarizes the argument. Kim insisted it was a necessity; I was emphatic that it was a luxury. We hadn't been married that long, and while our dating and engagement were somewhat turbulent, our marriage had pretty much been smooth sailing. But here we were at an impasse. We held diametrically opposed positions, and neither one of us would budge. She knew when we got married that I fancied myself a modern-day monastic. To say the least, I was disappointed that I was finding her to be a materialist.

My pastoral salary was a heaping five thousand dollars a year, and I couldn't believe she wanted to use the money in such a frivolous way. She wanted to buy a bed, and I wasn't having it. We would sleep on the floor. If God wanted us to have a bed, He would have to ship it from heaven. I look back now and realize the greatest miracle is that Kim is still with me.

I was unbending, but she was incredibly flexible. When I came home from work, she had spent the afternoon decorating the bedroom. It was a masterpiece of love and creativity. Right in the middle she had laid out every blanket and sheet we owned and had designed a makeshift bed for us. Not one ounce of bitterness on her part. No residue of anger or resentment. She has always been a marvel to me.

Other than one family member all the way in Florida, no one knew our dilemma nor our living situation. We had decided that if God wanted us to have a bed, He would make it happen. We both agreed that we wouldn't let the information leak. Those weeks on the floor were some of the most enjoyable nights of my life. We had such a great time enjoying that season together. I have to admit, my position changed with time. It wasn't so much the Scripture passages Kim would share with me or the strength of her arguments when we broached the subject. Really, the defining point of insight for me was when I couldn't bend anymore. I suppose sometimes if God can't get through to you from the head or the heart, he just comes at you from the back. I was quickly being won over to the view that a bed was more necessity than luxury. Nevertheless, I wouldn't surrender my stance. Maybe I was just too cheap to buy a bed, but in the midst of that, there was genuine, noble intention.

Then we got the strangest phone call. It was Jim Beals, whom Kim and I had met in Fort Worth years before when we were among the throngs of starving seminarians. Jim and Neva Beals served at a nearby church and adopted students while they were pursuing their education. They were our angels, and I had the privilege of mentoring Jim in the process.

It had been several years since I had taken Jim through the book of James, and then we had moved away. As so often happens, our contact had become sparse and intermittent, so his phone call came as a surprise. He was on a business trip, he explained to Kim. Sitting in his hotel, he picked up the Gideon's Bible that was placed in his room, and just happened to open to the book of James. Reading those familiar passages rekindled memories of our times together, and as he prayed for us, he had the strangest thought. He suddenly felt compelled to buy us a bed. Jim is essentially sane, so this peculiar inspiration seemed odd to him. But instead of ignoring it, he pursued it as if it were a direct mandate from God. When he called and shared his experience with Kim and then asked her if by chance we needed a bed, she was ecstatic—not because a bed might potentially be on the way, but because God had unexplainably made our need known to someone who could know from no other source.

In his profession Jim sold hospital furniture, and beds were a part of his inventory. He simply told us to choose whatever bed we wanted and that's what we would get. As committed as I was to sleeping on the floor, I was now equally committed to sleeping on the best mattress available. That Sealy Posturepedic queen-size mattress lasted us for nearly seventeen years. This experience has given new meaning to the concept that God is watching my back.

There is a verse that tells us that God gives sleep to those He loves, yet I have become convinced over the years that God was doing more than just ensuring me restful nights for many years to come. I was striving to be a monastic, convinced it was the only option if I were not to be a materialist. I knew that greed was a corrosive, and that endless wanting is one of the surest ways of corrupting your soul. I wanted to be free from greed and live freely. In my sincerity, I misdirected the trajectory of my life course. I had concluded that the opposite of greed was poverty and that the solution to wanting was not having. But I would soon discover that the opposite of greed is not poverty, but generosity. While it is no small challenge to learn how to live without, it is an even greater challenge to learn to live with. A part of my pursuit of poverty was an abdication of responsibility. If my sole pursuit was to have nothing, I was in the end the most selfish of all people. Even here my life must not be just about me, and at the same time I must not be afraid to enjoy the life that God has given me.

It is here we begin our quest for nobility. Not nobility by virtue of royal birth, but nobility that is defined by the character of the person. A *noble* was understood to be a person of great wealth. His nobility was expressed not by all he possessed, but through the generosity he displayed. Nobility was more than social class. It was a call to live a life of the highest quality. In fact true nobility is demonstrated best through selfless sacrifice. If all that you have is simply for your own pleasure, you are not a noble, but a glutton. The noble use all that they are and all that they have for the good of others. And in this, they find great pleasure.

THE NEGLECT OF GREAT THINGS

I've seen this tension in the lives of many people as they are working out what it means to be a follower of Jesus Christ. On one particular occasion during worship, by chance I overheard a husband and wife singing among the congregation. Even amid the other voices, I could tell they were amazingly gifted. We were really struggling to find musical talent as we moved toward a more progressive approach in music. I knew they could really help us and wondered why they had not stepped up to the challenge. They were not new to the church. They had come to faith through the church and had been there for almost a decade.

The husband explained that they had come to Los Angeles with an ambition for the music industry. They knew they had God-given talent, but concluded that they loved the limelight too much. In his own words they struggled with pride and arrogance and so decided not to sing publicly. I tried to help them see that two sins are not better than one. If their self-evaluation revealed that they struggle with the sin of arrogance, the solution is not to hide their talent, but to choose humility. Negligence is not a virtue.

Their conclusion was similar to my earlier conclusion that the solution to greed is poverty. What they needed was a change of heart. God entrusted them with these resources not so they would hoard or ignore them, but so they would use them for the good and enjoyment of others. The solution is not to stop doing good in order to ensure that we don't do evil. That's like adding insult to injury. God frees us from sin not to leave us empty, but to fill us with life. His goal is not to replace sin with inaction. In other words you don't fill a vacuum with a vacuum. You overcome selfishness with servant-hood and greed with generosity.

I wonder how many of us are neglecting the good we could do to avoid the evil we might do. It is tempting to ignore our responsibil-ity for others, to neglect the contribution God intends for us to make in the name of our own personal holiness. Is it right to choose a life of abject poverty if in fact God has entrusted you with the capacity to generate great wealth? If our entire lives are given to the salvation of our own souls, haven't we simply spiritualized a life that is essen-tially self-seeking?

As tempting as it may be to live detached from the world around us, it is not in keeping with the heart of God. Jesus did not come into this world and live His life on a mountaintop isolated from human suffering. He walked among us, ate with us, and shared in our humanity. He did not heal lepers from a distance, but touched them into wholeness. He pressed His disciples and prayed for them to be in the world but not of the world. The focus of their three years together was not the salvation of the Twelve, but their ministry to the entire planet. Jesus constantly pushed them to think outside the box. He commanded them to feed over five thousand people when they had no more than five loaves of bread and two fish; He healed on the Sabbath, violating the traditional interpretation of the religious lead-ers; He commissioned His Twelve to make disciples of all nations; He continuously inspired them to dream great dreams and chal-lenged them to trust God to do unimaginable things through them. He seemed determined to teach them that if they would commit themselves to the care of humanity, they would discover the endless reservoir of God the Great Provider.

John describes how a multitude had gathered around Jesus as He taught on the mountainside. He tells us:

When Jesus looked up and saw a great crowd coming toward him, he said to Philip, "Where shall we buy bread for these people to eat?" He asked this only to test him, for he already had in mind what he was going to do.

Philip answered him, "'Eight months' wages would not buy enough bread for each one to have a bite!"

Another of his disciples, Andrew, Simon Peter's brother, spoke up, "Here is a boy with five small barley loaves and two small fish, but how far will they go among so many?"

Jesus said, "Have the people sit down." There was plenty of grass in that place, and the men sat down, about five thousand of them. Jesus then took the loaves, gave thanks, and distributed to those who were seated as much as they wanted. He did the same with the fish.

When they had all had enough to eat, he said to his disciples, "Gather the pieces that are left over. Let nothing be wasted." So they gathered them and filled twelve baskets with the pieces of the five barley loaves left over by those who had eaten. (John 6:5–13)

THANKS FOR NOTHING

The generosity that God intended to display through His disciples went beyond their own capacity. Soon the disciples would learn that God's favorite context for miracles is sacrifice.

It is so easy to confuse Christianity with Buddhism, especially on this particular journey. We know that greed corrupts and destroys, so we conclude the only way to be free is to detach ourselves from all human desire until we withdraw ourselves from the world in which we live. Jesus, on the other hand, was accused of being a glutton and sinner. He clearly enjoyed the life that He lived. He was chastised for not living a monastic existence. Even His disciples were authorized by Him to break the rules. Jesus was having way too much fun for the religious observers who watched Him with disdain. I think they were also envious.

Is it possible to be a genuinely holy person and indulge in the pleasures of this life? Sometimes we forget that God created the world for man's pleasure and enjoyment. The Garden of Eden was a garden of pleasure, not of obligation. God put man into a deep sleep, took a rib from his side, and created woman, not because man didn't have enough responsibility, but because God saw how He could enhance man's enjoyment of living. The Scriptures tell us that God concluded it was not good for man to be alone. Laced within the concept of goodness are enjoyment, pleasure, and especially love. I wasn't there, but I am certain that the fruit on the trees tasted great.

We were created to enjoy God's world, and the world was created not only to declare the glory of God, but to satisfy our desires and meet our needs. From the design of our planet's atmosphere to the aroma of a good latte, creation is here for our good and pleasure. When we replace greed with generosity, we exchange a black hole for a wellspring. The goal is not so much to have less, but to give more. Generosity is the result of a life in continuous overflow. It is the exponential result of wholeness. What begins at 51 percent will continue to increase as we grow in the fullness of Christ.

We will find on our quest for nobility that God is the ultimate expression of wholeness. That's where this journey will take us, but where does it begin? What is the path to wholeness? We will see this path more clearly if we recognize that greed's ugly stepsister is ungratefulness. Greed always wants more. When we are greedy, we are never satisfied. Whatever we receive from others, we conclude we deserve. And in whatever quantity it may come, it is never enough. Lack of gratitude is a manifestation of an abundance of greed. From the vantage point of the taker, it is his or her justification for always demanding. He is endlessly disappointed in others. No one ever comes through for him. No one ever keeps his promises. Everyone always falls short of his expectations. There is no need for thanks, except thanks for nothing.

No truth, no matter how profound, will find its way into a heart that is absent of gratitude.

The dilemma in our pursuit for wholeness is that brokenness is often laced with ungratefulness. In fact I am convinced that perpetual brokenness is defined by a lack of gratitude, and this is the key to the path of wholeness. Whatever else we may need, whatever support systems might be helpful to us, whatever insights or truths may aid us in the journey, nothing will heal us if we are ungrateful. No truth, no matter how profound, will find its way into a heart that is absent of gratitude. Gratitude is the singular characteristic that will determine how far we travel on this quest for nobility. It is gratitude that nurtures wholeness and expresses itself as generosity in the end. Gratitude is the pathway of love. It unleashes the healing power of love. It increases our capacity to experience love and to give it.

UNLEASHING GRATITUDE

He had incredible potential, a keen intellect, and a passionate heart for the things of God. But as substantial as his gifting was, it was equally matched by his brokenness. I was more than happy to invest in his life, and certainly his promise and eagerness were motivation enough. I was mentoring a small community while working a full-time job and trying to be faithful as a good husband and father of two. It caught me by surprise the day he sat me down and reprimanded me. It was no small rebuke. He told me I had let him down. I had not followed through on my commitment. I was not giving him enough time and investment.

I considered arguing with him, but experience reminded me it would be no use. So I just took him home. We sat in the living room with my wife, Kim, who has a wonderful way of cutting through everything and just getting at the truth. I only asked her one question. "Honey, who do I spend more time with, you or him?"

I'll never forget Kim's response. "Are you kidding? I thought you were married to him." The conversation was over. The point I couldn't make was made with emphasis.

When we lack wholeness, our ability to perceive the investment of others is damaged. Our perception is that we're just not getting what we need. The truth is, nothing sticks because our hearts lack the proper texture for the investment to mature. This is the mystery of gratitude. Without it, all the investment in the world will not result in wholeness. Thankfully, this particular individual had a dramatic change of heart. A decade later it's my privilege to know him and I am always amazed at the level of his servanthood. It certainly wasn't the result of learning something new.

Sometimes the simple truth is the most profound. That we will never become whole without gratefulness probably doesn't seem complex enough to be true. For whatever it's worth, I have always found the greatest mysteries of life to be hidden in simplicity. The quest for nobility is a journey that takes us from gratitude to wholeness to generosity. There is no other path that leads us to the freedom that makes us complete. There is no way to circumvent the process. It all begins here. And as we will discover, it also ends here. It is a life of gratitude that makes us whole, overwhelms us with love, and moves us to live generous lives.

In Luke, Jesus has an unusual encounter with a Pharisee and a sinful woman, and out of it comes one of the most unorthodox teachings you'll find in the Bible. The event goes like this:

> Now one of the Pharisees invited Jesus to have dinner with him, so he went to the Pharisee's house and reclined at the table. When a woman who had lived a sinful life in that town learned that Jesus was eating at the Pharisee's house, she brought an alabaster jar of perfume, and as she stood behind him at his feet weeping, she began to wet his feet with her tears. Then she wiped them with her hair, kissed them and poured perfume on them.
>
> When the Pharisee who had invited him saw this, he said to himself, "If this man were a prophet, he would know who is touching him and what kind of woman she is—that she is a sinner."
>
> Jesus answered him, "Simon, I have something to tell you."
>
> "Tell me, teacher," he said.
>
> "Two men owed money to a certain moneylender. One owed him five hundred denarii, and the other fifty. Neither of them had

the money to pay him back, so he canceled the debts of both. Now which of them will love him more?"

Simon replied, "I supposed the one who had the bigger debt canceled."

"You have judged correctly," Jesus said.

Then he turned toward the woman and said to Simon, "Do you see this woman? I came into your house. You did not give me any water for my feet, but she wet my feet with her tears and wiped them with her hair. You did not give me a kiss, but this woman, from the time I entered, has not stopped kissing my feet. You did not put oil on my head, but she has poured perfume on my feet. Therefore I tell you her many sins have been forgiven—for she loved much. But he who has been forgiven little loves little."

Then Jesus said to her, "Your sins are forgiven."

The other guests began to say among themselves, "Who is this who even forgives sins?"

Jesus said to the woman, "Your faith has saved you; go in peace." (Luke 7:36–50)

This story is pretty straightforward. While Jesus is at the house of Simon the Pharisee, this exclusive gathering is interrupted by an immoral woman. The assumptions made are that she was most likely a prostitute, perhaps even Mary Magdalene. Simon is incensed and sees Jesus' lack of indignation as proof that he is not the Messiah. In response to Simon's thought, Jesus begins to teach through a parable. It translates something like this: Two guys were in huge debt (each makes $50,000 a year). One guy owed Visa somewhere in the range of $150,000. The other guy owed about two months' salary on the same card. Mr. Visa, in an act of generosity, decided to forgive them both. Wouldn't it be great to get your Visa bill back after Christmas and find it zeroed out?

Then Jesus asked the question that was essentially a no-brainer: "Which one of these two would love the creditor more?" Simon, the renowned teacher answers, "I suppose the one who had the bigger debt canceled," and Jesus affirms his conclusion.

Then Jesus moves toward application. He begins to describe the reception Simon gave him when he came to his home in contrast to the actions of this unnamed woman. Simon didn't even give Jesus the traditional greeting of a kiss, but the woman, from the time Jesus entered, had not stopped kissing his feet. Simon did not extend the common courtesy of offering a bowl of water and towel to cleanse Jesus' feet, but the woman wet his feet with her tears and wiped them with her hair. Simon chose not to honor Jesus by anointing his head with oil, but the woman lavished Jesus by pouring an entire alabaster jar of perfume on his feet. Then Jesus draws the oddest conclusion, "Therefore, I tell you, her many sins have been forgiven—for she loved much. But he who has been forgiven little loves little" (v. 47).

How would you have heard this if you had been Simon? Jesus was telling him that he lacks her capacity to love because he's only had a few things forgiven. What for Simon was a condition that brought judgment and condemnation, for Jesus it seemed to be a source of benefit. Is he really saying that the reason she could lavish him with such shameless love is because she has been such a horrific sinner? Is his deficit in love the outcome of a life well lived? What exactly is he suggesting? Is it really necessary to be a great sinner to be a great lover?

At face value the application seems insane or inane. What am I supposed to do? If I lack the ability to love, am I supposed to just close my Bible, throw caution to the wind, and go on a rampage of unrestrained hell-raising? After all, if her capacity to love was greater than Simon's because she had so much more sin forgiven, wouldn't this be the most expedient solution? I could come back after a year with an expanded capacity to love as the result of my greater need for forgiveness.

On the other hand, it's quite possible Jesus meant something different. In fact let me encourage you not to apply the former suggestion. Isn't Jesus really saying that Simon's capacity to love is directly related to his depth of gratitude? The woman knew she was a sinner. She understood the grace that had been extended to her. Her heart was filled with gratitude. She could do nothing less than lavish her worship and thanks on Jesus.

Simon just didn't get it. He couldn't see the depth of his own sinfulness. He was in denial concerning his need for mercy and grace. He believed he was righteous in the sight of God. He saw it as Jesus' privilege to be in his presence rather than his privilege to be in Christ's presence. His self-righteousness clouded his thinking. He would agree with Jesus that he needed very little forgiveness. While the woman may have been the worst of sinners, he was the best of people. His standard was how much one had sinned; Jesus' standard was how grateful one was for forgiveness. The woman's gratitude unleashed an irrepressible love. Simon was uncomfortable not only around overt sinfulness, but also around genuine expressions of love. Her gratitude left her with a promise of peace; his lack of gratitude left him in pieces.

Gratitude is the healing ointment for brokenness. It is central to the entire experience and journey of the Christian faith. Gratitude and grace share the same etymology and root meaning. When we properly connect to God, our lives become an endless expression of thanks and praise.

INSANELY HAPPY

Paul said, "Rejoice in the Lord always. I will say it again: Rejoice! Let your gentleness be evident to all. The Lord is near. Do not be anxious about anything, but in everything, by prayer and petition, with thanksgiving, present your requests to God. And the peace of God, which transcends all understanding, will guard your hearts and your minds in Christ Jesus" (Phil. 4:4–7).

Paul lived a life of celebration, finding contentment in every circumstance of life. He described himself as the worst of all sinners. I don't really think this is accurate. I think there were individuals far more wicked than Paul ever was. Certainly the likes of Adolf Hitler and even Charles Manson would vie for the title. Paul was indeed wicked before God, a self-righteous murderer who needed forgiveness; nevertheless he most likely wasn't dealing with facts when he spoke of himself as the most notorious of all people, even in his own time. He was expressing the sentiment of his heart as he embraced the profound nature of forgiveness. Paul, like the unnamed woman who showered Jesus with affection, could only live his life as an expression of love for God. He, too, had been forgiven much.

Maybe this is what Jesus meant when he said the last will be first and that the least will be the greatest. Is it possible that the worst of all sinners, the one who has the most forgiven, will be found the greatest lover in the kingdom of God, not by the measure of who sinned the most, but who embraced the most forgiveness? In this case, I, too, want to be the worst of all sinners, the one who sees himself as needing and receiving the most forgiveness. Forgiveness unlocks gratitude and gratitude unleashes love.

Forgiveness and gratitude are inseparable. When we receive forgiveness, we grow in gratefulness. When we grow in gratefulness, we are more willing to give forgiveness. Our ability to receive forgiveness is directly related to our willingness to give it. Beyond that our model for forgiveness is Jesus Himself. Paul reminds us, "Bear with each other and forgive whatever grievances you may have against one another. Forgive as the Lord forgave you. And over all these virtues put on love, which binds them all together in perfect unity" (Col. 3:13–14).

When we are grateful, we forgive freely. A direct benefit of gratitude is the freedom from bitterness. When we are grateful, we are not bound to grudges or vengeance. Gratitude enables us to be generous with love. Forgiveness is a significant part of this. When there is a deficit of love, there is also a reluctance to forgive. This is a significant dilemma for us in our journeys toward emotional well-being in that an unwillingness to forgive will circumvent the process of becoming whole.

In the same way that gratitude is intertwined with forgiveness, brokenness is often perpetuated by bitterness. It's not that bitterness is the cause of our brokenness, but that bitterness will circumvent the healing process. What makes this even more complicated is that oftentimes a broken person is more than justified to be embittered. Sometimes when I hear the tragic stories and the horrific experiences others have gone through, it's hard not to take on their offenses and become embittered with them. It's not an easy thing to tell someone who has been deeply hurt that her own road to healing is to forgive those who hurt her.

Aside from the fact that offenders need forgiveness, to forgive is essential in the process of healing. You cannot remain embittered and find wholeness. Even when those who have hurt you neither seek forgiveness nor desire it, it is still necessary that we forgive. In a reminder that we should not grieve the spirit of God, the Scriptures call us to "get rid of all bitterness, rage and anger, brawling and slander, along with every form of malice. Be kind and compassionate to one another, forgiving each other, just as in Christ God forgave you" (Eph. 4:31–32). This passage beseeches us to replace bitterness with forgiveness. In a conversation between Peter and Simon the Sorcerer, Peter makes this assessment of Simon's heart: "I see that you are full of bitterness and captive to sin" (Acts 8:23). When we forgive, it sets us and others free. Bitterness on the other hand holds us captive. When someone desires forgiveness, it is your gift to give out of the generosity of your spirit. Even if one does not desire your forgiveness, it is critical to be free from the bitterness that will enslave you.

Again, even as gratitude and forgiveness are inseparable, so are ungratefulness and bitterness. When we are grateful, we see and experience life with a healthy optimism. When we lack gratitude, we move toward pessimism and even cynicism. An ungrateful heart always sees what's wrong with life. The longer we live without gratitude, the more embittered we become. The more embittered we become, the more we find ourselves overwhelmed with depression. Bitterness in the end leads to hopelessness. If we are to enjoy lives of gratitude, we must break free from the gravitational pull of bitterness. For in the same way that gratitude leads to wholeness, bitterness will leave us shattered and broken. In this condition we will find ourselves unable to experience the life God dreams for us, and at the same time we will leave others cut and bleeding as they press against our sharp edges.

Bitterness creates an illusion of control and power. Bitterness is a form of hate. It is anger facing backwards. When we are embittered toward someone, we hold him prisoner to an experience or action in the past. In our minds our bitterness holds him captive and does not allow him to move forward. The reality is that our bitterness traps no one but ourselves. If the offender genuinely seeks forgiveness, even when you are unwilling to give it, he or she is made free. The only person you keep trapped in yesterday when you are unwilling to forgive is yourself. If you remain bitter long enough, you will eventually move to despair. Bitterness requires that you live in the past; hope requires that you live for tomorrow. Gratitude not only allows you to enjoy the present, but keeps you looking forward to the future.

THE NOBLE MIND

The concept of nobility has as much to do with how a person sees things as the status to which he is born. In its origins to be noble meant to be "high-minded." This does not imply being arrogant, but describes a person whose mind was focused on those things that were most honorable. The person with a heart of nobility focused his or her mind on the highest thoughts, principles, and motivations. In this sense our quest for nobility presses us to see life from God's vantage point, to recognize God's activity even in the midst of life's darkest moments. We are called to take a gauntlet that challenges us to see the light when there seems to be none. Gratitude accomplishes this very thing. Gratitude fuels optimism and inspires hope. Paul tells us in Romans that the quality of hope can only exist in relationship to the future. Concerning hope he explains, "Hope that is seen is no hope at all. Who hopes for what he already has? But if we hope for what we do not yet have, we wait for it patiently" (8:24–25).

Paul is giving us insight into the quality and nature of hope and optimism. Hope cannot exist in the past. When hope is directed toward the past, it becomes despair. Hope cannot exist in anything that we have already obtained. Even something that once generated hope loses that capacity once it is received. Hope can only exist in the future. Living in the past is a graveyard for hope. Existentialism—living for the now—in the end will lead us to the same dead end—a hopeless existence. When you refuse to let go of the past, you lose all hope. When you walk backwards into the future, you cannot see anything to hope for. This is one reason why a person who is embittered ultimately cannot be encouraged into a new frame of thinking. Until he is willing to let go of the past, he is not ready to take hold of the future.

Bitterness will not only rob you of the joy of the present, but will steal from you all the promise of tomorrow. When we refuse to forgive because we do not want to let those who have hurt us move on to a fresh future, we sacrifice our own future in the process. Forgiveness is like a breath of fresh air. You must inhale it and receive it and also exhale it as you give it. As we grow in gratitude, we find ourselves forgiving more quickly and more freely. Our readiness to forgive will draw others to ourselves in that we will be known as a safe place to fail. When you are grateful, to not forgive is unthinkable. How could you even consider holding something against another when you yourself have had so much forgiven? When you are the worst of all sinners, to withhold forgiveness from another is inconceivable.

Jesus makes it clear that the evidence of gratitude is not that you receive forgiveness, but that you're willing to give it. In Matthew 18 he gives us a parable in response to Peter's question, "Lord how many times shall I forgive my brother when he sins against me? Up to seven times?"

Jesus answered, "I tell you, not seven times, but seventy-seven times.

"Therefore, the kingdom of heaven is like a king who wanted to settle accounts with his servants. As he began the settlement, a man who owed him ten thousand talents was brought to him. Since he was not able to pay, the master ordered that he and his wife and his children and all that he had be sold to repay the debt.

"The servant fell on his knees before him. 'Be patient with me,' he begged, 'and I will pay back everything.' The servant's master took pity on him, canceled the debt and let him go.

"But when that servant went out, he found one of his fellow servants who owed him a hundred denarii. He grabbed him and began to choke him. 'Pay back what you owe me!' he demanded.

"His fellow servant fell on his knees and begged him, 'Be patient with me, and I will pay you back.'

"But he refused. Instead, he went off and had the man thrown into prison until he could pay the debt. When the other servants saw what had happened, they were greatly distressed and went and told their master everything that had happened.

"Then the master called the servant in. 'You wicked servant,' he said. 'I canceled all that debt of yours because you begged me to. Shouldn't you have had mercy on your fellow servant just as I had on you?' In anger his master turned him over to the jailers to be tortured, until he should pay back all that he owed.

"This is how my heavenly Father will treat each of you unless you forgive your brother from your heart." (vv. 22–35)

To receive forgiveness cannot be our ultimate end. When we are genuinely grateful for forgiveness given us, we will in turn extend grace and forgiveness to others. This is what it means to live in grace, to live in an unending stream of forgiveness. Grace both receives and gives forgiveness without measure. To receive the grace of God and yet treat others ungraciously is an act of wickedness. No matter how much we are required to forgive in others, it pales in comparison to what God has forgiven in relationship to us.

God's expectation is that you get rid of all bitterness, rage, brawling, slander, and malice and "be kind and compassionate to one another, forgiving each other, just as in Christ God forgave you" (Eph. 4:32).

In a preemptive strike against any excuse or justification we might have for holding on to our bitterness, Jesus demonstrates His ultimate act of forgiveness while dying on the cross. Bitterness always feels justified. We are often certain that no one could possibly understand how we feel. We convince ourselves that no one has gone through what we have gone through. Yet we are left with no room for escape. In His moment of greatest abandonment and suffering, Jesus exercised the full extent of His grace. His prayer for us is not judgment or condemnation, but instead, "Father, forgive them, for they do not know what they are doing" (Luke 23:34).

Instead of bitterness, Jesus chose forgiveness. He calls us to do the same, not only for the sake of others, but for the salvation of our own souls. When we are free from bitterness, we are once again free to pursue the life God dreams for us. Only forgiveness holds the key to this dungeon that keeps us living in the dark. Like a cancer, bitterness destroys every relationship in our lives. You can't just be bitter toward one person. It is impossible to compartmentalize corrosive emotions of this kind. When we are bitter toward one person, it adversely affects every relationship in our lives. Bitterness clogs the arteries and hardens the heart. It limits our capacity to love even those who have never wronged us.

We are warned in the book of Hebrews, "Make every effort to live in peace with all men and to be holy; without holiness no one will see the Lord. See to it that no one misses the grace of God and that no bitter root grows up to cause trouble and defile many" (12:14–15).

When we embrace bitterness, we reject grace. When we allow a bitter root to take hold of our hearts, we literally miss the grace of God. Bitterness destroys our relationships, impairs our judgment, skews our perspective, and distorts our memories.

GAINING PERSPECTIVE

Have you ever noticed that two people can have a dramatically different perspective on the same situation? It's the old adage about whether the glass is half-empty or half-full. The distinction is more than just a difference of personality types. It's more significant than simply whether a person is a pessimist or an optimist. Perspective is not shaped in a vacuum; it is formed in the context of gratitude. An ungrateful person sees the glass as half-empty and wonders who is holding out on him. The grateful see the glass as half-full knowing that someone has shared with them more than they deserved. Our perspective is a good indicator of where we fall on the continuum of greed to generosity and a good barometer for our level of gratitude.

Several years ago a large group of us from Mosaic were given tickets to a UCLA football game. The entire student ministry would be able to go and enjoy the game. I was also given four other tickets in a much better section where I could invite a few friends. I decided to share these with my son, Aaron, and invited him to bring one of his friends. I would bring one of mine. He was excited about not having to sit in the nosebleed section and having a great view of the game.

Just before the Saturday of the game, I had gotten better news. I was invited to watch the game from the sidelines. I would get to hang with the players and actually be in the locker room during their pregame and halftime debriefings. That day I shared with Aaron that he could bring another friend with him. In fact two more, since I would be joining the team on the field. I'm not sure if it was my unbridled euphoria that set him off, but Aaron did not respond well to my good fortune. "What about me? Why can't I be on the sideline?"

I explained I had only been offered one sideline pass. The solution seemed easy enough for him. "Well then, give me your pass."

I told him I had thought of that and asked, but he was too young, and they would not allow me to transfer the pass to a minor. This only seemed to upset him more. In the heat of the moment he blurted out, "Well then, I'm not going."

We have a mantra in our home that was created just for moments like these. I looked at Aaron and said, "Aaron, what do you deserve?" And in proper McManus fashion, he said, "Nothing." It's our way of reminding ourselves that we don't deserve anything, that all of life is a gift. We should see everything from the place of gratitude. This vantage point will always allow us to see the world from a perspective where the glass is half-full.

Aaron's response was more facetious than sincere. His follow-up after "Nothing" was, "And because I deserve nothing, I'll take nothing." He decided he would not go to the game. I left for work with no small tension between us. Sometimes the best thing you can do for someone is give him or her time for reflection. By the time I came home that night, Aaron had had a dramatic change of heart. He asked me if those four tickets were still available and expressed how grateful he would be if he could have them back. In the end he did get to come on the field, meet Coach Toledo and hang around the players, an experience he would have missed if he had been satisfied with nothing.

A New Optimism

Gratitude generates optimism. The grace of God not only frees us from sin, but from pessimism. When you trust God with your future, hope naturally abounds. Even in the worst of circumstances, the grateful of heart are able to find sources of joy and inspiration. Gratitude changes your perspective about life. You see the future, experience the present, and remember the past in a dramatically different way.

A part of the process of moving toward wholeness for me was remembering my past differently. I had established memory ruts. I would go back to the same places over and over again. Like the open wound you can't help but touch, I would continuously take myself to a place that resulted in self-inflicted pain. The original wounds were not of my doing, but no one but me kept choosing to go back there. My whole life seemed to be defined by less than a half dozen memories, but the memories I had chosen were all negative. I remembered a life filled with pain and disappointment, not because that was all I experienced, but because it was all I had brought with me.

Memories have a way of defining not only who you were, but who you are and who you will become. One experience can become pervasive. It can shape your entire view of reality. It can become the filter through which you experience everything in life. I started to re-remember. There were great memories in my past, but I had to blow the dust off them. I journeyed back and found some wonderful places and experiences. You will be amazed how many wonderful memories are trapped behind the avalanche of the few negative ones. The painful memories were no less real but no longer dominant.

There's an old saying that you need to "forgive and forget." You do need to forgive; you can't really forget, but you don't have to always remember. The negative does not have to be the primary source from which to draw. Remember the good and the good will grow. Of course, if you keep traveling back and returning empty, there is one other thing you can do: Create new memories. Make today memorable, even unforgettable. And then look back on this moment. Treasure this experience. Let it become a defining memory for your life. Live this moment to the fullest and let gratitude flow.

There is something even greater that God longs to do with your memories. It's important to remember all the good that has happened in your life and there is great healing power in creating new, positive memories. Yet the real miracle comes when you can look back at even the most painful experiences in your life and find the good that God has brought out of it. Until you can see the work of God in the worst of circumstances you have not yet begun to see your life from the eyes of God. When gratitude does its greatest work within us, we are able to celebrate who we are becoming even when we have passed through experiences we would wish on no one. No tragedy or hardship can rob from us the joy that is always before us when our eyes remain on Jesus.

> *Memories have a way of defining not only who you were, but who you are and who you will become.*

THE BEAUTY OF LIVING

When we are grateful, we are most fully alive. Gratitude allows us to absorb every possible pleasure from a moment. It is the grateful who suck the marrow out of life. When your heart is full of gratitude, life paints itself in far brighter and more vivid colors. The aromas, flavors, and textures of life are so exhilarating that they take you to places of indescribable pleasure. Life becomes an endless celebration. Your laughter and joy is the applause of your soul as you marvel in the goodness of God and the wonder of His creation. There is always something that fills you with joy and unleashes hope and inspiration. Gratitude doesn't lead to monasticism; it leads to hedonism, not a hedonism absent of holiness, but one that erupts out of wholeness.

We were hiking up Mount Wilson one beautiful Southern California afternoon. Kim, the kids, a friend of ours named Barb, and I were working our way to the top. I don't remember exactly why, but I was lagging way behind. I refuse to believe this was the result of my lack of athleticism. Whatever the case, they traveled in a cluster and I followed far behind on my own. I came to a cliff that was rocky and barren, and as I looked carefully, I saw a small flower that had broken through the hardened ground. I yelled ahead and exhorted everyone to rush back and see what I had found. In response to my shout, they all began to laugh. I was a bit confused. I hadn't said anything funny. I had no idea what was going on. But they had all seen the flower first and had made a bet that when I passed it, I would force them all to come back and admire it.

I don't like being predictable, but I am a compulsive enjoyer of life and beauty. What began as an exercise in praise has resulted in a life of continuous astonishment. I look for the flower breaking through the rock. I stop to appreciate the beauty and artistry of every sunset I have the opportunity to experience. Life is an adventure to be explored and excavated for its endless unexpected surprises and treasures. There is so much to enjoy. How could even one moment be lived without overflowing with gratitude?

When we recognize that life is a gift and we are overwhelmed with a sense of gratitude, when we fill every moment with praise for God's goodness and thanks for His generosity, we find wholeness, and our hearts increase in their capacity to experience and give love. Receiving is only one part of the process of healing. It is only when we return to give thanks that we are truly made whole. By faith we turn to Jesus to be made clean. It would be a tragedy if out of lack of gratitude we missed the opportunity to be made whole.

Now on his way to Jerusalem, Jesus traveled along the border between Samaria and Galilee. As he was going into a village, ten men who had leprosy met him. They stood at a distance and called out in a loud voice, "Jesus, Master, have pity on us!"

When he saw them, he said, "Go, show yourselves to the priests." And as they went, they were cleansed.

One of them, when he saw he was healed, came back, praising God in a loud voice. He threw himself at Jesus' feet and thanked him—and he was a Samaritan.

Jesus asked, "Were not all ten cleansed? Where are the other nine? Was no one found to return and give praise to God except this foreigner?" Then he said to him, "Rise and go; your faith has made you well." (Luke 17:11–19)

7

Wholeness from a
Black Hole

What for some would be childhood memories are for me mere shadows of a former life. When I remember back, it's both fuzzy and disjointed. Some things I remember as clearly as if they were yesterday. The details have remained with me over the four decades of my life. Fortunately the best of memories have held their greatest clarity. They remain vibrant and alive, treasures from days gone by. Other parts of my past are more elusive. I'm not sure if it's because I can't remember or I tried to forget. In either case it requires me to reach so deeply into my memory that it seems almost locked away.

I was twelve years old when I found myself on the proverbial couch. You know, the one where someone does surgery on your mind. Not brain surgery—soul surgery. This kind of surgery is far more intrusive than the other and perhaps even more complex. I remember an endless battery of tests from inkblots to timed reconstruction of puzzles.

He had the classic Freudian look, full beard, eccentric eyes. I had been terrified just by the idea of the meeting, but the actual experience was more interesting than anything else. I didn't know what he would find as he searched through my psyche, but I had concluded it was better to know, whatever the result. I wasn't even thirteen and I stood at risk of being labeled as crazy. It seemed unfair that I could be out of my mind before I could even get out of the house. I knew I was neurotic, but now I might find out I was also psychotic. Upon reflection it's kind of funny that some of my favorite movies have been *One Flew over the Cuckoo's Nest*, *As Good As It Gets,* and *A Beautiful Mind.*

The conversation was inevitable, but it still came as a surprise. My mom and stepdad calmly approached me and carefully asked me if I would consider going to a doctor. Not a medical doctor, but a shrink. Not helping my case, I reacted with emotional hostility, screaming at them, "You think I'm crazy." I was emphatic that I would not go. I felt betrayed and condemned by their suggestion. I look back and realize they were desperate to help me, but didn't know how.

After a cooling-off period, they came and assured me that I didn't have to go. It was just a suggestion. They just wanted me to get better. Somehow their words made it easier for me to see this as a good option and I decided that the worst thing was not knowing. There could be only a good result. I would either find out I was messed up, but not crazy, or that I was crazy. Maybe they would find a way to fix this mess.

I don't remember how much time I actually spent in and out of doctors' offices and hospitals; I just know this season of my life is entirely defined by this memory. I was sick all the time. Some kids get just sick enough to get excused from school. It had gone far past that for me. I could almost convince myself that none of this actually happened.

The scar that decorates my abdomen reminds me that it was more than just a bad dream. It was called exploratory surgery. That was a nice way of saying, "We have no idea what's wrong with you, so let's take a look." They found nothing wrong, but they took my appendix out while they were there. Why waste a good surgery? You might as well take something out. There is a difference between a hypochondriac and suffering from psychosomatic illnesses. I've learned the distinction the hard way. A hypochondriac is sick only in his imagination. He or she lives in an imaginary world disconnected from reality when it comes to disease and sickness. Psychosomatic illness is also born in the imagination, but it has real contact with life.

SOUL SICK

More and more doctors are discovering the connection between our mind and emotions and their relationship to our physical well-being. Your mental and emotional health has a dramatic impact on your physical health. The opposite is true too. Your physical health can directly affect your emotional and mental health.

The words of John, "Dear friend, I pray that you may enjoy good health and that all may go well with you, even as your soul is getting along well" (3 John 1:2) are sounding less like sentiment and more like science. He had keen insight into the fact that there is a relationship between the prosperity of our souls and the health of our bodies. When your heart is sick, it can spread everywhere. Like a cancer, despair in the human soul can cause all kinds of malfunctions.

While there is an unexpected leap that has to be made from spirit to flesh when diagnosing this kind of trauma, it is possible to find the trail back to the initial contact or wounding. Before the surgery there were recurring and vivid nightmares. They would not let go of me even after I was awake. And before the nightmares there was the reality. I was disintegrating from the inside out. Even when things were good, I was fighting back an overwhelming sense of despair.

There were days when just getting out of bed and facing a new day was a challenge. I was as close to failing as a passing student could be and kept my relationship with the outside world to a minimum as much as possible. The best way I can describe it is that I got lost inside myself. The outside world seemed so distant from me. Between us was a chasm of angst and confusion. Looking back, I realize I was trying to make sense of life, and the process just seemed overwhelming.

I share this with you for only one reason: I want you to know that I was lost in the black hole and that there is a way out. I'm convinced that there are more of us out there than we care to acknowledge, women and men who would give everything they have just to become whole. I continually meet people who have learned how to function while hiding their dysfunction. At times it's difficult to believe that not much more than a generation ago emotional health was the norm. For some of you that statement will seem more like a myth. My observation is that most people born after 1960 see wholeness as propaganda. It's hard to believe that some people are actually healthy from the inside out. Certainly if you don't believe something exists, you will not strive for it, unless of course you're crazy. But then again, most of us probably are.

In *An Unstoppable Force* we examined the phenomenon that when cultures have more of something, they have more words to describe it—more words for *snow* when you go north toward the pole, more words for *green* when you go south toward the equator. Certainly this is true when it comes to wholeness. Fifty years ago we had a limited vocabulary when it came to mental and emotional health. Someone might be "insane," "mad," "out of his mind." Popular language would just call you "crazy." Or if you're a fan of Daffy Duck, you might be "loony."

In a relatively short amount of time, we have expanded our vocabulary considerably. We now talk about function and dysfunction, neurosis and psychosis. No advanced training is needed to be familiar with the terms *bipolar, schizophrenic,* or *manic depressive.* So common is the language of brokenness in our culture that we even readily understand initials such as ADD and ADHD. We have quickly become versed in the vernacular of dysfunction. We have outgrown fear and replaced it with phobia, and we are phobic about everything. We have become a culture that diagnoses and medicates our children from a template that reduces antisocial behavior rather than one that nurtures and develops the wholeness they need. It might be fair to say that we have given up on well-being.

PIECING OUR LIVES TOGETHER

In the midst of our growing fragmentation, we have never been more focused on the individual than we are today. This focus plays itself out in unbridled consumerism. While materialism is certainly an outgrowth of consumerism, it isn't its primary focus. Consumerism's primary product in our culture is narcissism. Remember, narcissism is a life in which everything is about us. It may seem like a contradiction to say that we have given up on becoming genuinely whole and are consumed with lives that are about ourselves, but strangely, these two go together.

Even the language of pop psychology betrays us. We are told that the most important thing is to take care of yourself. The secret to personal well-being is that you must love yourself. Everything begins with you. "You can't love anyone else until you love yourself" is the mantra we are invited to embrace. We are given professional permission to put ourselves above everyone and everything else. In this scenario love is all about consumption. You've got to take what you need before you can give. The belief is that once you've taken enough, you'll be satisfied and begin to give to others.

Yet the reality is very different from this scenario. When we are broken, there's never enough. When we are emotionally fragmented, we leak. No matter how much we consume, how much we take for ourselves, we always find ourselves empty in the end. This in turn leaves you only more frustrated and embittered. You stop believing that what you are searching for is really out there. And how can you give what you don't have enough of? Or why would you give something that has left you unsatisfied and unfulfilled?

When we are broken, wholeness can seem either elusive or illusory. Our desperate search for it often takes us on a journey to find that which we have never known. Our determination to find what was lost only causes us to lose our way. The search for wholeness is counterintuitive and requires us to let go of what we so long to take hold of and to begin a pilgrimage that leads us to an entirely different path. Wholeness is not found through receiving, but through giving. This is why wholeness and generosity are inseparably linked.

It is easy to conclude, I cannot give what I do not have. While it is true you cannot give what you do not have, you can give what you have not experienced. From a purely human perspective, you can serve even if you've never been served; you can forgive even if you've never been forgiven; you can express compassion even if you've never received compassion. Yet when most of us conclude we have nothing to give, it is based on an evaluation of what we've experienced.

Generosity is not contingent on what you receive, but on what you are willing to give. What we have to give is not the sum total of what others have given to us, but what genuinely emerges from our hearts. To be truly generous, we must be generative. If we only give what we have received, we are nothing more than relational and emotional barterers. We see everything necessary for human community as a limited resource. This kind of scarcity mentality leads us to hoard and keep things for ourselves.

When you reduce generosity to its primal essence, what you have is love. All generosity, whether in the area of economics or emotions, comes down to the same core. When we are broken, we become an emotional black hole. No matter how much is poured into us, its light is absorbed and never finds its way back out. When we are whole, we are nurtured by what is invested in us, and at the same time, freely give of ourselves to others.

THE HEALING ESSENCE

Again, while the giving may have specific applications—time, money, trust, concern, listening, encouragement, forgiveness, and endless others—what is really being given is love. When a person is whole, he or she does not see love as a limited resource; he or she sees love as limitless. Those who are whole know love to be an ever-expanding commodity. We were created by God to be generative when it comes to love. Love is always intended to flow freely to us and from us. We were designed to be conduits of love. The problem is that we've been disconnected from the source of love.

John reminds us that we love because God first loved us (1 John 4:19). God is not only the source of all love, but He is the instigator of our own need for love and desire to love. Love is so central to who God is that it is a primary test of our own relationship to the Creator.

John writes, "Dear friends, let us love one another, for love comes from God. Everyone who loves has been born of God and knows God. Whoever does not love does not know God, because God is love" (1 John 4:7–8).

John also connects the relationship between love and wholeness. He explains, "God is love. Whoever lives in love lives in God, and God in him. In this way, love is made complete among us so that we will have confidence on the day of judgment, because in this world we are like him. There is no fear in love. But perfect love drives out fear, because fear has to do with punishment. The one who fears is not made perfect in love" (1 John 4:16b–18).

John introduces the idea of being made perfect. This theme runs throughout the Scriptures and has at times been greatly misunderstood. James addresses the same outcome when he describes us becoming mature and complete, not lacking anything (James 1:4). Paul describes this as becoming mature, attaining to the whole measure of the fullness of Christ (Eph. 4:13).

The Scriptures describe us as being perfect and complete in this life. The best parallel word would be *wholeness*. The promise of God is not that we will be flawless in this world, but that we can be whole in this life. We have wasted too much effort trying to become perfect in our actions and invested too little energy in becoming healthy in our spirits. The perfection God promises flows out of the wholeness that only Christ can form in us by the love of God. It is a perfection that drives out fear and unleashes love.

Has it ever occurred to you that God intended you not only to receive and give love, but to literally generate love—that you were designed specifically to be a love machine? Listen to the expansive language the Scriptures use in regard to love:

> May the Lord make your love increase and overflow for each other and for everyone else, just as ours does for you. (1 Thess. 3:12)

> And this is my prayer: that your love may abound more and more in knowledge and depth of insight, so that you may be able to discern what is best and may be pure and blameless until the day of Christ, filled with the fruit of righteousness that comes through Jesus Christ—to the glory and praise of God. (Phil. 1:9–11)

> I pray that out of his glorious riches he may strengthen you with power through his Spirit in your inner being, so that Christ may dwell in your hearts through faith. And I pray that you being rooted and established in love, may have power, together with all the saints, to grasp how wide and long and high and deep is the love of Christ, and to know this love that surpasses knowledge— that you may be filled to the measure of all the fullness of God. (Eph. 3:16–19)

In each of these passages, the desired outcome is an expanded capacity and resource of love. The last of these paints a picture of a person drenched in the love of Christ to such an extent that he experiences the full measure of the goodness of God. This person doesn't leak; he overflows. This is the ultimate secret of moving toward wholeness. The process begins with gratitude. Remember, a significant aspect of unleashing the healing effect of gratitude is the willingness to forgive and move forward. The heart of gratitude focuses on all that is good rather than all that is absent. At the same time we find ourselves placing others above ourselves—moving from self-absorption to servanthood. When we redirect our energies in this way, we find ourselves giving away even those things we have not received from others. Once we are doing this, the healing process has already begun.

This, of course, can only take us so far. We all need to be loved. We all need compassion. We all need forgiveness. We all need acceptance. And this is why, above all else, we need God. We were created to bask in the unending and unconditional love of God. Every good thing our soul requires we will find in Him. All that we have not experienced from others we can experience in Him. All that our souls long for can be satisfied in Christ. While we may never find or receive the love from others that our hearts are desperate for, we can receive a love even greater than that of which we were deprived.

My wife, Kim, and our little girl, Mariah, were having a conversation one day when, in a moment of affection, Kim said, "Mariah, I love you to pieces." Mariah, a bit confused by the imagery, looked at Kim and said, "Mommy, I love you whole." Sometimes children have keener insight into profound issues than we do as mature adults. Human love all too often loves us to pieces.

There is an old Nazareth song entitled "Love Hurts." How many of us haven't found ourselves hurting most deeply the ones we most deeply love? Divine love always loves us to wholeness. Again I think our language betrays us when describing the struggles of daily life. We are "brokenhearted" when love comes to an end. We find ourselves "falling apart" when we are overwhelmed. Sometimes the best we can do is "hold it together." Each of these common phrases betrays our sense of fragmentation. Is it possible that we're only in danger of "losing it" because we're trying to hold so many pieces together? As innocuous as it may seem, maybe we should stop loving each other to pieces and start loving each other whole. Only the love of God is free from all self-serving motivation. Only His love comes without reservation or condition. We find in Jesus Christ the only love that makes us truly whole. He passes that love to all who would trust their hearts to Him. This is the quest for nobility, to live and to love in a manner worthy of God. This is why ultimately wholeness cannot be defined by our ability to *experience* love, but our ability to *exercise* love.

GIVERS AND TAKERS

The most basic definition I've used for wholeness is simply 51 percent. You know, where you give more than you take. Not too much more, just a two percent difference. Sometimes ideals are difficult to measure, but most of us have a sense of whether we're making a contribution or a withdrawal. If there are a hundred one-dollar bills and a hundred people take one, what are you left with? That's right, nothing. On the other hand, if there are a hundred people and each contributes at least one dollar . . . Well, you get the point. What if in every situation you made a commitment to make a greater contribution than withdrawal—whether financial, relational, emotional, or the investment of your time? It's hard for us to picture what wholeness looks like in its perfect state. Of course Jesus is our best example of 100 percent—a person whose entire life was given to giving. Imagine living every moment of your life for the contribution you can make in the lives of others.

Picture with me just for a moment a person whose every motivation, every word, and every action was intended for the good of others. This is essentially the life of Jesus. It was not that He was absent of needs. In fact we find the love and encouragement of His friends was both appreciated and desired. Yet in spite of the actions and responses of those around Him, He always made the decision to give of Himself to others. Jesus always gave more than He took.

No one could ever rightfully accuse Him of consuming more than He contributed. Everyone who genuinely engages Jesus in a relationship receives far more than they ever give. The more dramatic examples in the life of Jesus are that He made the sick well, gave sight to the blind, cleansed lepers, made the lame walk, and even raised the dead. Every environment Jesus entered was touched by His healing nature. Wherever Jesus' influence was invited and received, health resulted. Jesus not only forgave sins, but He made people well. He explained to His disciples that He came to serve, not to be served. Translated into this context, Jesus was saying that He came to give and not take. His was a journey of true nobility.

Understanding the nature of wholeness is more than just an interest for me. It was an issue of survival. For over a decade I invested a great deal of my life working with individuals and families who were trapped in a cycle of poverty and addiction. Those two don't always come together, but they quite often do. When I began working with the urban poor, I had a rather romantic view of poverty. The rich were evil, and the poor were good. I attributed a nobility to the poor that I found sometimes to be merited, but most often to be misplaced. I met some amazing people in the most difficult of circumstances. Even in the darkest situations, there would always be at least one person whose life would light the room. When you consider everything that was going against him and the resilience that it took to rise above his environment, he was nothing short of heroic. But I also learned the hard way that poverty is not a virtue.

I also learned that I couldn't buy a person's way out of a self-destructive pattern. P. T. Barnum talked about the sucker that's born every minute. Time and again I proved I had my minute covered. I nearly drove Kim and the church broke. I couldn't believe how many people's cars kept running out of gas, how many people lost their wallets or couldn't pay their rent just this month. It may have taken me longer than most, but I quickly began to realize that I was pouring the limited resources I had into a black hole. I wasn't meeting needs; I was feeding an insatiable appetite of want. I wish I could at least say I was describing those outside of the church, but that wasn't the case. Believing in Jesus just didn't seem to tip the scales in the direction of giving rather than receiving. We were deluged by a tribe of Christian consumers. They saw the church as just one more venue from which to take rather than a community where they could serve and invest in others.

One family in particular forced me to see things from a more honest perspective. They had been participating in the church for several years. They were vocal in their faith and were loved by the congregation. But every six months or so they would be facing eviction from the apartment they were living in. Like many others, they had an established pattern of paying the first few months' rent and then living for several months rent free knowing the eviction process would take some time. On four or five different occasions, I made the decision to pay their rent. It was hard for me to see this single mom and her children put on the streets. It was probably the sixth time that we faced the same crisis that I had to make the decision not to intervene. It wasn't just that I concluded it was wrong to do so; we just didn't have the money to help her.

Since it wasn't an issue of lack of concern, I personally went to her home, sat down, and explained to her that we were unable to help. I also felt that after several years I had earned the right to speak to the continuous cycle that was clear in her life. I suggested that even if we paid the rent this time, without a change in her decision making, she would soon find herself in the same situation again. I was in my mid twenties and still a fairly young believer, and I was totally caught off guard by her response. She became hostile and started cussing me out. I don't mean a mild use of colorful language, but the kind of conversation that would make the Sopranos blush. Then she threw me out of her house and told me never to come back.

I suppose I'm a slow learner, and it may take me longer than most to catch on to some things, but I left that day knowing that, while I had put a shelter over their heads again and again, my efforts had resulted in no change in her life whatsoever. My approach just wasn't working. In fact, if anything, it seemed I was feeding the beast.

Was I only an eager participant in a codependent relationship? Was I trying to be Jesus to people in all the wrong ways? Was I in fact circumventing a process that is absolutely necessary in the journey of transformation? Was I feeding brokenness rather than nurturing wholeness? I came to the painful realization that I was.

PATH TO WHOLENESS

I was living in Dallas at the time. From my vantage point, Dallas was the mecca of Christian psychotherapy. It was the '80s, and organizations like Minirth-Meier and Rapha were thriving due to the overwhelming need for counseling among churches. Most of the programs that were available were extremely expensive. They required either significant personal wealth or really good insurance. My community had neither of those. If professional counseling was the best hope for broken Christians, the followers of Christ in my neighborhood were hopeless.

After four years of seminary and seven years in the Christian faith, I concluded that the unspoken policy was to give Jesus the small stuff and leave the real problems to Freud. The sad truth is that the church didn't know how to help people get better. Wholeness was as much a mystery to us as it was to anyone else. Modern psychiatry is the totality of the study of human dysfunction. Its expertise is in identifying, describing, and defining expressions of human brokenness.

The path to wholeness cannot be discovered by concentrating on the signs of fragmentation. This is why Jesus is our best and only hope. Jesus was truly whole. He was a pure expression of a healthy human being. While we can learn about God by studying His divinity, we can equally learn about man by studying His humanity. In Jesus we unlock the mystery of wholeness. From His choice to make Himself nothing to His willingness to die on our behalf, Jesus points the way. His prayer at Gethsemane to His Father, "Not my will, but yours," illumines for us the mind of Christ. His life wasn't about Himself. He calls us to choose the same path. He promises the life we long for can be found if we will lose ourselves in Him. He invites us to find our purpose and our healing in serving others. It is here He unwraps for us the human side of divine change. God fully intends to make whole disciples out of broken people. Wholeness is a promise for all of us. While it goes against everything we feel, we must trust Him that His process is the only one that heals us. His love unleashed in us is our only hope for the process of wholeness to find its completion.

Love in its purest expression is not something that is received, but something that is given. God is love not because He is most loved, but because He is most loving. We love Him because He first loved us. In the same way, human love is most purely expressed and experienced when it is given more than received. To properly pursue love, we must strive to give it away rather than simply find it. When we begin to love in this way, we begin to find the wholeness God promises. Until we embrace this reality that what we need will only come when we give it away, we endanger ourselves by becoming the ultimate consumers.

When you consume things, you are a materialist. When you consume people, you are a cannibal. At least things are inanimate; people are real flesh and blood. It's my understanding that one of the reasons the Tyrannosaurus rex was so notorious was its insatiable appetite due to its accelerated metabolism. Rex was always hungry. Anytime was a good time to eat, and everyone Rex met was a potential candidate. Rex was the ultimate consumer.

Unfortunately, sometimes Rex is a picture of the most dysfunctional of human relationships. We see people as existing for our benefit. We are so desperate for friendship, so longing for love, that every time someone risks getting close to us, we consume him or her. We are so busy devouring that person's kindness that we are virtually oblivious to our lack of contribution. We don't even consider taking time to feed or nourish the other person. Pardon the phrase, but we become emotional leeches. We attach ourselves to the hearts of unsuspecting and compassionate individuals who hope to help us get better. We suck them dry of every ounce of their emotional reserve until they are emaciated beyond the point of recognition. After they've gone from grape to raisin, we detach and look for our next victim. Just before we leave, to make sure we leave no good deed unpunished, we pronounce this judgment on them: "You told me you'd be there for me when I needed you. You let me down. You're just like everyone else."

When you are the victim of this scenario, those final words are the crippling blow. Gasping for breath, you watch them walk away and quickly attach themselves to another unsuspecting caregiver. You would warn them except for one thing—you're free—and better them than you.

Over the years I've become wary of anyone who begins a conversation by building me up and speaking badly about the last person who invested in his or her life. This is a sure sign of a relational and emotional consumer looking for the next prey. There is a reason why everyone disappoints such a person. The person would tell you no one has been there for him or her, and even that no one loves him or her. Any outside observer would know this is not true, yet for that individual, this is an honest evaluation of past experience.

FILLING THE HOLE

He's seventeen and destroying his life. His weapon of choice is first drugs, then alcohol. His sexual recklessness is leaving a barrage of human shrapnel all around him. Between the trajectory of his life and the pace at which he is getting there, he probably won't live to see his twentieth birthday. In a moment of anger, after explaining he's not hurting anyone but himself, he adds that no one loves him anyway. He is unconvinced and unmoved by the tears being shed just inches from him by his mother. The anguish on the faces of his friends is translated by him to be judgment rather than concern. Though stoic, even the pain of his father cannot be hidden. Even cursory observation would see a young man surrounded by a community of concern, yet he is certain he is unloved.

While an unwillingness to love is an outcome of choice when we are emotional consumers, an unexpected consequence is the inability to experience love. Often when we are broken, we perceive that we are unloved even when we are surrounded by love. We conclude no one cares because we have desensitized ourselves to the concerns of others. We become numb and lose our sense of touch. We lose our ability to feel because we are unwilling to love, and when we close ourselves to the experience of giving love, we close ourselves to the experience of knowing love.

In the midst of his poetic discourse on love, Paul makes this critical observation: Love is not self-seeking. Genuine love is never self-motivated. It is always about the good of others. Love always places others above itself. Love remains elusive when we're only willing to get it and not to give it. We can become so self-seeking that the experience of love becomes absent from us. When we open ourselves to love, we open ourselves for love.

As contrary as it may seem, the person who gives away the most of himself will have the greatest experience of love. The depth and profound nature of love can only be known in the context of personal sacrifice for others. This is why wholeness comes only in the act of giving rather than the pursuit of getting. We are most whole when we are most free to give. When we approach the Scriptures with the understanding that holiness and wholeness are inseparable, even the commandments appear in a new light.

While wholeness is often thought of as a personal reality, its essence is far more communal. Wholeness is a spiritual condition that affects both our emotional and relational well-being. Your emotional health (internal) and your relational health (external) are inseparable. Both the Ten Commandments and the Great Commandment are fundamentally about relationships. In Mark 12 one of the teachers of the law came and asked Jesus a question: "Of all the commandments, which is the most important?" If you boil this question down, what he's really asking Jesus is, "What is the most important thing to God?" We might hear the question in the context of only Ten Commandments, but this student of the Torah would understand that there were at least six hundred different commands that needed to be considered. Jesus' answer was this: "The most important one . . . is this: 'Hear, O Israel, the Lord our God, the Lord is one. Love the Lord your God with all of your heart and with all your soul and with all your mind and with all your strength.' The second is this: 'Love your neighbor as yourself.' There is no commandment greater than these'" (vv. 29–31).

The teacher of the law responded, "Well said, teacher. You are right in saying that God is one and there is no other but him. To love him with all your heart, with all your understanding and with all your strength, and to love your neighbor as yourself is more important than all burnt offerings and sacrifices" (vv. 32–33).

Jesus believed that the teacher had answered wisely and said, "You are not far from the kingdom of God" (v. 34).

In response to what was the most important of all to God, Jesus' answer could be summarized in one word: relationships. There is nothing more important to God than your relationships. You are never closer to the kingdom of God than when relationships are your priority. First, of course, is your relationship to God. Inseparable from this relationship with your Creator is your relationship to others.

LOST IN A LOVE TRIANGLE

For years I interpreted the second part of this command as meaning that you could not love others until you loved yourself, that you had to first love yourself and then you could love your neighbor. I have become convinced this is exactly what it is *not* saying. The second commandment is not sequential. There are not three commandments—just two. It is not love God, then love yourself, then love others; it is love God and love others as yourself. It is a command to give yourself away, to take your focus off yourself and to make others the focus of your life. There is a difference between loving yourself and being in love with yourself. When you have a proper relationship with God, you have a healthy sense of yourself. God's love allows you to find fulfillment in the person He has created you to become. God's love becomes the measure and basis of your personal value. When you love God with all your heart, you just have to accept what He says about you—which, by the way, is that you are wonderfully and marvelously made!

All that said, God is inviting us to focus on loving rather than on being loved. God knows that only when our hearts are in this position are we able to experience the love we long for. Are you willing to love God with all of your being, love others, and trust that you will not be left wanting? If you pursue loving God and loving others, love will pursue and find you.

Even the Ten Commandments establish the same framework. The first four commandments are related to our relationship to God to ensure that we treat God properly and love Him in a manner worthy of who He is. The last six commandments are all about how we relate to others. The fifth calls us to not live as takers in relationship to our parents, but to honor them; the sixth tells us not to take someone else's life; the seventh commands us to not take another person's spouse; the eighth, not to take one's possessions; the ninth, not to take someone's good reputation; and the tenth, not to *want* to take what is our neighbor's and not ours. You could legitimately summarize the last six commandments as: Don't be a taker.

Israel was commanded by God to be givers. They were to lend freely, share their abundance with the poor, give 10 percent of their income to the worship of God, live on less than they made, and be a blessing to the nations. They were to be a people who demonstrated wholeness. They were to give themselves away and trust that God would supply them in abundance. Even the Sabbath was a slap in the face to consumerism. Let the rest of the world slave away seven days a week trying to gain more for themselves. You work six, rest on the seventh, enjoy God, and astonish the world as you thrive.

It is clear to me that just as there are healthy families and unhealthy families, there are healthy cultures and unhealthy cultures. God established at the heart of the nation of Israel the framework for communal wholeness. They were to be a generous people, a nation of givers. Taking opposes the very nature of God. They were to reflect the generosity of God and expose the emptiness of a life of selfish pursuit. This is exactly the invitation that is given to us when we are invited to become followers of Jesus Christ. We are told to "be imitators of God, therefore, as dearly loved children and live a life of love, just as Christ loved us and gave himself up for us as a fragrant offering and sacrifice to God" (Eph. 5:1–2).

In essence we are challenged to love on a divine level, to see if it's possible to love too much. It's as if through His death Jesus threw down the gauntlet. He was determined to prove that love cannot be killed, or if crucified, would certainly rise from the dead. The more of ourselves that we give away, the more whole we become. The more completely we love, the more complete love makes us. This is our quest for nobility—to live the quality of life God had in mind when He created us.

I am struck with the first half of the Great Commandment and how it relates to our specific dilemma in regard to wholeness. We are called to love God with all of our hearts, all of our souls, all of our strength, and all of our minds. Have you ever loved anything with all that you are? Have you ever risked giving the totality of your being, entrusting it to the care of another? Is it possible that it's not God who needs all of us, but it is we who need to give all of ourselves to God? For those of us who are followers of Christ, we know that we need all of God, but do we know as clearly that our wholeness is dependent on our giving all of ourselves?

I don't know if I fully understand what it means to give all of myself in every dimension as Jesus describes. I do know what it is like to love halfheartedly or to be double-minded. I am far more acquainted with holding back, playing things close to my chest, and keeping the most vulnerable part of me guarded. Love requires trust, and trust always requires risk. Yet God is inviting us to give all of ourselves, a most frightening proposition in the safest of all contexts. God can be trusted with the most fragile of hearts. He knows we will never fully experience love unless we give all of ourselves away. Even for those who have been hurt and betrayed, there is a person to turn to. He will not betray your trust. As the apostle Paul discovered through his own life experience, everyone who trusts in him will never be put to shame (Rom. 10:11).

MADE WHOLE IN THE ONE

In John 17, Jesus prays for His disciples. In His prayer He describes His unique relationship to the Father, and He requests that the disciples may be one as He and the Father are one. Jesus is not in this particular case reinforcing monotheism. Certainly that God is one yet expresses Himself in three persons is an extraordinary mystery. Yet Jesus is speaking of something else. He is pointing to an expression of God that is intended to reach us. This is not a prayer for unity, but a prayer for wholeness. There is no fragmentation in God, no dysfunction in the relationship of the Godhead. Each seeks to honor the other. No part of the Godhead is self-seeking. Love is always the motivation, the intent, and the outcome. Everything about God is good, and everything flows from God. He is the eternal giver, the source of every good and perfect gift, of all that is to be desired.

We were designed to live in this way. We were created to be expressions of the goodness and wholeness of God. Good is to flow from our lives. Love is generative. It becomes an unlimited resource flowing from our hearts. We were created to know the full experience of love. When God made mankind, it was very good. We were a continuation of God's goodness. Apart from Him, there grows an all-consuming vacuum in the midst of our souls. In Him we are made complete and find that elusive state we describe as wholeness.

8

Incurable Romantics

They were in their teens when they first met. Both of them were involved with other people at the time. He was a student at USC and she was studying at Cal State L.A. She was beautiful and energetic, with a magnetic personality that drew him right in the first time he saw her. She was also off limits. Her uncle was a pastor, and she was a devoted follower of Jesus Christ. Greg had never dated anyone quite like her and couldn't imagine it would ever happen. It seemed pretty clear to him that he was not the quality of person she would even consider.

Nearly three years went by after that first encounter before they started dating. Though he was also a Christian, she was the first Christian he ever dated. From his vantage point she was as beautiful on the inside as she was on the outside. Debbie was the love of his life, and it seemed inevitable that they would be together forever. Two years of dating, one year of engagement, and then they were married. It was storybook except for one detail—Debbie was sick. At first it was fatigue, then minor aches and pains, but the symptoms progressed as her condition worsened. Debbie had lupus, a systemic disease that attacks the body in unpredictable patterns. The diagnosis came before their engagement, and while it complicated the situation, it in no way diminished Greg's growing love for Debbie. An unscheduled trip to the hospital seemed determined to interrupt their schedule between engagement and marriage.

Yet in spite of everything, they were married as planned on November 14, 1981. Debbie remembers how bad she looked as a result of her medication and treatment. Greg remembers how beautiful she looked. Their descriptions are so different, it makes one wonder if they were at the same wedding. Shortly after their engagement the chemo began. Debbie then suffered from an inflammation of the heart. Soon after, she found herself covered with shingles. And then the crisis culminated when her illness chose a new target—her kidneys.

From 1983 to 1988 Greg and Debbie walked together and grew in their love for each other even while her kidneys began to deteriorate. In 1987 Debbie was placed on a donor list where kidneys were made available according to highest need. Ironically, this list is called a cadaver donor list. Someone would have to die for Debbie to live. But Debbie was unsuccessful on the cadaver list, so doctors begin looking for a living donor. By the next year they suggested that they begin testing family and friends. A successful kidney transplant requires such a high level of compatibility that the most likely prospects are first siblings and then perhaps parents. The probability of finding a suitable match becomes very low once you move outside the family. Some in Debbie's family were simply unwilling to be tested for compatibility. Those who were willing were not suitable candidates. Debbie's sister also had lupus—that eliminated her. Of those closest to her with the highest potential for a successful match, there was no one to be found.

In the midst of all this, Greg suggested that he be tested. He was the most unlikely of candidates, and at best would have been considered a long shot. The chances of someone's spouse being a perfect match are slim. Yet that's exactly what happened. Though they were only related in marriage, Greg was an almost perfect match. Now

Greg had a choice to make. Would he give up one of his healthy kidneys out of love for his wife? His own family reminded him of the risk and even raised the scenario that he might give her his kidney and she might leave him. No divorce settlement in the world would redivide the assets such that he would get his kidney back. Even his doctor privately offered him a way out. Concerned that Greg might be acting under duress, he assured him that he could give him many valid reasons why he would not be a good candidate if he needed them. On top of all this, there was a history of diabetes in Greg's family, and he could someday be on a waiting list too. But for Greg the answer was an easy one: He was more than willing to give his kidney for the love of his life. Before he was allowed to do so, he was forced to undergo psychiatric evaluation to ensure that he was not insane or suffering from what is described as the Martyr Syndrome. Greg wasn't crazy— he was just crazy in love. He was an incurable romantic.

When I ask Greg why he did it, I expected him to tell me it was necessary to save Debbie's life, but he never said that. He actually never let it get to that. He gave Debbie his kidney long before her life was in real jeopardy. He explained that after nine years of relationship with his best friend, knowing how difficult each day had been for her, he longed to change her quality of her life. He believed that through his sacrifice, he would be providing a dramatically different life for her. I have to tell you this bothered me. A sacrifice this significant deserved a life-or-death scenario. I asked him bluntly to make sure I fully understood. "Greg, are you saying that you gave up your kidney not to save her life, but to change her quality of life?" He immediately shot back at me, "I wanted her to live!" For Greg the opportunity to change the quality of Debbie's life was the gift of life. He didn't want her to simply survive; he wanted her to enjoy life to the fullest.

Thirteen years later Greg bears an eighteen-inch scar on the left side of his abdomen that serves as a daily reminder to him of the choice he made for the one he loves. Debbie and Greg share a life together that is dramatically different because they laid together in Cedars-Sinai Hospital in September 1989, side by side in surgery. And while the

Bible tells us that when a man and woman are joined together they are made one, Greg and Debbie SooHoo have taken this metaphor beyond its reasonable expectations. It is interesting that before a transplant can take place, this surgery requires that a rib be taken from the man's side to access his kidney. They are almost a contemporary picture of man and woman's first encounter in a garden called Eden. Out of curiosity I asked Greg, "How did they choose which kidney to take?" He laughed and said, "They took the best one."

A NOBLE CAUSE

There is a place where very few of us ever aspire to go, where the measure of our worth is not how much we have, but how much we give—of ourselves. This place is entered only by those who risk the dangerous quest for nobility, a quest that leads to a place of endless generosity. *Generosity* is one of those interesting words that has evolved over time. Its ancient meaning speaks to the nature of our birth. Specifically, it refers to those of nobility; the *generous* are those of noble birth. The implication is that those who are born into wealth are born with responsibility. It is assumed that wealth is a gift from God, and that if you are born into a position of nobility, you have been entrusted by God with the care of many. The poor are dependent on your generosity.

Over time this word became more generically applied to those who *acted* with nobility than those *born* in it. When a person would use his resources as a means to bless others, he was then considered generous. Generosity soon was seen not as a product of position, but of disposition. It doesn't take long to recognize that a person can be born into great wealth and not be generous. The fact that great wealth is often accompanied with even greater greed is not lost on any of us. At the same time the best of humanity has reminded us that even great poverty cannot extinguish great generosity. Some of the world's most generous people would be counted poor in the eyes of this world.

Esperanza lived in what many casual observers would describe as a shack. Her sons, adult men bound by addiction, would take from the little she had. Her husband, hardened and unbelieving, left her virtually alone in this world. Yet week after week, she would bring a jar of pennies to the small church she attended because she was determined to give something. *Esperanza,* by the way, means "hope." Her small gifts complemented hope with love, the kind of small sacrifices that could easily be overlooked by people but were smiled upon from heaven.

There is a poverty that kills generosity, but it is never economic. This kind of impoverishment can be readily hidden behind six figures and endless possessions. At the same time great wealth does not mean lack of generosity. Some of the world's wealthiest individuals are also undeniably generous. Those who understand know that generosity goes far beyond their financial contributions. The generous see the world differently. They also experience life differently. While the greedy see the world with limited resources, the generous always operate from an abundance mentality. The greedy take to ensure that they will never be without; the generous give without fear. The greedy are convinced that for them to have, someone else has to have less.

The generous invest their lives in the prosperity of others. It isn't simply that the generous are unconcerned for their own lives and well-being; it is that they have discovered an unexpected secret: Life is most enjoyed when we give ourselves away. In that sense the generous could be described as hedonistic. They experience indescribable pleasure in serving the good of others and knowing that someone else's life was enriched as a secret indulgence. It is Greg SooHoo's laughter when he explains that his wife has his best kidney. Fortunately they're both working fine. Greg also illustrates the essence of true generosity. The generous give more than their things; they genuinely give themselves. In the most marvelous of ways, those who give most freely live most fully.

Generosity is the natural overflow of love. Love not only expands our hearts, but increases our capacity to give of ourselves. Jesus reminds us, "Greater love has no one than this, that he lay down his life for his friends" (John 15:13). The apex of generosity is sacrifice. Generosity isn't about how much we give, but how much it costs us. The same action, the same contribution, may be of significantly different value in relationship to two different people. For one person to give $1,000 is extraordinary if he only has $2,000, but incidental if he has $2 million.

Yet this is beside the point. Generosity isn't about counting what you've given in comparison to someone else. Generosity is about being free. The generous are free from the things of this world. While they own possessions, their possessions do not own them. They are free from taking for their own benefit and are free to give, even when it results in personal sacrifice. Generosity is love in action, and love is measured in giving, not taking. The generous change the texture of every environment. They engage every dimension of human experience from a dramatically different vantage point. Their agenda is always to make a contribution. They are committed to leaving every encounter having given more than they have taken. They are investors rather than consumers.

In the most marvelous of ways, those who give most freely live most fully.

To see this best, let's move out of the arena of finances and into a dramatically different context. Have you ever been around someone who is emotionally greedy? Every relationship is intended for her own benefit. Every time she's with you, she takes from your emotional reserve while never even considering contributing to your own emotional well-being. You may not even understand what is happening; you just know that every time you meet with her, you leave drained. You may have been sitting the whole time, but you're exhausted when you get up to go home.

Thankfully, the world is also filled with people who are emotionally generous. You don't identify them as such; you just know you love to be around them. You enjoy their company and cannot spend too much time with them. There is an economy of human emotions, and you have just been invested in by a generous giver. At times you may even feel guilty, wondering what you can do in return, yet no matter how diligently you try, you always feel as if you've received more than you've given. You are both indebted and made free by a generous giver.

Generosity flows in so many directions. Few investments are as important as our time. How many fathers have lost their sons when they were generous with their resources and yet were never there for them? You can never overestimate the importance of being generous with praise. A person's self-esteem can be nurtured through encouragement and crippled through continuous criticism. Generosity creates an environment for emotional health. Those who have had the privilege to grow under the nourishment of someone who is truly generous reap immeasurable benefit.

Psalm 112 gives a brief picture of the world of the generous person:

> Praise the LORD. Blessed is the man who fears the LORD, who finds great delight in his commands. His children will be mighty in the land; the generation of the upright will be blessed. Wealth and riches are in his house, and his righteousness endures forever. Even in darkness light dawns for the upright, for the gracious and compassionate and righteous man. Good will come to him who is generous and lends freely, who conducts his affairs with justice. Surely he will never be shaken; a righteous man will be remembered forever. He will have no fear of bad news; his heart is steadfast, trusting in the LORD. (vv. 1–7)

THE NOBILITY OF LOVE

While the Scriptures remind us that the greedy stir up dissension; the generous nurture wholeness. While generosity is motivated by love, greed is fueled by lust. Greed is narcissistic; generosity is Christlike. Greed is a product of self-love. Generosity is the product of selfless love. The latter knows Jesus to be the greatest lover who ever lived. The former would mistakenly attribute that person to the likes of Casanova. This contrast is critical in that the greatest application of generosity is not financial, but relational. This is perhaps the best and truest measure of nobility. Do we treat people as objects to be used or gifts to be treasured?

We were sitting in one of the busier Starbucks in the city of

Monterey Park. Our meeting was inspired by a question he asked the previous Sunday night. On occasion I have those attending Mosaic simply write out questions on three-by-five cards, and I spend the evening working through the responses. His question leaped to the top: "What do you do if you have no hope?" The card was unsigned, and I had no way of knowing who it was. I made a public appeal to whoever asked the question, encouraging him to talk to someone that night. He came and spoke to me. We agreed to meet for coffee.

He's a writer in the industry, having moved from New York just a few days before to work a project. In the middle of pursuing a career, he was trying to find a reason to live. Our conversation that day didn't go all that well. Every time the conversation would begin to move to anything substantial, he would get distracted. At first it was subtle, but soon enough it was more than obvious. I didn't say anything, but I kept wondering why I couldn't hold his attention. He finally blurted out something about all the fine-looking women in the place. He apologized, explaining it was hard for him to concentrate because he loved women. All this didn't bother me as much as what he said next. He said he supposed he was just a romantic. Now, I'm a Latin, and we Latins take pride in being true romantics. I wanted the word back. In my mind he had just defiled it.

I told him he may be a lot of things, but he wasn't romantic. Lust was not an act of love. There is nothing unique about wanting what you cannot have or wanting to take something that has not been offered you. I went on to tell him that Jesus was history's true and incurable romantic. His life and death are the standard by which all romance should be measured. His was an act of unconditional love; His life, the greatest love story ever told. To want to take is not romantic. To long to give, now, that's romance. His is a story of unrequited love. Every writer whose retelling found its way into the pages of the Scripture tells the story of Jesus as God's ultimate act of love. With love as God's motive, it should not surprise us that the events of Jesus' life culminated in His ultimate sacrifice. It should also not surprise us that God, who is love, acts with such immeasurable generosity.

As strange as it may seem, God's generosity has generated considerable controversy. You would think that the generosity of God would be received with open arms. We find in the Scriptures this is actually not the case.

When speaking of the kingdom of heaven, Jesus tells a parable of a landowner who goes out in the morning to hire workers for his vineyard. He agrees to pay each worker one denarius for a day's work. The parable continues:

About the third hour he went out and saw others standing in the marketplace doing nothing. He told them, "You also go and work in my vineyard, and I will pay you whatever is right." So they went. He went out again about the sixth hour and the ninth hour and did the same thing.

About the eleventh hour he went out and found still others standing around. He asked them, "Why have you been standing here all day long doing nothing?"

"Because no one has hired us," they answered.

He said to them, "You also go and work in my vineyard."

When evening came, the owner of the vineyard said to his foreman, "Call the workers and pay them their wages, beginning with the last ones hired and going on to the first."

The workers who were hired about the eleventh hour came and each received a denarius. So when those came who were hired first, they expected to receive more. But each one of them also received a denarius. When they received it, they began to grumble against the landowner. "These men who were hired last worked only one hour," they said, "and you have made them equal to us who have borne the burden of the work and the heat of the day."

But he answered one of them, "Friend, I am not being unfair to you. Didn't you agree to work for a denarius? Take your pay and go. I want to give the man who was hired last the same as I gave you. Don't I have the right to do what I want with my own money? Or are you envious because I am generous?" (Matt. 20:3–15)

Jesus summarizes the parable by reminding us that the last will be first and the first will be last. Jesus is giving us insight into how God makes decisions. He is allowing us to look straight into the heart of God and understand His divine motivation. God is motivated to be generous through His unending and unconditional love.

Throughout the parable, the landowner continues to find those who are just standing around doing nothing. Even one wasted life is a tragedy to God. Like the landowner in the parable, God's intention is to move us out of the paralysis of existence and bring us into a life that is productive and meaningful. There is no hierarchy or merit in regard to admission into the kingdom of heaven. All of us, regardless of how much we do, participated in His purpose only in response to His generosity. We receive God's grace because He is gracious. Not one of us can earn a relationship with God. It is easy to feel righteous if you spend your life looking at someone more broken or sinful than you. This kind of arrogance might lead you to conclude that you deserve more than someone else.

Yet all who enter the kingdom of heaven must be certain of one thing: Admission is a gift. Why should we be envious of the generosity of God in the grace that He bestows on many? Why would it bother us that His generosity would extend beyond us? Shouldn't we celebrate when the most sinful of humanity turn their hearts toward God and find forgiveness? When you understand the generosity of God, you know that God finds no pleasure in the death of the wicked, but in fact finds pleasure when they turn from their ways and live (Ezek. 18:23).

DIVINE GENEROSITY

There will be times in our lives when what we want is vengeance, but we actually find ourselves opposed to God because of His generosity. Peter reminds us that when we think God is acting too slowly, He is in fact simply being patient, not wanting anyone to perish, but everyone to come to repentance (2 Peter 3:9). It bothers us to think that someone could live an evil life but then sincerely turn to God as he approached death and find mercy in God's sight, especially if we've struggled to live admirable lives. For that individual to find forgiveness rather than judgment seems entirely unfair. I've even heard educated individuals use this as an attack against the Christian faith. That God would be this generous can be more than troubling. The exception, of course, is if you or I were that person or if that person were someone we deeply loved. Then we would long and perhaps even cry out for the mercy of God.

God is more just than any of us will ever be. He will not pretend or close a blind eye to our sinfulness. His holiness requires more than our brokenness can provide, yet He generously offers us life. When we turn to Him regardless of our condition, His gift to us is the same. In this regard He does not treat us differently. He loves us all with an everlasting love. You can choose to hold God's generosity against Him, or you can receive the abundance of the life He offers.

God is not only generous in how He receives us to Himself; He is also generous in how He relates to us. God loves to pour out His gifts on His children. James reminds us that "every good and perfect gift is from above, coming down from the Father of the heavenly lights, who does not change like shifting shadows" (1:17). The Scriptures are resplendent with promises of blessing from God to His people. When we live in a proper relationship with God, it has a dramatic effect on every area of our life.

The Scriptures tell us that God desires to bless our relationships, our marriages, our children, our work, our finances, and our very lives. Many of the characters and personalities written about in the Bible demonstrate this dynamic relationship with God Himself. Some other stories illustrate the dramatic turnaround that can take place when our lives are placed in the hands of God. At the same time, what God promises, what God guarantees, has been greatly misunderstood. The popular teaching on God's relationship to our economic well-being deviates not only from what God promises, but who God is in His character. The message is pretty straightforward—God is like a divine stockbroker. You give your money to the church or some Christian organization, and God guarantees to return it ten- or even a hundredfold. The subtext, of course, is that God wants you to be rich. If you are not rich, it's because you lack faith. Wealth is mystically connected to an act of belief. All of this is with the certainty that God's intention is always to change our economic status upward.

The most difficult falsehoods to correct are the ones that walk closely to the truth. The irony of this particular teaching is that it uses biblical promises to advocate unbiblical virtues. The underlying motivation, even in the giving in this system, is greed. Giving is never an act of true altruism. It is instead a temporary loan with a certain expectation that God will return it, plus interest.

Even the application of the story of the seed multiplying is moved from stewardship to selfishness. In the parables of the seed, the talent, and the mina, everyone who multiplied what they had were servants increasing the *master's* investment. The increase was not what their master was giving them, but what they were able to return to their master. Pleasure was found in faithfulness and productivity, not in endless personal gain.

The focus of generosity is the contribution we make in the life of others; it is not about investing in a system that increases our own economic standing. This is one important place where the prosperity gospel misses its mark. God's goal for all of us is not that we become affluent. God's goal is that we become generous. When your pursuit is for wealth, you leave generosity behind. When you live generously, God pursues you with His riches. You are never poor when you live to give. You are never rich in the sight of God when you hoard things to yourself. There is a relationship between living generously and being entrusted by God. God searches for those individuals through whom He can bless the world.

Paul speaks to this principle of generosity:

Remember this: Whoever sows sparingly will also reap sparingly, and whoever sows generously will also reap generously. Each man should give what he has decided in his heart to give, not reluctantly or under compulsion, for God loves a cheerful giver. And God is able to make all grace abound to you, so that in all things at all times, having all that you need, you will abound in every good work. As it is written: "He has scattered abroad his gifts to the poor; his righteousness endures forever."

Now he who supplies seed to the sower and bread for food will also supply and increase your store of seed and will enlarge the harvest of your righteousness. You will be made rich in every way so that you can be generous on every occasion, and through us your generosity will result in thanksgiving to God.

This service that you perform is not only supplying the needs of God's people but is also overflowing in many expressions of thanks to God. Because of the service by which you have proved yourselves, men will praise God for the obedience that accompanies your confession of the gospel of Christ, and for your generosity in sharing with them and with everyone else. (2 Cor. 9:6–13)

A careful reading of this passage will make clear that Paul's purpose was not to give us a venue for all to be rich, but to call us to live generously. Paul uses the metaphor of sowing and reaping not to establish a principle for prosperity, but to call us to a life that properly reflects God in His character. Paul was certain that if we choose to live generous lives, others will be moved to praise God. The attitude of our hearts is to be one of a cheerful giver, not an eager recipient. When we give for future gain, we are simply acting on deferred gratification.

This is not what Paul is advocating. He is teaching us a principle of investment. If we give sparingly of our lives, the return will be minimal. When we give generously, the return will be commensurate. He is not making a disconnected relationship between cause and effect. When we take this passage and conclude that giving money to one place will result in God miraculously bringing money from somewhere else, we are misapplying the Scriptures. He is certainly not saying if you put a hundred dollars in an offering you'll find one thousand dollars on the sidewalk. There is a direct correlation between what you reap and what you sow. And by the way, the process for every farmer between sowing and reaping can best be described as work. It is important to remember that God is the provider of the seed for the sower and through that He provides bread for food, which results in an increase and expansion of the harvest.

But here again the harvest that Paul speaks of is a harvest of righteousness. Our guaranteed increase is the good that we are able to do. Our generosity guarantees that we will more marvelously reflect the God who created us. The more good we do, the more good we are able to do. Generosity increases our capacity to bless others. When generosity is unleashed, it flows to every area of our lives. We become generous not only with our money, but also with our time, effort, gifts, talents, passions, every part of us. When you choose to live generously you can know that "you will be made rich in every way so that you can be generous on every occasion."

THE GENERATIVE SPIRIT

While not all of us will find ourselves in positions of great affluence, we are all entrusted with the stewardship of our wealth. To those who are not rich by the measure of this world, God's instructions again are clear:

> Command those who are rich in this present world not to be arrogant nor to put their hope in wealth, which is so uncertain, but to put their hope in God, who richly provides us with everything for our enjoyment. Command them to do good, to be rich in good deeds, and to be generous and willing to share. In this way they will lay up treasures for themselves as a firm foundation for the coming age, so that they may take hold of the life that is truly life. (1 Tim. 6:17–19)

It is important to note that there is nothing wrong with having great wealth. In fact there is nothing unethical or improper about enjoying the wealth you have. We are reminded that it is God who richly provides us with everything for our enjoyment. God *wants* us to enjoy our lives. He finds pleasure in our pleasure. There is no call here for a monastic life. All too often the Bible has been misrepresented regarding this end of the spectrum as well. Jesus did not call His disciples to reject a life of affluence and embrace a life of poverty. He simply called them to follow Him. For each one the implications were distinct but significant. The Scriptures always call us to reject a life of greed and to embrace a life of generosity. In fact when we choose the first condition, we abdicate any responsibility we may have to provide for the needs of others. To choose personal poverty is not always a decision for the greatest good. Often it's an abandonment of the full stewardship of your God-given capacity.

I took one of our interns on a short trip to the office supply store. These are the best kinds of trips for informal conversations that have long-term impact. As we were casually looking for the supplies we needed, I asked this highly intelligent UCLA graduate what he was planning to do with his life. Looking for clarification, he asked, "You mean to pay the bills?" I answered with no small amount of passion, "No, not to pay the bills." I went on to explain to him that if his only goal was to pay his bills, he would be living a nauseating, self-indulgent life. I reminded him that some people lived in the kinds of conditions where survival was a daily struggle. Others, at their best, could barely hope to pay the bills. Those who have the privilege of a healthy upbringing and a great education have to embrace more responsibility than simply paying their bills. If it were within his reach to produce great wealth, to create jobs for the unemployed, to provide income so that meals could be put on a table, if he had been entrusted by God with the skills and capacity to improve the quality of life for hundreds, if not thousands, it would be sin for him to do anything less.

It is not incidental that the words *generosity* and *generative* share a common etymology. When we are committed to being generous, we are inspired, and in fact at times required to be generative. About four years ago we were in a capital fund-raising program, and Kim and I committed to give Mosaic $30,000. Since this was nearly our entire income, we had to start thinking in new ways. It would be fair to say that we began developing and honing new skills along with praying desperately for a miracle. Our willingness to move to a new level of generosity created the opportunity for God to do even greater things in our lives. While I had thought about it many times, the urgency of our commitment forced me to move my desire to write from idea to reality. Gaining greater wealth for ourselves was not nearly as inspiring as making a greater contribution to the movement of Christ. Through this experience God has reminded me that we will be held accountable not just for the gifts we use, but for those we neglect.

We must be careful that our desire to escape from materialism does not lead to an abdication of responsibility. Yes, God calls some to a life of poverty, yet even there James reminds us that God chooses those who are poor in the eyes of the world to be rich in faith and to inherit the kingdom He promised to those who love Him (2:5).

If Jesus calls you to sell all your possessions and follow Him, there is nothing else you should do. God will, without a doubt, call each of us to relinquish everything that stands between us and Him. The apostle Paul knew what it was to live in both abundance and poverty. Kim and I have known both too. It is true that God brings true contentment regardless of circumstance. Yet for many of us, our calling is not to a life of poverty, but a life of generosity.

Sometimes the simplicity of poverty becomes romanticized in our minds when we feel the weight of responsibility that comes from prosperity. We must remember that poverty is not a virtue any more than wealth is a sign of godliness. The rich are called—in fact, commanded—to do good, to be rich in good deeds. It is God's expectation that the rich be generous and willing to share from their abundance. To do anything less is to put your trust in the possessions of this present world. To live for riches is to live a life of greed, arrogance, and foolishness. When we embrace prosperity as a gift from God entrusted to us for the good of many, we are laying up for ourselves treasures in heaven, not born out of greed, but born out of the very heart of God. This is the essence of the quest for nobility: to become like God in His generosity.

The generous see themselves as stewards of God's treasures. They are not cautious in giving themselves away, for God Himself is their source of replenishment. They understand everything to be the Lord's and thus are free to give without reservation. It's not that they give carelessly or without thoughtfulness, nor is it that they give without consideration of need. They are the contributors of life. They are the true investors in the human spirit. Wherever they are, there is more. They never leave a place or a relationship having taken more than they have given. Yet somehow they never leave empty. In giving they find themselves enriched. They are an anomaly in the human economy.

The takers of this world always need more. They are always hungry, always craving. The givers are unexplainably full. Those who refuse to believe in God's economy never understand the endless flow of their resources. The takers are always looking for happiness, convinced somehow that the next thing they grab will be their source of joy.

The giver is always open-handed, yet never empty-handed. Each has taken hold of what Paul describes as the life that is truly life. As simple as that may sound, the generous have found the secret to happiness. They have found the joy of living through serving others. They receive in disproportionate measure as a result of their unselfish giving of themselves. When we become generous, we become like God. Every creative act of God is created not out of selfishness or self-indulgence, but out of His generosity. We demean the nature of our God-given creativity when we use it for anything beneath His character. Creativity and generosity are to be identical sisters, always expressing and resulting in a work of beauty. Greed and ungratefulness caustically make nothing out of something; generosity and gratitude creatively make something out of nothing.

This is the end goal in this quest for nobility. For too long our goal has been to simply stop the thief from stealing. When more inspired, we strive to help the former thief find legitimate work and at least pay his own bills. A more industrious community of faith might even be committed to helping the one-time thief discover his greatest talents with the hope that he will do something useful with his life. God calls for more than all of this. His intent was never to neutralize the greedy, nor is he satisfied by simply making us functioning human beings. His intention is that the thief becomes the benefactor, that the person who once lived life taking from others will now give his life for the benefit of others. We see this entire journey summarized in one verse from the apostle Paul, "He who has been stealing must steal no longer, but must work, doing something useful with his own hands, that he may have something to share with those in need" (Eph. 4:28).

THE GRACE OF NOBILITY

We were sitting by the fireplace in a seminar at our house. Several times a year those who are considering becoming a part of Mosaic spend an evening with us, share a meal, and allow us to share our core values. There are several commitments we ask of those who consider moving from Mosaic's community at large to volunteer staff, where they will join at a higher level of commitment.

A middle-aged man sat down next to me and asked me a question that I knew was a setup: "Is this a grace church or a law church?" Sometimes all you can do is walk into the trap, so I answered, "This is a grace church." He responded with relief and said, "Good. I was concerned that you would require me to tithe."

I said, "Oh, no. We're definitely a grace church. The law says do not murder; grace says that we are not even to hate our enemies, but to love our enemies. The law says do not commit adultery; grace frees us even from having lust in our hearts for another man's wife.

The law says to give 10 percent to tithe; grace says be generous. We would never stop you at 10 percent. You can give 20, 30, 40 percent of your income if you'd like."

Grace is never less than the law. Grace is not freedom to live beneath the law, but to live beyond the law. It shouldn't startle us that Jesus tells us that we cannot love both God and money, that where our treasure is, there our hearts will be also. He, better than all of us, understands that greed imprisons us and generosity sets us free. He pleads with us to believe that if we try to save our lives, we'll lose them. But if we will give our lives away, we will find life. God is generous in giving life away, and the life of God always makes us generous. This is the real meaning of having life and having it in abundance—so much life that it cannot be kept to ourselves, but must be given away. This is the genius behind generosity.

A QUEST FOR ENLIGHTENMENT
UNLOCKING THE DIVINE IMAGINATION

An uprising against a self-absorbed life.

A revolution of the soul overthrowing foolishness and despair.

This gauntlet leads us through faithfulness

to perseverance and ultimately to wisdom.

Coming out of nowhere through the power of hope!

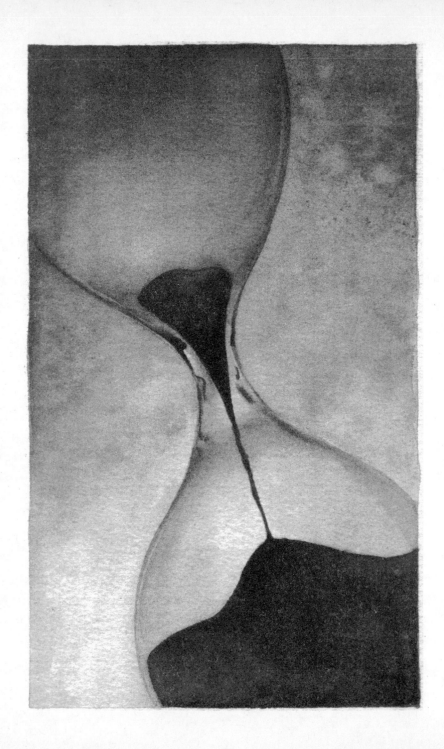

信 *f*
 a
 i
 t
 h
實 *f*
 u
 l
 n
 e
 s
 s

9

The Weight of Small Things

It was a hot, summer Friday afternoon. Kim and I were living in Dallas at the time, and I had just come home from teaching at a summer camp. It was the summer of 1988, and for the last six years we had been working among the urban poor in the middle of south Dallas under the shadow of the Cotton Bowl. Camp consisted of a couple hundred little girls from fourth to sixth grades under the umbrella of GAs—Girls in Action. Some organizations are improperly named, but this group earned their title.

I had been prepared for an endless stream of energy, but nothing could have prepared me for this experience. It wasn't that I didn't have the energy to keep up with the girls; I just didn't have the emotional reserve. At a boys' camp you connect through sports and competition. With these girls this just wasn't enough. I had to know their names, every one of them. They wanted to talk all the time. An endless barrage of questions awaited me every time I risked showing myself in public.

After five days I was exhausted. The experience was great, the kids were wonderful, but I was drained. When I got home that afternoon, all I wanted to do was take a shower and go to sleep. In the midst of my exhaustion, I had forgotten a commitment I had made for that night. That's where being married can be so helpful. As soon as I told Kim all I was going to do was stay in, she reminded me that wasn't going to be possible. That night was the beginning of the Youth Evangelism Conference. Every year Reunion Arena was packed with students who were eagerly waiting to have God speak to them, and many would come with their friends who did not have a personal relationship with Jesus Christ. My role for the past several years was to work backstage. Technically, my title was "directional advisor," which basically meant I just pointed to which direction they needed to go to find the counseling rooms. My wife worked for the organization that hosted this event, and she wasn't about to have me stand them up.

I enjoyed serving at this event, but I had been doing this for several years and was ready for a break. I told Kim that I wasn't going to go. She insisted that I was. Her argument was that it would be irresponsible to back out at the last minute. I reminded her that the only skill that was necessary to fulfill the function of my work would be to point in two different directions. Surely they could find someone else competent enough to take up this monumental task. Besides, I just spent five days in the wild jungles of Girls in Action. Even God would understand my need to stay home and recover. No, I was clear. I had every right and justification to withdraw. But Kim is a very passionate person and was unrelenting. It would be fair to say that she commanded me to get up and get ready to go. Since I'm the spiritual leader of our home, I would make the decision . . . so I changed my mind, got in the car, and drove to the event.

Going under duress only made me want to do it less. I really didn't want to go, and now, I really didn't want to go even more. I didn't have any clean clothes, so on the way I stopped by Miller's Outpost and bought a pair of jeans. I was so tired and frustrated that I didn't even bother to check the size of the pants that I picked off the shelf and took with me. They were at least two sizes too big around the waist and two sizes too long, but I didn't care. After all, I would spend the whole night backstage. Did I mention that when you're backstage, you don't get to enjoy any of the experience? You really can't hear the music or enjoy the message, but I was resigned to being faithful to my commitment. Though Kim served as my conscience in partnership with the Holy Spirit, I knew this was the right thing to do.

As the time for the event began to approach, something curious began to transpire. The well-known national youth speaker who was scheduled for that evening was not going to arrive in time. The speaker who was scheduled for the next day was on a golf course and could not be reached. The event had begun. The kids were fully engaged in a worship concert and were completely unaware of what was happening. About forty-five minutes before the message was to be delivered to nearly twenty thousand students, the director, Carlos McLeod, approached me. He quickly explained to me what was going on and simply summarized by saying, "Erwin, the Lord wants you to speak tonight."

I have to confess I didn't take him seriously. I thought he was just joking. I had two good reasons to come to this conclusion. First of all, it wasn't that long before this that Dr. McLeod and I had at least a minor conflict. I was a long-haired pastor who wore blue jeans, T-shirts, and tennis shoes. He felt pastors should be dressed appropriately in suits and ties. When he confronted me and insisted that I change how I dressed, to put it mildly, I said, "No thank you." Secondly, Dr. McLeod was surrounded by an entourage of young preachers waiting for such an opportunity. It would seem to me that he would naturally invite one of them. So when he told me he was convinced God wanted me to speak, I just laughed. I figured this was some form of male bonding.

It was on the third time when he grabbed my shoulders and began to shake me that I realized he was more than serious. As far as I knew he had never heard me speak, and he was more than aware that the congregation I pastored had an average attendance of about fifty people. I didn't even have a Bible with me. I suppose it was a subtle rebellion, my statement that what I was going to do that night didn't even require that I bring the Scriptures. It was humiliating that my first response to his request was, "I guess I'll need a Bible then." He didn't blink an eye. He just looked at me and said, "Son, we'll get you a Bible. What translation would you like?"

I went and found Kim, who was working at one of the desks in the arena. I frantically explained to her what was happening and that I had been asked to speak in just a few minutes. Kim looked at me so calmly with a combination of *I am so proud of you* and *I told you so.* She softly explained, "I've known all day that you were to speak tonight." At first I thought she meant someone had told her, but quickly I realized she was simply saying that God's Spirit had some-how made this known to her. She knew before everyone else knew, but she did not feel it was appropriate to say anything to me. I can only imagine what was going through her mind as I was telling her that I wasn't going.

If all this were not strange enough, one more thing happened to move this experience into the surreal. I decided to go out to my car and see if I could find my Bible. As I was praying, I felt impressed to speak from Daniel. Independently, Kim had come to me afterwards and suggested that if I could remember the particular message, I should speak from this exact same passage in Daniel. I heard only one line from the MC as he was speaking onstage stage, and it was simply, "like Daniel . . ." As I searched my car, I opened the trunk, and there was about a half sheet of paper there alone. I rarely write much down for my messages, and what was sitting there were my handwritten notes from my message on Daniel. So Daniel it was.

I remember slipping into a private room, falling prostrate on the ground, and weeping for the longest period of time. In less than thirty minutes, I would speak to more people than I had ever spoken to in my entire life combined. It seemed so strange that God would choose someone whose entire work was with the homeless and the impover-ished to step into this moment. And I almost missed it. The equation was so simple; the connection was so clear. If I had not been faithful in the small thing, I would have missed the greater opportunity.

SWEAT THE SMALL STUFF

The words of Jesus have echoed inside of me ever since that event: "Well done, good and faithful servant! You have been faithful with a few things; I will put you in charge of many things. Come and share your master's happiness!" (Matt. 25:21).

Most of us, when we think of this statement from Jesus, focus on the celebration, "Well done, my good and faithful servant!" Many of us have even found not only inspiration, but motivation from these words. Yet while these words focus on the final outcome, the words that follow them unlock the process. The quest for enlightenment leads us to the wisdom of God. Wisdom is forged through the crucible of perseverance. But how is perseverance developed? Where does the resilience to see the journey through to the end come from? What is the key for unlocking greater opportunity, responsibility, and productivity? If perseverance unlocks wisdom, what develops perseverance?

The great things that we long for and search for are found among the small things we may ignore or even discard.

In this parable and its parallel story found in Luke 19, we find the answer: The great things that we long for and search for are found among the small things we may ignore or even discard. The quest for enlightenment begins in what may appear as the mundane. The journey toward wisdom passes through perseverance but begins with faithfulness. Both parables end with the same spiritual principle emphatically declared, "For everyone who has will be given more, and he will have an abundance" (Matt. 25:2, cp. Luke 19:26).

Jesus is laying out for us a principle for life that is so simple it is easy to miss: If Rome wasn't built in a day, neither is character formed in one moment. There is a process in our becoming all that God created us to be. This is the human side of divine change. While becoming like God in His character is nothing shy of a gift from God Himself, being able to express that as a part of who we are is a process. This is the surprising journey to holiness. Transformation is both the miracle of God and the stewardship of man. Godliness is a result of divine activity and human action. God promises to do what we cannot do for ourselves and commands us to do that which He will not do for us. There is both miracle and responsibility. In both the parable of the talents and the parable of the minas this truth is central. God entrusts us with His resources, and then holds us accountable for what we do with them.

> Again, it will be like a man going on a journey, who called his servants and entrusted his property to them. To one he gave five talents of money, to another two talents, and to another one talent, each according to his ability. Then he went on his journey. The man who had received the five talents went at once and put his money to work and gained five more. So also, the one with the two talents gained two more. But the man who had received the one talent went off, dug a hole in the ground and hid his master's money.
>
> After a long time the master of those servants returned and settled accounts with them. The man who had received the five talents brought the other five. "Master," he said, "you entrusted me with five talents. See, I have gained five more."
>
> His master replied, "Well done, good and faithful servant! You have been faithful with a few things; I will put you in charge of many things. Come and share your master's happiness!"
>
> The man with the two talents also came. "Master," he said, "you entrusted me with two talents; see, I have gained two more."
>
> His master replied, "Well done, good and faithful servant! You have been faithful with a few things; I will put you in charge of many things. Come and share your master's happiness!"

Then the man who had received the one talent came. "Master," he said, "I knew that you are a hard man, harvesting where you have not sown and gathering where you have not scattered seed. So I was afraid and went out, and hid your talent in the ground. See, here is what belongs to you."

His master replied, "You wicked, lazy servant! So you knew that I harvest where I have not sown and gather where I have not scattered seed? Well then, you should have put my money on deposit with the bankers, so that when I returned I would have received it back with interest.

"Take the talent from him and give it to the one who has the ten talents. For everyone who has will be given more, and he will have an abundance. Whoever does not have, even what he has will be taken from him. And throw that worthless servant outside, into the darkness, where there will be weeping and gnashing of teeth." (Matt. 25:14–30)

This parable and the other in Luke establish a framework for how the kingdom of God works. The master distributes his resources among his servants not proportionately or equally, but as he chooses. Nevertheless, each servant is entrusted with the master's property. He leaves on a journey to one day return and settle accounts with them. In this version he gives to his three servants respectively first five talents, then two, and finally one. The first two servants essentially double the master's investment.

It is important to note that the master does not tell them how to manage the money or what to do with it. It does say that he distributed the resources according to each individual's ability. He didn't give them more than they were capable of managing well. Each one was effectively positioned to succeed. Yet the third servant, after receiving his one talent, dug a hole in the ground and hid his master's money.

After a long time the master returned. The first two he commends with the popular declaration, "Well done, good and faithful servant!" His evaluation was simple: "You have been faithful with a few things." As a result of their faithfulness, he determines that they could be entrusted with more. Their faithfulness had two immediate results: They were now put in charge of many things, and beyond that, they were invited to come and share in their master's happiness.

THE DIVINE SIFTING PROCESS

Luke puts a different spin on this part of the story. In the parable of the minas, a man of noble birth was going to a distant country to have himself appointed as king and then return to his people. So he called ten of his servants and gave them ten minas. He gave them these simple instructions, "Put this money to work until I come back." Again, he left it to their discretion as to how they would invest the money they were entrusted with.

This parable has a side note that some of his subjects hated him and did not want him to become king, but he became king anyway and soon returned home. Upon his arrival he sent for his servants to see what each had gained with his money. The first came, and with one mina he earned ten more. The second came, and with one mina he multiplied it five times. To the first one the master answered, "Well done, my good servant! Because you have been trustworthy in a very small matter, take charge of ten cities." To the second he responded, "You take charge of five cities."

This scenario reinforces two aspects also affirmed in the first parable. Each servant was measured not in comparison to the other, but by his own God-given capacity. In both scenes a test was necessary to ascertain the level of responsibility each servant could be entrusted with. In both cases the master intended to administer greater opportunity and privilege but waited for them to pass the test. It is also important to note that these parables assume that people are not the same. While our constitution is correct in declaring that all men are created equal, we would be mistaken to conclude that all of us are created the same. People just have different capacities. I don't know why; I just know it's true.

Some people, when they paint, create art that actually looks like or gives the impression of the subject. Not me. Some people, when they sing, hit every note, and it is melodious to the listening ear. Not me. Some people can solve complex mathematical computations and it is as simple as one, two, three. Not me. Frankly, I have been greatly encouraged by all the new research in multiple kinds of intelligence. I'm hoping that further study in this field will discover a dimension of intelligence where I shine.

The truth of the matter is that it isn't very difficult to see that we are not all the same. Some people seem to have gotten an overload when God was handing out talents. You may not feel you fall into this category but be assured there is divine talent in you. It is both waiting to be unleashed and dependent on your being a faithful steward of what you've been entrusted with.

The master's basis for evaluation is summarized in his statement, "Because you have been trustworthy in a very small matter . . ." His bottom line was that the small stuff matters. While we may be unable to perceive it, the great things of God come out of the small acts of faithfulness. The master began by entrusting his servants with minas and concludes by giving them charge over cities. When he found they could be trusted with things, he then gave them responsibility over people. Their stewardship with the less significant revealed their trustworthiness with those things of greater importance. How they served exposed how they would lead. The wisdom to lead a city, much less the wisdom to lead five or even ten, is found in the ones who can be trusted with the smallest of matters.

The great things of God come out of the small acts of faithfulness.

The parables choose two different words to paint a picture of the kind of person God desires for us to become: *faithful* and *trustworthy*. When we are faithful, we are trustworthy. The person who is

unfaithful cannot be trusted. These two characteristics are inseparable. Perseverance is the ability to remain faithful for the duration.
However long the master is gone, however long before the king
returns, those who are trustworthy will persevere to the end and find
pleasure in his return.

Then there is the other servant, the one that neither parable can
ignore. Both describe a servant who did nothing with what was
entrusted to them. Both had an improper view of the master. Their
conclusion was that their master was a hard man, a thief who took
what was not rightfully his and reaped profit from it. They both
claimed they were paralyzed by fear and this led them to only hide
what had been given to them. The servant given the one talent
buried his talent in the ground. He didn't steal the talent, and without being asked he quickly returned it, yet his master condemned
him with the indictment that he was wicked and lazy.

Lazy I can understand. Here's a guy who did nothing with what
he had been given all the time the master was gone. You would think
he could have done *something* with what he had. The master
reminded him that he could have at least put the talent in the bank
to draw interest. But he called him more than lazy. He said he was
wicked. When I think of something being wicked, it's usually pretty
extreme. I would be more likely to describe an act as sinful long
before I would describe something as wicked, especially in this situation. At face value this guy is unindustrious, passive, and paralyzed
by fear. If he had taken the talent and hired an assassin, I would have
thought that wicked. If he had used it to solicit a prostitute, I would
have considered that wicked. If he had stolen the money, made millions and kept it for himself, I would have condemned that as
wicked. But he didn't do any of that. In fact he returned exactly what
was given him. Why would that be wicked?

Is it possible that God views negligence of human capacity differently? The servant was declared wicked when what he could have
done was measured against what he did. When we think of human
talent or gifting, we tend to put it in a category of value added. If a

person does not achieve his or her God-given potential, we might consider it a tragedy, but we would never think of it as wickedness. Our pursuit for holiness has historically been all about the elimination of sin. At best it focuses on keeping the Ten Commandments, which of course strongly focus on what you shouldn't do. From our common view of holiness, the third servant in both these parables did nothing wrong in regard to his actions. He just didn't do anything.

Yet this parable gives us an inside view of legalism at its best. This man was paralyzed by an improper view of God. There is a difference between the fear of God and being afraid of God. We have seen that the fear of God sets us free to live. Being afraid of God paralyzes us and reduces us to existing. His wrong view of God's character led him to a wrong conclusion of what God would require of him. At the same time, his wrong view of God led him to lose both the potential of his life and the pleasure of his master.

This parable establishes God's measure for our lives. God sees not only who we are, but who we can become. When we neglect our God-given capacity, when we refuse to maximize our God-given potential, it is wickedness in the sight of God. How would it change the work of the church if our measure of effectiveness was not how little sin was being done, but how much good was being accomplished? We have seen with clarity that a life lived against God is wicked, but have we ever seen as clearly that to live a life beneath our divine capacity is equally dishonoring to God? To not have that opportunity is tragic. To relinquish it, to neglect it, to reject it is wicked in the sight of God.

UNLEASHING DIVINE POTENTIAL

You are created for more than just existing. While we have redefined mediocrity as normal and far too often expect nothing more than that from ourselves, God will not have it. He did not create us to be average, but to be unique. Being human was not intended to be a curse, but a gift. While you may dream of a better life or the better person you could be, only God really knows the person you were intended to become. Only He sees the full measure of what is neglected or lost.

In both parables the servant was fearful and in neither parable was his apathy found acceptable. Sin is what happens when we have too much time on our hands and too little purpose in our lives. Sin fills a vacuum that is not supposed to be empty. To give our lives to the elimination of sin is like trying to fill a black hole. The Bible tells us that the reward of sin is death. Sin and life cannot coexist. They are like darkness and light.

Jesus reminds us that the thief comes to rob and to kill, but that He came to give us life and life abundant. When you begin to live, sin falls off like pounds in a sauna. Some of the more difficult sins only come off when you run the treadmill. Still, when you begin to live, you become free from sin. The vacuum is filled with life. The outcome is stewardship, and all of us have gifts for which God demands our stewardship. Whether you are a one-, five- or ten-talent servant, you have not been left empty-handed.

I was once sitting in a meeting with about twenty leaders from around the country. Each led his own organization, and we came together to see if we could coalesce our efforts on a common project. The facilitator for the day asked everyone to share their names and to describe in some way the unique contributions they were asked to bring to the meeting. As awkward as it was, each person took a moment or two to describe what essentially came down to their God-given talents as related to this project.

The last person stated his name and summarized, "I don't have any talent. I just work hard." My first reaction was, *Boy, do I feel stupid.* His answer was by far the most humble, yet at the same time I felt something was lost. I'm pretty sure everyone in the room worked hard. Very few people ever accomplish significant things without labor. In fact the very best in any discipline only make it look easy because of all their hard work. I am also equally sure that while he was a very hard worker, he was also very gifted. To say you don't have any talent is to contradict God.

Every one of us has God-given talent. Beyond this, God pours into each of us His gifts. Each is unique in the contribution he or she can make. All of us are complex and represent a composite of intelligence, passions, personality, skills, talents, and gifts. The dynamic interaction of all of these are the material from which we draw our potential. Yet potential and productivity are not the same.

In *Chasing Daylight,* we unwrapped the dilemma of untapped potential.

There's so much talk about potential in our culture, as if it's the end-all of success. Has anyone ever said about you, "He has so much potential"? If you're under twenty—let's give you twenty-five—consider it a compliment. Potential—your untapped or unlocked capacity. Potential—the hint of greatness not yet developed. "He has so much potential"—a statement of praise and maybe even adoration. And then you're thirty, and you still have all this potential. Pressing forty, and you're still full of potential. If you're forty-five and someone looks at you and says, "You have so much potential," pause, excuse yourself, step into a closet, and have a good cry.

What once was a statement of promise is now an assessment of lost opportunity. There is a point where you're not supposed to be full of potential; you're supposed to be full of talent, capacity, product. Potential is a glimpse of what could be, yet there must be a shift from where we have potential to where we are potent.

You're not supposed to die with your potential. A life well lived squeezes all the potential placed within and does something with it. When potential is harnessed, we become potent. Potential, when it becomes potent, always produces results. We are born with potential, but we are called to live productive lives. The fool squanders his potential. He is not faithful with what has been given him.

When it comes to potential, the parable of the talent exposes how unequally talent is distributed by God. It's more than the fact that some people are simply more talented than others. Once you recognize that even in this case no one is left without talent, this is not so difficult to accept. What's more critical to this process is how the master takes the talent from the wicked servant and gives it to the servant who gained the most. When I first saw this, it was extremely troubling to me. When the master commanded, "Take the talent from him and give it to the one who has the ten," my immediate thought was, *No, give it to the one who has the five. He was faithful too. Besides, the other guy has ten already. If you give it to the one with five, he'll have six, and it will be more even.*

The master explained his action when he declared, "For everyone who has will be given more, and he will have an abundance." This reality is accentuated by whom he chose to give the unused talent to. Those who are most faithful with the most resources will find an expanding role in God's Kingdom. When I looked to the text in Luke 19, I realized the parable literally speaks on my behalf. Here the master commanded, "Take his mina away from him and give it to the one who has ten minas." Same thing. He doesn't give it to the one with five, but to the one with ten. In verse 25, the servants interjected, "Sir, he already has ten!" That's exactly how I felt. Again, the master made the same point. "I tell you that to everyone who has, more will be given, but as for the one who has nothing, even what he has will be taken away."

I'm convinced more people think like me than like God. We want equity. Most of us would be more than happy to see everything in life sort of even out. We don't want less, but we would like to have as much as the guy who has more than us. It's disturbing to think that God would be so disproportionate. Yet this is absolutely true. If God can help more people by entrusting you with far more than He gives to me, He will. It's not about how much you or I get; it is about what we will do with what we have.

For some dark reason the human heart inclines us to want to

bring others down to wherever we are if we cannot bring ourselves up to where they are. Some cultures call it "crab antics." Others use the phrase "cutting the tall poppy." When this framework shapes social structures, it results in forms like communism or socialism. The kingdom of God will never be like this. Whoever is faithful with what God has given them will be candidates for expanded responsibility in the kingdom. If they are the only ones who are faithful, they get to jump to the front of the line. Healthy corporations understand this principle. If they have one division that is thriving and another that is losing money, they know it's foolish to pour their money into the division that is struggling rather than to invest supplemental resources in the section that is growing. With one you invest in health; with the other you magnify the loss.

When we are unfaithful, we are a bad investment. We may find ourselves blaming others for our failures, but in the end, it's all us. Too often organizations have placed unfaithful people in positions of responsibility hoping to inspire a transformation of character. These have been both costly and painful decisions. When a person is placed into a position of leadership on the basis of talent, even though known to be untrustworthy, a great travesty has taken place. Power does not make a person trustworthy. Authority does not make a person responsible. When we are trustworthy, we can be entrusted with power. When we are faithful, our influence in the lives of others will naturally expand. Talent without character is a dangerous thing. Talent fueled by character is a gift from God.

Character is formed in the crucible of faithfulness and refined through the gauntlet of perseverance. Remember, the shape of our character is the shape of our future. It is through the transformation of our character that God both points the way and lights our way. The character of Christ fuels us with a passion that moves naturally in the direction God desires for us. The character of Christ also illumines us to see things with the eyes of God. The quest for enlightenment begins with faithfulness. It is here where the wisdom of God is formed in our hearts.

FAITHFULLY SEEKING WISDOM

We tend to seek wisdom only when we face an overwhelming crisis. We tend to treat wisdom as if it is a rare commodity—pulling it out only when we really need it. Often it is only when we find ourselves up against the wall that we turn frantically to God in the hope that He would give us divine insight. For everything else in life, we find our own decision-making process more than adequate. Yet we miss a very important truth. There is wisdom in the small things, the small choices. The seemingly minor decisions require wisdom just as much as the monumental ones. In fact, the reason we find ourselves in so many crisis moments is exactly because we lacked wisdom at an earlier stage in the process.

Not every crisis we face is a result of lack of wisdom, but this is many times the case. It's just too easy to discard the importance of small things. We are convinced that if we were entrusted with great responsibility, we would address it differently. Yet the reality is the same kind of intentionality we demonstrate in the little things is precisely how we will handle issues of great weight. When we've been entrusted with something, whether great or small, it is not inconsequential. Even when the responsibility itself has minimal scope, the pattern we establish for ourselves has long-term ramifications. More than the work itself, it is the work in us that makes it significant. When we demean the importance of any task for which we have accepted responsibility and are negligent in doing our best, we are choosing to become a certain kind of person.

Even in the smallest of things our character is being formed. In fact, in the smallest of things, the deepest aspect of our character is shaped and developed. The implications of faithfulness cannot be overestimated and must not be underestimated. Rather than concluding that we don't have any talent but that we just work hard, we should recognize that it is when we work hard that our talents begin to be harnessed. While it is helpful to know the unique talents you have been entrusted with, our talents are not to be the focus of our lives. Serving others through the gifts and talents that we have is far more important. There will be times when we will find ourselves called to serve even when it is outside of our most significant abilities. Even when our work is not focused on our talents, the effect can be both positive and substantial.

The development of our talents is critical to maximizing our life impact; yet more important than this is the development of our character. Faithfulness is about making significant those tasks entrusted to you that further the common good. You may be a gifted musician but working behind the scenes on the tech crew may be the most important thing for you to do at this juncture in your life. You may be a skilled communicator, but if you're asked to stack chairs, you should treat that with the same importance. You may one day run the company you work for, and your present assignment may seem beneath you, yet your future success may be entirely dependent on how eagerly you embrace the job in front of you right now. Today you may only be making decisions of little weight, but how you make those decisions will be the very same methods you'll use in your greatest moments of decision. Every wise person is marked by the scars of perseverance. Perseverance is the fruit of faithfulness. All of us would love to find a shortcut to wisdom. Wisdom does not have to come slowly, but it does not come frivolously. Faithfulness accelerates wisdom.

On one of those afternoons when we decided to journey down to Orange County and visit Disneyland, I noticed there were two lines in which people were standing. There was the really fast-moving line with all the happy people in it and the line we were standing in. I couldn't figure out what was going on. We didn't notice two entry points, but there were clearly two ways of getting in. Then one of us saw the signs. The two lines had clear designations. Our line was designated "Standby." The other line had the very exciting and promising designation "Fast Pass." I had no idea what they did to earn Fast-Pass class; I just knew I wanted to be upgraded. I was pretty ticked off that the couple hundred dollars I paid to get us in only allotted me the privilege of going standby. I was a citizen of the Magic Kingdom. This kind of class warfare seemed so unfair. Did I pay all that money just for the privilege to hope I could get in?

Quickly my children figured out how this whole thing worked. You had to stand in line to get a Fast Pass ticket that upgraded you from standby to the more elite status. After that, we changed our entire approach on our journey through the kingdom. We had joined the multitudes of smiling faces, smugly passing by the waiting throngs. We were nobility with reservations that separated us from the masses.

If you're anything like me, you don't like waiting. If there's a faster way, I want to find it. It's not that I'm impatient; I just don't like standing around. Wasting time is a waste of time. Some things you have to wait for. Sometimes to hurry the process threatens the quality. With wisdom you don't have to be worried about trying to get it too fast, but you need to be very concerned about getting it too slow. No matter what you do, you're not going to rush God in this process. Tragically though, you can hold God up.

When we are unfaithful in the small things, we relegate ourselves to the standby line. Whenever we are faithful with little, when we are found trustworthy in the small matters, we accelerate our journey to wisdom. This is not to say that we will ever find a quick fix in this process. Faithfulness by its very essence implies time. Faith you can have in a moment; faithfulness takes a bit longer, which may be why so much of our God talk focuses on faith and neglects faithfulness.

THE FAITH TO PERSEVERE

A casual listener to Christian teaching across the airwaves would conclude the solution to every problem is to have more faith. If you have a problem, all you need to do is believe. If you can't overcome the problem, you're just not believing big enough. The metaphor of the mustard seed is thrown into this mix of faith talk. We are told that Jesus said all we needed was faith the size of a mustard seed and we could speak to the mountain, "Be removed," and it would be cast into the sea. Jesus' words are interpreted to mean that what we have is a faith problem—we just don't believe enough. This spiritual journey becomes an endless cycle of trying to muster up more belief, bigger faith. But Jesus is pointing us to the very opposite conclusion. He's not saying we need to have more faith; He's actually telling us we just need to have some. It's not about making your faith bigger. All you need is mustard seed-sized faith. The implication is any less is none at all. Jesus was not calling us to work up our faith. He was calling us simply to put our faith in God. It is not our faith in an event that is critical, but our faith in God Himself. It is not about believing in a miracle or believing for a miracle; it is about an unshakable confidence in the character of God.

In Matthew 11, John the Baptist sent his disciples to ask Jesus a question: "Are you the one who was to come, or should we expect someone else?" Jesus sent back this response: "Go back and report to John what you hear and see: The blind receive sight, the lame walk, those who have leprosy are cured, the deaf hear, the dead are raised, and the good news is preached to the poor. Blessed is the man who does not fall away on account of me" (11:3–6). It is curious that John, who was the cousin of Jesus, was doubting who Jesus was. If anyone should have been sure, it was John. The Bible tells us he leaped in his mother Elizabeth's womb when she was in the presence of Mary, who was pregnant with Jesus. Interesting that while in the womb, John was convinced Jesus was the one but was confused about it later.

On another occasion, John saw Jesus walking in a crowd and boldly declared, "Look, the Lamb of God, who takes away the sin of the world!" (John 1:29). Even in the midst of a crowd, John knew who He was. While John was baptizing in the Jordan, Jesus came to him asking to be baptized, and John insisted that it was Jesus who should be baptizing him (Matt. 3:14). Once again John had absolute clarity that Jesus was the One. But when John acquiesced and baptized Jesus, John saw the heavens open, witnessed the Spirit of God descending on

Jesus like a dove and heard a voice from heaven declaring, "This is my Son, whom I love; with him I am well pleased" (vv. 16–17).

In this situation, like the rest, John didn't pause and ask, "Now, I was wondering, are you the One that we are waiting for or should we look for another?" There is only one reason John asked this question when he did. He was in prison, and Herod was about to have him beheaded. If you are about to lose your head over God, you want to make sure He's the right one. Yet even in this crisis, John's doubts came as a result of Jesus' inactivity on his behalf. He was the one preparing the way for Christ. While everyone else wondered who He was, John was declaring who He was. Yet this moment was different. His life was now at stake. It was becoming clear to John that Jesus would not intervene on his behalf.

What John needed was not the faith to be released from prison, but the faithfulness to see God's mission for him fulfilled. Jesus' response was one of astonishing credentials—the blind were made to see, the lame were made to walk, lepers were cured, the deaf could hear, and even the dead were raised. What's more, the good news was proclaimed to the poor. All this John already knew. Jesus' résumé brought no surprises to John except for His final statement, "Blessed is the man who does not fall away on account of me."

This is an odd saying at the end of such a miraculous description. Why would anyone be tempted to fall away from a God through which there was so much miraculous intervention? Because though He is the God who can do all that was described, He is also the God who calls you to the greatest level of sacrifice. There are moments when our greatest act of faith is to remain faithful. There will be times where no level of faith will change our circumstance. Faith is not always a way out of a crisis. In fact I am convinced it rarely is. Faith gives us the strength and confidence to see every challenge and crisis through to the end. There is a resilience that erupts out of faithfulness where you just won't quit! You learn to never give up. Faith is a confidence in God that results in faithfulness. That faithfulness gives us the power to persevere. In the midst of our perseverance, we find the wisdom of God to help us understand and see our way through. When Jesus calls us to be faithful and even to endure great things, we are blessed when we do not fall away from Him but continue to follow closely at His side.

THE FAITHFULNESS OF GOD

Even Jesus found no shortcuts on His journey while He walked the earth. In Isaiah the series of passages known as the servant songs describe the coming and life of Jesus generations before His birth. When you read them, you can hear the events in Jesus' life in detail. Without being told you would never know their antiquity. Perhaps one of the most famous of these verses is in chapter 53:

> He was despised and rejected by men, a man of sorrows, and famil-
> iar with suffering. Like one from whom men hide their faces he was
> despised, and we esteemed him not. Surely he took up our infirmi-
> ties and carried our sorrows, yet we considered him stricken by
> God, smitten by him, and afflicted. But he was pierced for our
> transgressions, he was crushed for our iniquities; the punishment
> that brought us peace was upon him, and by his wounds we are
> healed. (vv. 3–5)

Another of these songs is in chapter 50. Listen to verse 6: "I offered my back to those who beat me, my cheeks to those who pulled out my beard. I did not hide my face from mocking and spitting." Back a couple verses, it reads, "The Sovereign LORD has given me an instructed tongue, to know the word that sustains the weary" (v. 4). Sounds like wisdom, doesn't it? What a gift to always know the right thing to say. This is more than just finding the appropriate words but having the words that bring healing and life. Have you ever felt someone's pain so deeply that you were genuinely at a loss for words? Have you ever felt anguish over someone's life being so entangled and shattered, yet you had no idea what to do or say? Isaiah 50:4 continues and unlocks the process from which Jesus gained this kind of wisdom: "He wakens me morning by morning, wakens my ear to listen like one being taught."

For Jesus, wisdom wasn't just the result of a download from heaven. In other words when He became man, He didn't cheat. He gained wisdom from the same process that we are invited to employ. He knew what to say because morning by morning He opened His ears and heart and became a student. The words of God come to those who listen carefully to the voice of God. The wisdom of God comes to those who walk with God. And the path is not easy or safe.

The passage continues, "The Sovereign LORD has opened my ears, and I have not been rebellious; I have not drawn back" (50:5). Even for Jesus the path was difficult. It would have been easy to justify turning another way. Yet in His faithfulness, He found the strength to persevere and through perseverance He gained the wisdom of His Father. I know it's difficult to think of Jesus as having to gain wisdom. We tend to think of Jesus as always complete in every way. To see this clearly, we only need to remember that Jesus came into this world as an infant. He had to learn everything from scratch—how to eat, how to walk, how to speak, how to read, how to live.

Luke reminds us of this dynamic in the one small description of Jesus at the age of twelve. His summary of Jesus' childhood is simply this: "And Jesus grew in wisdom and stature, and in favor with God and men" (2:52).

We all like the destination, but not as many of us are excited about the process. Even fewer of us are convinced of where the journey begins. The quest for enlightenment begins with faithfulness. Before David was king, he was a warrior. Before he was a great warrior, he was an obscure shepherd. Before Joseph became second only to Pharaoh in the empire of Egypt, he endured the life of a slave. Before Ruth found a life filled with joy and promise at the side of Boaz, she endured the death of her first husband, but gave her life to serving Naomi, her mother-in-law. She chose faithfulness to the family of her deceased husband above her own personal good. It was only on this journey that she found the future God planned for her. It was only through faithfulness that each of them discovered the life God held for them. But first there were times of great uncertainty.

As with Jesus, no one journeys this path without significant obstacles and hardship. We will all face the temptation to rebel or perhaps draw back, yet if we hold fast, we will find the light of day. If the journey draws you to it, but you find yourself overwhelmed with its weightiness, then do just two things: Look to the end and see the promise of enlightenment, then look straight ahead and focus on taking one step at a time. God loves to entrust even more to men and women who are faithful with what they have.

PRESERVING YOUR CHARACTER

I've been in some of the world's most hostile environments, but never felt closer to death than in this moment. We were in the Middle East just days before September 11, 2001, and I felt as though I was going to die. In fact it looked as if the whole group of us was in danger. I always imagined the closing chapter of my life would have a more noble or romantic end. I could see it now—cause of death: bad mayonnaise.

We had decided to take a day and travel to the interior of Lebanon. We were rushing out of Beirut on our way to Baalbek. I wanted my wife and kids to experience the wonder of these ancient Roman ruins. I have a vague memory of Mimi mentioning to her husband, Nabil, that we should pick up some ice. We never did. Did I mention it was August? A half day later when we sat down to enjoy our picnic lunch, we gave little thought to this small, insignificant detail. But by the next day, every one of us who chose to enjoy the mayonnaise discovered that Montezuma's revenge is an international phenomenon. In the end we lost hours because we saved minutes.

Stopping to get ice would just slow us down. But neglecting to get ice would shut us down.

Just as ice keeps mayonnaise from spoiling, faithfulness keeps your character from going bad. The small things don't seem very important in the moment, but they have huge ramifications in the future. It's not the great challenges that cause successful leaders to fall; it is the ignoring of the small things. When it comes to character, the details really do matter. In your quest for honor, you have to sweat the small stuff. Great leaders in a very real way come out of nowhere. We must never underestimate the weightiness of small matters. To this day, I still can't eat mayonnaise.

堅持不懈

p e r s e v e r a n c e

10

Waiting Game

Paris in the summer. We were finally there. The capital of romance. We'd been all over the world, but Kim always wanted to go to Paris. And there we were. It would have been like a second honeymoon except everywhere we went we were followed by two smaller human beings who insisted they were our children. Well, there went the romance.

Paris in the summer. We were all there. A city filled with history. Our highlight would be the Louvre, an endless wealth of treasure. What a wonderful opportunity for learning. Museums are not usually the dream vacations for thirteen- and nine-year-olds, but we knew this would be the memory of a lifetime. We took the Metro early that morning from La Defense, where we were staying. From the Metro we would board one of the double-decker tour buses that would circle the city throughout the day.

We arrived at the Louvre early that Thursday to make the most of our opportunity. Our time in line was relatively short as we waited for the doors to open. Just about the time we arrived at the ticket counter,

I reached for my wallet. It wasn't there. This happens to me all the time, so I began looking in my other pockets. It didn't take long to realize my wallet was gone. I had everything in my wallet—all the money, the credit cards, even the bus passes. It would not be an understatement to say my whole body was overwhelmed with panic.

I quickly turned to Kim and explained my wallet was gone. I immediately concluded that I had left it on the bus. We were on the top floor of the double decker. I looked back at the street where passengers load and unload and the bus was still there. I told Kim and the kids to wait, and I ran to the bus in hopes that my wallet would still be somewhere on board. There was an attendant there who organized the passengers as they were boarding, and I explained to her my dilemma. She eagerly gave me permission to look on board, but I found nothing. Then I noticed our driver had changed. Even his race had changed. I quickly discovered this was not the same bus. It looked the same, was parked in the same place, but was not the same bus.

They explained that there were over thirty buses that ran similar routes. The bus we had been on was at least two buses ahead. After my pleading wore them down, they let me ride the bus in hopes of catching the bus I had left my wallet on. I asked if they could call ahead. They explained they had no central communication system. I couldn't even imagine a company of this size not being able to communicate with each other. But I was in Paris, not Los Angeles.

I rode the bus to the other side of the city feeling like a character out of *The Bourne Identity*, in desperate search for "the package." In futility they let me out for what must have been nearly an hour's journey on foot. I had no idea where I was, but somehow found my way back to my family waiting outside the Louvre. We decided to try a different approach. We waited at the one stop as bus after bus made its drop. We searched every bus looking to see if it was the right one. Our entire day was spent—or should I say wasted—on this futile search.

Hours later we found the bus that we had been on. We knew it was the same one. Our driver had returned to us. We searched the bus thoroughly, but no wallet. He assured us nothing was on board, and no one had turned anything in. The French we had interacted with were not hopeful of the recovery of my wallet. It seems pickpockets run in abundance in Paris. Some even suggested that we would be hard pressed to find an honest person returning the lost merchandise. We certainly found the French extremely helpful to us and gracious in our dilemma. Nevertheless, there was no wallet.

In a final act of compassion, the attendant and bus driver allowed our family to ride the bus back to the central terminal, even though we didn't have tickets. We were exhausted and disappointed. We spent the whole day at the Louvre and never saw a thing. We had no idea how we would get back to our hotel or what we would do for the rest of our travels. We were to go to the Middle East from France, and we were still at least two weeks from returning home. The bus finally came to its destination. The day was now overtaken by the night, and we were about to find ourselves stranded in the heart of Paris. But at least the experience had brought us together. We were all moping and discouraged.

Then the strangest thing happened. An Italian man followed us off the bus. It had to be obvious to everyone that we were on a desperate search. I pretty much had everyone in the upper deck searching with us or moving out of the way to let me look. It was quite a scene, as sad as it was funny, so it caught me by surprise when he stopped me and asked if I had lost something. I answered, "Yes, I've lost my wallet."

I can't even begin to describe what it was like to see this man pull out my wallet. He briefly had me identify what he would find inside and quickly turned it back over to me. The best I can tell, he had found it hours before and was on his way to turning it in to the police. His name was Roberto Priore from Salerno, Italy. The one honest man we needed in Paris was Italian. But even if you can see that there are honest people in the world, how in the world can you explain our chance encounter? Paris is a big city. What is the mathematical probability that a guy from Italy would find the wallet of a guy from El Salvador while they're both staying in Paris and actually meet so he could return it?

While I searched frantically that day, Kim and the kids prayed earnestly. Aaron reminds me that it was hot and uncomfortable. While the details of this event begin to fade away even in our memories, the miracle of it remains with us. How could it be an exaggeration to say that God returned my wallet? My children experienced the power of prayer and persistence working together. I am convinced that one without the other would have left us stranded. It would have been all too easy to have given up right away. After all, giving up was more than rational and pressing on would have easily been attributed to unreasonable hope. Yet this experience and many others like it lead me to an important observation: Often we miss the undeniable work of God because we give up too soon.

Often we miss the undeniable work of God because we give up too soon.

DETERMINATION

It's maddening to think that our efforts might only be failures because we quit. It's not that there aren't times we shouldn't cut bait or close the chapter on an enterprise, but there are certain things we must never quit on. While projects can be dispensed with, virtues are indispensable. Strategies come and go. They are not intended to be permanent. Character is quite different. If we treat who we are as being of the same quality as what we do, we are structured for failure. It's easier to replace a wallet than it is to regain your integrity.

Paris is a reminder to me not to give up too soon, that perseverance is often the only thing that separates failure and success. Life is a gauntlet that requires determination. I wonder how many times we have missed out on a unique God moment because we have given up on the journey. My kids never saw the Louvre, but they did see God come through. They missed a museum filled with the works of men, but they entered an experience filled with the work of God. It is the same way with wisdom. The wisdom of God comes like a gift, yet it is a gift born out of the womb of perseverance.

Wisdom is the treasure that awaits us on the other side of our quest for enlightenment. And while wisdom is not always the result of time or experience, wisdom is nurtured and formed in the context of trials and temptations. For wisdom to be properly forged in our hearts, it requires us to stand the pressure cooker of life.

James tells us, "Consider it pure joy, my brothers, whenever you face trials of many kinds, because you know that the testing of your faith develops perseverance. Perseverance must finish its work so that you may be mature and complete, not lacking anything. If any of you lacks wisdom, he should ask God, who gives generously to all without finding fault, and it will be given to him" (James 1:2–5).

James describes a process that each of us must go through to gain the wisdom that is necessary for life. He promises that God will give wisdom generously to all who ask, but that promise is preceded by a description of the journey we must take. Perseverance is the necessary link to wisdom. James describes perseverance as an active agent powerfully at work within us *and* in the process of finishing a work. When this work is complete, we would be described as mature and complete, not lacking anything. This sounds like a great state to be in.

Perseverance has multiple dimensions. In the Scriptures the same word can be translated as endurance or even patience. Perseverance is more than just waiting. It's more about how and why we wait. It is the ability to stand and thrive under pressure. When we hold out for the good, our perseverance is expressed as patience. When we hold on to the good, our perseverance is expressed as endurance. To persevere requires wisdom in the process and grows us in wisdom through the process. When we do not persevere, we do not grow in wisdom. Whenever God places us in circumstances where perseverance is critical, He is trying to birth wisdom within us. When we circumvent the process, it is a miscarriage of wisdom.

The quest for enlightenment requires a perseverance that results in patience. Patience ensures that we do not move faster than God.

It does not imply idleness. Waiting on God requires that we continue to do what is right even when our situation does not change. Patience encompasses a life that follows what God has asked even when it appears that God is not following through on what He has said. Patience holds out for the good.

Though Peter is specifically addressing the return of Christ, his words carry application far beyond even that particular context. He reminds us, "But do not forget this one thing, dear friends: With the Lord a day is like a thousand years, and a thousand years are like a day. The Lord is not slow in keeping his promise, as some understand slowness. He is patient with you, not wanting anyone to perish, but everyone to come to repentance" (2 Pet. 3:8–9).

Our need to persevere comes with an implicit understanding that there will be times when it seems God is moving far too slow in keeping His promises. When God moves slower than we'd like, there is a vacuum created. This is the vacuum in which our greatest temptations will come. If God doesn't act on our timetables, will we act apart from Him? Will we settle for less than what He desires for us? Will we conclude He is indifferent to our needs and seek another way of fulfilling the longings of our hearts?

James reminds us that suffering must not be used as an excuse for impatience. "Brothers, as an example of patience in the face of suffering, take the prophets who spoke in the name of the Lord. As you know, we consider blessed those who have persevered. You have heard of Job's perseverance and have seen what the Lord finally brought about. The Lord is full of compassion and mercy" (5:10–11).

The quest for enlightenment also requires a perseverance that endures. Endurance ensures that we do not lose our strength before the task is done. In some races only the one who finishes first is crowned champion. In this race everyone who finishes is proclaimed victor. The journey toward wisdom requires that we pass through a gauntlet. Endurance encompasses a life that follows what God has asked even when it appears that there is no advantage in maintaining your course. Endurance holds on to the good.

The writer of Hebrews reminds us that while it may seem impossible at times to finish the course to which we've been called, there are many others who have gone before us and have found success. He inspires us with this picture:

> Therefore, since we are surrounded by such a great cloud of witnesses, let us throw off everything that hinders and the sin that so easily entangles, and let us run with perseverance the race marked out for us. Let us fix our eyes on Jesus, the author and perfecter of our faith, who for the joy set before him endured the cross, scorning its shame, and sat down at the right hand of the throne of God. Consider him who endured such opposition from sinful men, so that you will not grow weary and lose heart. (Heb. 12:1–3)

THE PRESSURE COOKER

Our need to persevere comes with an implicit understanding that there will be times when it seems God is allowing us to experience far more than we are able to bear. Most of us have at least an unspoken expectation that if we do what is right, God will bless us for it. Not in the afterlife or in some obscure future date, but soon, if not immediately. It creates dissonance in us when bad things happen to us when we are striving to become the best of people. It only adds insult to injury when it seems that good things keep coming to bad people.

Though God promises He will never allow us to undertake more than we can bear and that He will always give us the strength to overcome whatever difficulty we may face, there will be days when we wonder if we can hold on even one more moment. Yet it should not come as a surprise to us that great suffering can accompany a life entirely given to God. Even, and especially, our Lord Jesus was not absolved from this path. Though He is exalted above all, His suffering surpasses us all. He endured not only the opposition of sinful men, but also endured the agonizing pain of death on the cross.

Perseverance is both the resolve to be patient and the commitment to endure. Perseverance not only holds out and holds on to the good, but finds the good in the worst of all circumstances. This may be the most miraculous element of perseverance as it produces wisdom. We are not called just to endure hardship. Our mandate is not simply to hold on for dear life, but to hold on to life dearly.

James tells us to consider it pure joy when we face trials of many kinds. Can you imagine that? He is inviting us to find pleasure in the midst of pain. In fact several times joy and suffering are bound together in the Scriptures. Without careful observation these two might create an unhealthy form of spiritual masochism. In fact historically it seems this is exactly what happened. Even in our materialistic environment you don't have to listen long to hear suffering described as a virtue. Maybe it's just because we feel so guilty when we don't do very much of it. But at the core it exposes a genuine misunderstanding of the role of suffering in our lives. Suffering is not a virtue; it is a reality. You are not to pursue suffering. I assure you, suffering will pursue you. Suffering is not the source of joy even for the most spiritual, yet suffering is not a joyless setting. And this is exactly the point that James was trying to make. It's not the trials that are the source of joy, but trials are the settings for our greatest opportunities for joy. When you belong to God, trials become not only a reminder of your need for God, but also a promise that God will meet you in the midst of it. If God is your greatest pleasure, then trials become your greatest joy. The key to experiencing this ultimate joy becomes perseverance. You don't want to turn to any substitute. You want to wait on God, and you can be certain that He will come through, even though it may not be the way you think.

The example of Jesus gives us our best insight into the relationship between suffering and joy. Hebrews tells us that Jesus endured

> *Perseverance is both the resolve to be patient and the commitment to endure.*

the cross for the joy set before Him. There was no joy in the cross. The cross brought Jesus only agony and death. It was not for the joy of the cross that Jesus allowed Himself to be crucified; it was for the joy He could see through the cross. It was a joy set before Him, and that joy remained with Him even through His crucifixion.

Paul reminds us that the road is the same for us as it was for Jesus. We are each called to carry our own cross and at the same time, we're invited to live a life of unspeakable joy. You can almost hear Paul shouting in his discovery:

> Therefore, since we have been justified through faith, we have peace with God through our Lord Jesus Christ, through whom we have gained access by faith into this grace in which we now stand. And we rejoice in the hope of the glory of God. Not only so, but we also rejoice in our sufferings, because we know that suffering produces perseverance; perseverance, character; and character, hope. And hope does not disappoint us, because God has poured out his love into our hearts by the Holy Spirit, whom he has given us. (Rom 5:1–5)

Followers of Christ suffer just like everyone else. The pain is just as real, the disappointment just as deep, the tears just as profound. Yet how we face suffering is quite different. God allows us to see through the suffering. We rejoice in our sufferings knowing our pain is not without meaning. We persevere in the confidence that we ourselves are being transformed. Perseverance produces character, and character, hope. And hope, we will discover, is the ultimate gift gained in wisdom.

WISDOM OF PERSEVERANCE

All this brings us back to James. Not only are we challenged to allow perseverance to work on us with the promise that wisdom will emerge out of us, but we are also then invited to see and experience trials in an entirely new way. James tells us to consider it pure joy when we face them. The only reason he gives us for this is the knowledge that the testing of our faith will develop perseverance. Of course, he does go on to remind us that if we will brave the journey, we will become mature and complete, not lacking anything. Without sounding irreverent, it just seems pretty stupid to consider trials the venue for indescribable joy. But this is exactly what he's calling for when he says "pure joy." He is describing the ultimate experience of aliveness.

If you were going to list the top-ten joy-producing experiences in your life, would trials even make it on the list? I can't even imagine including something as painful as suffering or hardship. Other than the compelling argument that God says so, why in the world should we equate the facing of trials with the emotion of joy? What does God have up His sleeve? What does He know that we don't know?

James says it so subtly that it can easily be missed. God longs to give us wisdom, and it is born out of perseverance. Only the testing of our faith develops the perseverance that we need on our quest for enlightenment. There are some things God desires to do in our lives that come no other way. Even the person you long to become when your heart is aligned with God's, you cannot become if you are unwilling to pass this way. To become like Christ, this ordeal must be faced. You can be filled with joy even in the midst of suffering when your pursuit is character and not comfort. You can consider trials as the perfect environment for indescribable joy when you embrace your circumstance as God's incubator to form you in His image.

Yet beyond that James tells us that what God is doing is testing our faith. What this doesn't mean is God is trying to figure out whether our faith is real. What this does mean is that God is trying to forge in us a real faith. God allows and at times causes us to go through the kinds of circumstances that strip away all falsehood and leave us with our real selves. God's ultimate intent is not to leave us faithless, but to leave us faith-full. There are few things as exhilarating as going through the fire and finding that you had the resilience to make it through. All of us wonder at times whether we have what it takes. God wants to bring us to a place where we have no doubt of the work He has done within us.

There is another aspect to trials that create for us a source of joy. Whenever we face a trial, it is a reminder of our own need for God. More than that, it is the context in which God meets our needs. The picture that James paints when he speaks of various trials is vivid in its variety. The word *various* literally means multicolored. He is opening our eyes to see that whatever the challenge, whatever the need, God is there, both able and willing to meet us at our point of need. This, too, should bring us unexpected joy. When you walk in intimate communion with Christ, a trial serves as a call to the banquet table of God.

God knows our needs, but sometimes we are oblivious to our need for God. Trials realign us with reality and position us for divine encounter. Our ability to persevere is critical in such cases. Even if God responds swiftly, we will find ourselves tempted to turn to another source of provision.

EATING ROCKS

The same word that we translate "trials" can also be translated "temptation." When God tests our faith, the evil one attempts to destroy our faith. While God sends us through tests to draw us toward Him, Satan tempts us to draw us away from God. In the same experience both dynamics are in play. We cannot be tested without being tempted. God longs for our victory; Satan plots our defeat. The evil one also knows that the place of our greatest vulnerability is the vacuum created between our need and God's provision. He is keenly aware that God fully intends to supply our every need through Christ Jesus. His best strategy is to invite us to choose another way before God meets us in the midst of our test. Satan knows when we're hungry that God intends to bring us bread. Yet he also knows if we lack perseverance, he can convince us to settle for something less. He tried to convince Jesus to turn stones into bread. With us he just tries to convince us to eat rocks instead.

The human condition begins to make sense when you realize that most of us are eating rocks rather than waiting on God to bring us bread. We keep trying to find a way to meet the deepest longings of our soul apart from the God who intimately created us. We all have our own version of eating rocks. For Carolyn, all she ever wanted was to be really loved, to have that one person who would commit his life to her and turn to no other. She wanted to be a wife, have beautiful children, and of course, have a career accompanied by secure relationships. She had a painful past, and it had left her broken. Unlike others who were more fortunate, she had not escaped the pain of abuse. This only added to her sense of insecurity and accentuated her longing to be loved for all the right reasons.

He seemed so much like Mr. Right. He had all the right moves and said all the right things. They were engaged to be married, and it seemed that the storybook life would finally be hers. Just weeks before the wedding day, she found herself pregnant with his child. Just days after that, she found herself alone.

Several years had passed, and all she longed for was to find Mr. Right. It's hard enough to find someone to share your life with when there are only two people involved. It's so much more difficult when he not only has to love you, but love you both. Being a single mom is strenuous enough without factoring in how it complicates future relationships. Yet as impossible as it seemed, Mr. Right finally came along. He loved them both. Carolyn was engaged again. Finally all the hurts of the past would be swallowed up in the joys of the future. She found herself pregnant again. But marriage was too complicated for him, or for some other unexplainable reason, he had a sudden change of heart. Once again she was alone, responsible not only for herself, but for two children. How would she take care of them and make ends meet?

It's so hard to find that special someone. It is especially hard to wait when you're so afraid it may never happen, and so easy to convince yourself that you have to take things into your own hands. To persevere is no easy thing. To hold out for the good and to hold on to the good sometimes just doesn't *feel* very good. Yet Jesus would not and we cannot turn stones into bread. If we're not careful, we might find ourselves eating rocks.

I guess it's here where I'm supposed to bring this story to a happy ending, but the story is still being written. One possibility is that she waits on God and through the most romantic of circumstances meets the man of her dreams and they live happily ever after. Another possible scenario is that she finds an unexplainable contentedness in her singleness. She discovers that being alone is not the same as being lonely. Her legacy becomes the life she models and passes on to her children. Of course, another real possibility is that she never believes that the bread is coming so she just keeps eating rocks.

TRUE LOVE WAITS

It was one of the highlights in Jesus' life on earth. He had just been baptized by John, and the heavens opened. The Spirit of God descended on Him like a dove, and a voice came from heaven declaring, "This is my son whom I love. With him I am well pleased." You would think after such a glorious moment that life would come easy to Jesus, yet quite the reverse is true. Immediately after this, Jesus entered a series of temptations spearheaded by the evil one himself. And this was no chance meeting. In fact, the Bible tells us that "Jesus was led by the Spirit into the desert to be tempted by the devil" (Matt. 4:1).

Have you ever been told that the reason you are going through trials or facing temptations is because you're out of God's will? Have you ever assumed that the spiritual pressure cooker was an indication of your lack of intimacy with God? How many times have we been told that if we're right with God, we'll be living in the richness of His blessing, that everything will go well for us when we're close to Him. Yet here we find Jesus being lavished with the pleasure of His Father, then immediately being driven into the desert to be tempted by the devil. This spiritual encounter was on God's timetable, not the evil one's. Matthew tells us the Spirit led Jesus into the desert. Mark uses far more forceful language, saying that the Spirit *drove* Jesus into this conflict. Trials and temptations are not the punishment of God, but the process of God. Yes, there are times our lives are in ruin, and we suffer needlessly as a result of our own foolishness. But we must not assume this is always the case.

In Satan's first temptation he came to Jesus after forty days of fasting. Jesus hungered. The cravings of his flesh were a new experience for God. Certainly Satan had been in no hurry. He didn't come the first day, nor the tenth, nor the twenty-fifth. He came on the fortieth day. His temptations were specific, targeted to where Jesus would be weakest. His temptation was simply, "If you are the Son of God, tell these stones to become bread" (Matt. 4:3).

The enticement was pretty straightforward. If you're God, or more specifically, since you are God, reject this needless suffering and meet your own needs. Why would your Father make you go through this? Circumvent the process and end this foolishness. Here's a thought: Just turn these stones into bread. Jesus' response unlocks for us the endless source of joy available in the midst of trials. He answered the devil, "It is written: 'Man does not live on bread alone, but on every word that comes from the mouth of God'" (Matt. 4:4).

This has to be one of the most misunderstood statements of Jesus in the Bible. It has all too often led us to a level of superficiality that borders on irrelevance. He was not saying, "Satan, I don't need to eat. All I need to do is read my Bible." Jesus was not living in denial. He was well aware of His own body's need to be replenished. He was not ignoring nor was He deaf to His body's demands. And He certainly wasn't sermonizing. He was unlocking a view of reality that is dramatically different from ours. He was quoting Deuteronomy 8, where God explained to Israel the purpose of the forty years of wandering.

Moses records these words to God's people:

Remember how the LORD your God led you all the way in the desert these forty years, to humble you and to test you in order to know what was in your heart, whether or not you would keep his commands. He humbled you, causing you to hunger and then feeding you with manna, which neither you nor your fathers had known, to teach you that man does not live on bread alone but on every word that comes from the mouth of the LORD. Your clothes did not wear out and your feet did not swell during these forty years. Know then in your heart that as a man disciplines his son, so the LORD your God disciplines you. Observe the commands of the LORD your God, walking in his ways and revering him. (Deut. 8:2–6)

Like Jesus, God drove Israel into the desert to test them. As with Jesus, He allowed them to become hungry. In the midst of this, God fed them manna, a waferlike bread that appeared on the ground like the morning dew. It was the bread of angels, a gift from heaven. The people asked, "Manhu?"—"What is it?" *Manhu* sounds like *manna,* and thus it gained its name.

The quality of the manna was unique. It would only last for a day. Once, out of fear that there would be no food in the days ahead, the people attempted to save some, but it rotted and was filled with maggots. On the Sabbath the bread miraculously lasted two days, but the rest of the time it would only suffice for one day at a time. God was teaching them literally to pray, "Give us this day our daily bread."

The composition of manna was unique. Have you ever been on a health kick and read the nutritional information on the side of a box? Most companies list for you the benefits of enjoying their product and which particular vitamins are gained through consumption, and even give you the percent based on recommended daily values. If manna had a container, its list of nutritional value would be beyond belief. Every vitamin necessary for good health was contained in the manna. It somehow served both as a protein and a carb. Manna was the sum total of a well-rounded meal. When Israel ate manna, they didn't even need to eat their veggies. Everything they needed to eat for life was in the manna. And God did this to teach them one thing: that it's not the bread that sustains you, but every word that comes from the mouth of God.

Manna became a physical manifestation of God's Word. God spoke into the manna, and it carried with it the capacity to meet Israel's every physical need for nourishment. God was determined to teach them that it was never the bread alone. To believe that it is makes you nothing more than a materialist. To separate the created thing from the source of its Creator is to demean the gift. God spoke, and all that is created came into existence. Water quenches thirst because God decided and declared that it would be so. The earth produces life because God announced it would be this way.

Creation was uniquely designed to meet our needs, not apart from God, but because of God. The converse would also be true. If God had not spoken, our needs would remain unmet. The Greek view of torment and hell was improperly elemental. It would paint a picture of the one dying of thirst because the water was always just outside his reach. The Scriptures give a very different picture. The glutton will eat and eat but never be satisfied. Apart from the Word of God, all the stuff of this world will leave us empty. We pray before we eat our meals as an acknowledgment not simply that God has provided us food, but that the food was created by God to meet our needs. When we eat and are satisfied, it is the direct result of God speaking this into reality. Even with the Israelites' clothes, God reinforced this during their journey. He reminded them that their clothes did not wear out during those forty years. Can you imagine having clothes that you could wear every day in the most extreme of environments, that would not wear out? God was determined to teach his people that all of life is spiritual. He would not allow Israel to dichotomize between the secular and the sacred. All of life is sacred. Because creation so naturally meets our needs, we must not for a moment think we have no need for its Creator. Creation is here to draw us back to God.

So Jesus told Satan, "What's the point of turning rocks into bread? If bread existed that was created without God's Word, it would be no more than eating rocks. At the same time, if it was my Father's will, He could simply speak, and all my hunger would be satisfied." Jesus chose to wait on God, His provider. However long He must wait, He would persevere. He would rather be hungry waiting on His Father's timing than to lose hope and be found eating rocks when the bread came. Of course, eating rocks is hard on the teeth, terrible for the digestion, and leaves one incapable of eating the banquet when the table is finally set.

DIVINE PROVISIONS

It was September of 1981. I had just graduated from the University of North Carolina at Chapel Hill and was on my way across the country to pursue my master's degree. A young relative of mine found himself in severe trouble, and helping him required most of the limited resources I had saved to continue my studies. With a detour to visit my family in Orlando, I found myself catching a ride with barely enough money to pay my first semester's tuition. After tuition and fees, I had just over ten dollars left. I had no place to live, no car, no job, and pretty quickly, no money.

I was placed on the waiting list for on-campus housing, but there were about 150 people ahead of me. I began by sleeping on someone's floor, praying like crazy and memorizing James 1. Each day I would check to see how close I was to getting a room. Each day was filled with as much uncertainty as excitement. I had no doubt this was where God wanted me to be and no regrets for the choices I had made that left me in my present state. Then somehow, while nearly a hundred other students remained on the list, I found myself getting a room.

That's when I began to experience a series of events that changed my life forever. I came home one day and found a bag of groceries waiting at my door. I can tell you that no one knew my financial situation. Besides, most students were struggling at best. But there it was, fresh groceries, sliced meats, fresh cheeses, fruit, juices, milk—every one of them perishable. I had no idea where it came from, but that didn't stop me from eating. I didn't have a roommate, so it couldn't be for anyone but me. I had far more than I could possibly eat. I didn't have a refrigerator, so there was no way that I could save the food that was brought to me that day, so I made some quick friends, and we shared the banquet. Though it was temporary, it was a much-needed and enjoyed relief from wondering how I would make it through the day.

Then the next day when I returned to my room after studies, there was another bag waiting there for me. More of the same: great meats and cheeses, beautiful fresh fruit, nice cold juices, a virtual feast. So I invited my new friends again, and we enjoyed another banquet. Then came the third day, and the fourth, and the fifth. Each day a new bag filled with groceries awaited me. After two or three days I didn't need to invite anyone. I was very popular and was visited often. I had no idea where the food was coming from. No one I knew could afford so generous an act.

Then one afternoon as I was returning to my room, I saw a man nearly twice my age quietly placing a bag at my door. When he saw me, he began to quickly leave, but then as if he were giving up, just turned and responded to my call. I couldn't really remember having met Roy before this moment. He was a kind and unassuming man who had chosen vocational ministry as a second career. I asked him why he was doing this, and he reflected back to a chance meeting we had had some time before. He explained that we had both been in an elevator going down to the basement when we first met. I vaguely remember both of us saying no more than a polite hello. He explained that in that short encounter God had spoken to him. Specifically, he said that God instructed him to start bringing me food every day. He didn't know why, and it didn't really matter. He simply did it because he sensed it was the leadership of God's Spirit to him.

He then acknowledged he had hoped to remain anonymous. I have to confess at that point I got a little worried. I was very grateful for the food, and I really did need it. It struck me suddenly that now that he was exposed, he might stop providing the food, but the opposite happened. I had more than a food supplier, I now had a friend. Boy, did we enjoy some great meals together—hot and juicy, the kind to be savored and remembered.

Then there was the job. There was a job board in one of the educational buildings with dozens and dozens of postcards advertising job opportunities. The jobs posted on this board were like guppies swimming among a school of piranhas. Just making the call before anyone else was no small miracle. I would go by on a semidaily basis trying to find something that would work for someone who didn't have a car, not to mention no observable, employable skills. My years of preparation in the fields of psychology and philosophy equipped me to ponder the higher thoughts of the cosmos while flipping the burger before it burned. It's pretty humbling to realize that at least four visits to Walden's Pond only prepared me to ask the most profound of questions: "Would you like fries with that?"

Then I saw the card. The perfect opportunity. It paid a lot of money—at least from my vantage point—and I would only have to work on Saturday. On that particular occasion I didn't have anything with me to write down the information, so I returned to my room and decided that before I would go back to the job board, I would ask for God's help in the process. Kneeling by the bed, praying specifically for this one job, it couldn't have been more than minutes before I heard a knocking on my door. Though I didn't know the person standing on the other side, he somehow knew my name. He went on to explain that he had posted a job on the board and had then gone to the athletic center to ask for recommendations. They sent him to me. I never had to go back to the job board. I never needed to write down the number. I didn't even have to apply for the job. The job came to me. It literally knocked on my door.

Now I had the precise job I wanted, if only I could get there. At that time I had a practice of keeping a prayer journal. It has never been one of my greatest strengths, but it's always been rewarding when I have attempted it. Throughout my spiritual journey I have tried to minimize the things I ask for personally and focus my intercession on the needs of others. I didn't want to be the kind of person always asking God for something else. So when I ask, it's usually substantial. In this case I had written down one item. *God, I need a car.* Now, I was perfectly fine if the answer was, *Yes, you do. Go get a job and earn it.* But I was trapped in one of those catch-22s; I couldn't get the job to earn the car if I didn't have the car to get the job.

Then the call came. Standing in the hallway talking to a stranger on the dormitory phone, I received the most astonishing news. The person on the other side, who did not know me and whom I had never met, had heard my spiritual journey from a friend and felt inspired to give me his car. Our first and only meeting was the day he transferred the title of his car over to me.

It is in the crucible that we not only discover who we are, but more profoundly, who Christ is within us.

I began this journey with everything I owned in a paper bag—plus a guitar. I had no place to live, no food to eat, no job, no transportation, and yet in a matter of days, every one of those needs was miraculously, if not spectacularly, met. It was like manna from heaven, as if God was trying to teach me that I was not created to live on bread alone, but on every word that comes from His mouth. What need in my life could God not meet? What longing was He unaware of? With each trial I faced, I encountered the grace and generosity of God. There were days when I wondered how it would all work together. I must confess there were even times I found myself in tears of frustration. Yet at each point, I discovered that if you hold on to the good and hold out for the good, you can find the good in even the worst of situations.

This season of my life contained both my most significant economic poverty and some of my most enjoyable memories. Time after time, in moments of uncertainty, I have experienced God's generous gift of wisdom. He allowed me to see life from an entirely new vantage point. Day after day the full weight of perseverance was called for. I needed both to be patient and to endure. Yet through all of this, joy seemed to flow in abundance. Hardship does not require famine of joy or enjoyment. It is in the crucible that we not only discover who we are, but more profoundly, who Christ is within us.

It is in the midst of these circumstances that we are brought to the same place that the apostle Paul celebrated: "I have learned to be content whatever the circumstances. I know what it is to be in need, and I know what it is to have plenty. I have learned the secret of being content in any and every situation, whether well fed or hungry, whether living in plenty or in want. I can do everything through him who gives me strength" (Phil. 4:11–13).

11

Unlocking Divine Mysteries

Wisdom calls aloud in the street, she raises her voice in the public squares; at the head of the noisy streets she cries out, in the gateways of the city she makes her speech: "How long will you simple ones love your simple ways? How long will mockers delight in mockery and fools hate knowledge? If you had responded to my rebuke, I would have poured out my heart to you and made my thoughts known to you." (Prov. 1:20–23)

"Everyone learns everything the hard way. And I don't mean it talking about him more so than myself. You kind of learn when you experience it, not when you hear it."

No, these are not the words of Dr. Phil to an eagerly awaiting audience looking for wisdom for life. They are the words of Chris Webber as he attempted to explain the ongoing personal saga of his teammate Jason Williams of the Sacramento Kings. Before Williams was traded away, he was a paradox of potential and problems. In the world of sports, Williams was one more example of unimaginable capacity combined with self-destructive tendencies. Always a phenom on the court, the only real question as to whether he would make it to the NBA revolved around his inability to stay out of trouble. Bouncing around to different schools after high school, he was suspended twice while playing at the University of Florida. Whether it was a disdain for structure or an appetite for pot, he seemed destined to never fulfill his athletic potential. Taken seventh in the NBA draft by the Kings, he began astonishing his peers from his first dribble.

Yet while Williams serves as a perfect metaphor for the dilemma that many of us find ourselves in, it is Webber's assessment that gives us the most insight. Webber's explanation for William's struggles is simple: Everyone learns everything the hard way. And of course, if this is true, we should neither be surprised nor judgmental. After all, this is the only way any of us can learn. We say it all the time: "I need to learn it for myself."

It has become common wisdom that the only way to learn is to go through it personally. We both assume and conclude that experience is the mother of wisdom. The mantra of our time is "You can't know if you don't try it." In fact if you don't try it, if you avoid certain experiences, you are considered sheltered and naive. Real learning only comes on the road of hard knocks. The rockier and more painful the journey, the more insight you have to share.

There are several subtle assumptions made from this perspective of learning that will leave us looking foolish. For one thing just going through something doesn't ensure that you will gain wisdom from the experience. How many of us haven't made the same mistake over and over again? Even when others around us are pulling their hair out because of our recurring life patterns, we seem to have an uncanny ability to miss the obvious. Rather than having to learn it for ourselves, just holding that perspective seems to inhibit our ability to learn from our own experience.

Another assumption from this perspective of gaining wisdom is that you can only learn from your own mistakes. If we can only really learn when we go through it, then we have essentially invalidated learning from anyone else's experience. Is it possible to learn from someone else's mistakes rather than just your own? Does everyone really learn everything the hard way, or do some people learn many things the easy way—through others? If personal experience is the only filter from which real learning can come, then what of the wealth of learning that is available through the composite history of all humanity? Is there anything to be gained by listening to others?

It should be obvious that those who live enlightened lives have demonstrated a unique ability to learn from everyone and everything around them. This characteristic is an essential component of living wisely. Not only is it possible to learn from others, but it is impossible to be an effective learner without relating our experiences to others. When you are your own reference point, you destine yourself to an endless cycle of foolishness. If you are determined to only learn the hard way, you will find it hard to learn. In the end you will find yourself falling hard. You can have a wealth of experience and die wisdom poor.

If you are determined to only learn the hard way, you will find it hard to learn.

It was 1981, and I began giving my weekends to working with the homeless in downtown Fort Worth. A small group of us would bring coffee and donuts and a couple of guitars and would provide a worship experience in the water gardens. One of my first conversations was with an ex-con who was nearly three times my age. His opening remark was that he had killed his wife and gotten away with it. Yeah, he served some time, but now he was back on the streets, free from any consequence.

I didn't have a lot of experience dealing with someone like him, and I still remember that my response was just, "You really shouldn't have done that." If I could have that moment back again, I would have said something more profound, but it was the best I could think of at the time. Our conversation continued and became more intense.

I admit I was making a strong effort to try to help him see that his life was proof that he had not escaped the consequences of his actions.

He became angry and sneered, "Son, I am twice your age, and you're trying to tell me how to live." I remember nervously pointing out to him that it strikes me that he has lived twice as long as I have, and I have found more meaning for life in half the time. I walked away knowing that time was no guarantee of wisdom. You can grow old and die a fool. Experience is no guarantee of enlightenment. If you're learning everything the hard way, you might want to ask yourself if it's possible that you're hardly learning.

A QUEST FOR WISDOM

The path to wisdom is less journey and more quest. It doesn't come simply by traveling. You have to pursue it. If the life of God is an adventure, the life of godliness is an odyssey. Yes, much of the learning will come as you travail down the hard roads. Life is the context for growing in wisdom, not simply when you experience something, but when you extract it from your experience. In fact wisdom and experience are uniquely interconnected. Not only can wisdom be gained from experience, but the quality of your future experiences will be shaped by your wisdom.

The life that God calls you to cannot be lived without wisdom. I am thankful that God calls people like me, who have lived foolishly, to follow Him. But the journey cannot be engaged if we choose to remain the fool. While many of us long for God to give us a map so that we can simply follow it, He instead gives us a compass that points the way. What we continually ask for is to know God's will for our lives; what God continually offers us is His wisdom for our lives. So critical is wisdom to the journey that God offers it as a gift to all who would desire it. James, the half brother of Jesus, tells us, "If any of you lacks wisdom, he should ask God, who gives generously to all without finding fault, and it will be given to him" (James 1:5).

Thousands of years ago a young prince named Solomon discovered the pleasure that God finds when we long for wisdom above all things. First Kings records the encounter between God and the son of David:

> At Gibeon the LORD appeared to Solomon during the night in a dream, and God said, "Ask for whatever you want me to give you." Solomon answered, "You have shown great kindness to your servant, my father David, because he was faithful to you and righteous and upright in heart. You have continued this great kindness to him and have given him a son to sit on his throne this very day. Now, O LORD my God, you have made your servant king in place of my father David. But I am only a little child and do not know how to carry out my duties. Your servant is here among the people you have chosen, a great people, too numerous to count or number. So give your servant a discerning heart to govern your people and to distinguish between right and wrong. For who is able to govern this great people of yours?" The Lord was pleased that Solomon had asked for this. So God said to him, "Since you have asked for this and not for long life or wealth for yourself, nor have asked for the death of your enemies but for discernment in administering justice, I will do what you have asked. I will give you a wise and discerning heart, so that there will never have been anyone like you, nor will there ever be. Moreover, I will give you what you have not asked for—both riches and honor— so that in your lifetime you will have no equal among kings. And if you walk in my ways and obey my statutes and commands as David your father did, I will give you a long life." Then Solomon awoke— and he realized it had been a dream. (3:5–15a)

Solomon, feeling the weight of the future of an entire nation on his shoulders and given the opportunity to ask God for anything he desired, asked only for wisdom. The focus of his desire was on the good of his people rather than on any personal benefit to himself. Solomon reduced wisdom to the practical application of leading people well and being able to discern between right and wrong. With the complexities of governing a nation, the ability to make right choices would be invaluable. When you or I make a bad decision, our sphere of influence might dramatically limit the ramifications. When one is king over a nation, even small decisions may have significant consequence or benefit. The strength and quality of his decision making is both public and highly visible.

Certainly the request itself distinguishes Solomon among the kings of history. How many kings have made the focus of their power the good of their people? History is resplendent with the abuse of power for personal greed and glory. Solomon's unique quest gives us tremendous insight into the texture of a heart that gains wisdom. The heart of a fool is motivated by personal gain. The heart of wisdom is motivated by the good of others. By desiring wisdom, Solomon placed the good of others above his own good. In return God gave him not only wisdom, but all the riches and honor that he had forsaken in his own heart. While wisdom does not always guarantee a life of riches and honor, wisdom always produces a rich and honorable life.

Wisdom unleashes our capacity to create the good. Wisdom not only sees the good that must be done now, but catalyzes such events that result in a good future. Wherever wisdom flows, good follows. Not that everything that happens *to* a person who lives wisely is good, but everything that happens *from* a person who lives wisely is good. Wise people have an unusual capacity to not only make good choices and to generate good results, but also to create healthy environments.

Stop for a moment and reflect on all the individuals you have known in your lifetime. Pick the person that you feel best exemplifies wisdom. (If you can't think of anyone, start hanging around a better group of people!) Does that person that you've chosen have immense wealth? Having asked this question in numerous situations, I've found that very few people who were selected as examples of wisdom were actually very rich. Some of them were, so we know that you can be both affluent and wise, but you can also be poor and wise.

Again, this person you were thinking about, how highly educated is he or she? Does the individual have a Ph.D. in some field of study? Again, my informal surveys have found that the great majority of women and men identified as wise did not have postgraduate degrees. There were some who were selected that were both highly educated and considered wise, but overwhelmingly the numbers were very few. What I have found is that one can be highly educated and also be wise, but it was not a given. Many of the people identified as wise had only average levels of education, and some of them in fact lacked significant formal education. It wasn't hard to conclude that you can be uneducated from a conventional standard and still be a person of great wisdom. The converse is also true. You can accomplish great things in the academic world and live a life of foolishness.

THE POWER WITHIN

Wisdom, as difficult as it is to define, is not that difficult to describe. Even when we are not sure what wisdom really is, we know it when we see it. As immeasurable as wisdom may be, a fool is difficult to miss, and a wise person always stands out when he or she is needed. For financial help we may turn to a financial planner, and to advance our education, we may sit under a professor, but when our life is falling apart, it's wisdom that we seek.

Wisdom enables us to heal broken relationships and create an environment of health.

For whatever else wisdom is or accomplishes, wisdom enables us to heal broken relationships and create an environment of health. Wisdom creates and produces good. When we act on wisdom, good things happen. This doesn't mean that walking in wisdom is painless. Doing the right thing can be extremely painful. It can come at a great price. Nevertheless the ultimate results of wisdom are health, freedom, and creativity.

An essential component of wisdom is the ability to get to the core. Wisdom always finds a way through the mess we make of life. It doesn't find the easiest way, but the way marked by the footprints of God. Wisdom knows that ancient paths will lead us into a divine future. Wisdom is the product of a sacred imagination. Wisdom knows the way to freedom. Where there is wisdom, there is always hope. Wisdom simplifies. Wisdom clarifies. Wisdom untangles. Wisdom unshackles. Wisdom illuminates. Wisdom liberates. In the end wisdom enlightens us to live lives of nobility.

We find this in another example from the life of Solomon:

Now two prostitutes came to the king and stood before him. One of them said, "My Lord, this woman and I live in the same house. I had a baby while she was there with me. The third day after my child was born, this woman also had a baby. We were alone; there was no one in the house but the two of us.

"During the night, this woman's son died because she lay on him. So she got up in the middle of the night and took my son from my side while I your servant was asleep. She put him by her breast and put her dead son by my breast. The next morning, I got up to nurse my son—and he was dead! But when I looked at him closely in the morning light, I saw that it wasn't the son I had borne."

The other woman said, "No! The living one is my son; the dead one is yours." But the first one insisted, "No! The dead one is yours; the living one is mine." And so they argued before the king.

The king said, "This one says, 'My son is alive and your son is dead,' while that one says, 'No! Your son is dead and mine is alive.'"

Then the king said, "Bring me a sword." So they brought a sword for the king. He then gave an order: "Cut the living child in two and give half to one and half to the other."

The woman whose son was alive was filled with compassion for her son and said to the king, "Please, my lord, give her the living baby! Don't kill him!" But the other said, "Neither I nor you shall have him. Cut him in two!"

Then the king gave his ruling: "Give the living baby to the first woman. Do not kill him; she is his mother."

When all Israel heard the verdict the king had given, they held the king in awe, because they saw that he had wisdom from God to administer justice. (1 Kings 3:16–28)

The story specifically serves as a demonstration of the wisdom Solomon received from God. His ability to administer justice was contingent on his ability to discern human motivation. The gift God had given him was the ability to get beyond the surface and move to the essential. In a profound way Solomon was given the ability to get to the heart of every matter. He created a scenario where the good and evil of the human heart would rise to the surface. He could easily rule against the one who would rather choose to destroy than to sacrifice.

Wisdom is more than simply the ability to see beyond ourselves, but even perhaps more profoundly, to see within ourselves. I don't know how many times I've sat in a room with a pregnant teenager who laments, "I don't know how this happened to me." Or how many times as a child, my parents would heatedly ask me, "Why did you do that?" and my answer was simply, "I don't know." I can tell you without any doubt that if you don't know how you got into it, you won't be able to find your way out. If you don't know how it happened to you, you will not know how to stop letting it happen. If you don't know why you did it, you will not be able to change your motivation.

Solomon's judgment reminds us that wisdom is the ability to cut to the core of complex issues. But before we begin applying wisdom toward the actions of others, it is always wise to examine our own hearts first. Wisdom not only allows you to move beyond living a senseless life; it helps you begin to make sense of life. The fool acts without reflection; the wise man reflects on his actions.

There is an elegance and beauty to wisdom. She brings simplicity out of complexity. While the fool strives to bring attention to himself, wisdom brings others to attention. Wisdom never claims to know everything, yet somehow she always seems to know what's most important. Without wisdom we choose to live in the dark. We become like a blind man running frantically through a dense forest. We can become embittered against the trees that block our way; we can conclude that everyone runs blind and only those with the hardest of skulls find their way through. Or we can hear the voice that invites us to open our eyes and discover that we were never intended to run blind. The promise of wisdom is that you can see if you want to. Yes, to run this course requires unlocking divine mysteries, but it is God Himself who offers us the key. Our quest for enlightenment will always lead us to wisdom, and wisdom will light our way.

Connecting the Dots

It was a small weekend retreat where we were focusing on a group of high-risk, high-potential teenagers. After several years of working among the urban poor, I made an observation of a unique disconnect among urban youth. There seemed to be either an inability or unwillingness to connect the dots. The relationship between cause and effect somehow seemed to be missing. In the middle of one of my lectures, I pulled out a tennis ball and invited one of the young men in attendance to help me with a demonstration. I handed him the ball and told him to throw it as hard as he could at the wall behind me. We were inside a building, and even he had a sense that this was inappropriate. He repeated my request in disbelief, and I invited him again to throw it as hard as he could against the wall. His body language screamed out, *You don't have to ask me twice.*

Aware of his audience, he seemed to gather all of his strength and heaved that ball as hard as he possibly could. His aim was perfect. The ball pounded against the wall and came ricocheting right back at him, hitting him somewhere on the head. All of his friends who were greatly skilled at public mocking began to ride him. He was half embarrassed and half mad. He looked at me and immediately began to indict me. "Why did you make me do that? Why did you make me hit myself?"

I calmly asked him, "Where did you think the ball would go? I didn't throw it; you did. Why didn't you throw it at an angle?" Upon reflection, he was clear before he threw it that the tennis ball would not go through the wall. He just didn't stop to think through the consequence of his action. There was a disconnect between cause and effect. He didn't factor in the bounce. Now if the wall had been covered in Velcro maybe his conclusions would have been merited. He would have been justified in an expectation that the ball would stop on the wall. But it wasn't Velcro, and frankly, I made sure the ball was loaded with bounce. I knew these kids. I knew them well. They kept making Velcro decisions and having to live with bounce consequences. They were constantly surprised that their actions would be followed by reactions. I was convinced that if they could just connect the dots, if they could see relationship between cause and effect, they would be free of so much unnecessary pain in their lives.

In this scenario, wisdom is the ability to see where the ball is going after the throw. It becomes the ability to see choice as cause and consequence and benefit as effect. All too often a crippling paradigm is to see our circumstances as isolated from our actions. When we do this, we abdicate personal responsibility for our lives. Taken to an extreme, we find ourselves holding God accountable for the consequences of our actions and becoming embittered toward Him in the process. It's as if we want the freedom to make any choices we like, but expect God to make sure that we don't have to live with the consequences of our choices. We want God to be our divine pooper-scooper, following us around cleaning up our mess. None of us want to give up our right to choose, yet we are more than willing to abdicate responsibility for our actions.

When we don't blame God and we don't take responsibility, we essentially become gamblers. We start seeing life as the arbitrary distribution of good and bad luck. At times we would rather believe in luck than in responsibility. When you break it down, superstition is nothing more than an improper connection between cause and effect. You do a rain dance convinced it will motivate the gods, and if you keep dancing until it rains, it works every time. You hit a home run using a certain bat, and suddenly it's all about the bat and not about your skill. You can't step on the cracks, walk under the ladder, or cross paths with a black cat, or you're in real trouble.

And then there's religion. Aren't our endless rituals often nothing more than meaningless superstitions? Isn't this at least in part why science has become an enemy to faith? If faith is based on truth, shouldn't a life in faith free us from superstition rather than bind us to it? Ironically, when we disconnect our circumstances from our choices, we make a choice to live powerless lives. When we embrace the interconnection between our present decisions and our future opportunities, we regain the power to set our course and to shape our journey. Something as simple as a proper view of cause and effect not only grows us in wisdom, but brings greater freedom to our lives.

If you genuinely don't know what's going on, if you cannot see the recurring destructive patterns in your life, you don't know how to stop them from happening again and again. This is at least one reason why we live in a culture of addiction. It is funny how we describe endless self-indulgence as "freedom." The truth of the matter is that very quickly our pleasures become indulgences and our indulgences become addictions. The final analysis reveals that our sin reduces us to living as slaves to addictive patterns, destructive habits, and unfulfilling ruts. Rather than living more creatively and with greater freedom, we find ourselves controlled by our cravings and tragically conforming to the pattern of this world. We should not forget that in Eden there was one option for evil and endless options for good.

A life without God is not a place of endless creativity; it only feigns uniqueness.

A life without God is not a place of endless creativity; it only feigns uniqueness. Without God in the end, we all find ourselves looking the same. In God we see the endless possibilities for good. Wisdom refuses to surrender the freedom of the future for a temporary indulgence. Wisdom recognizes that while some opportunities are captivating, beneath the surface they are ready to take you captive. Something as simple as connecting the dots empowers you to shape your future from the present. Wisdom recognizes that the inseparable relationship between cause and effect is more than a natural phenomenon; it is a spiritual reality.

Paul warns us not to take lightly the impact and significance of cause and effect:

> Do not be deceived: God cannot be mocked. A man reaps what he sows. The one who sows to please his sinful nature, from that nature will reap destruction; the one who sows to please the Spirit, from the Spirit will reap eternal life. Let us not become weary in doing good, for at the proper time we will reap a harvest if we do not give up. Therefore, as we have opportunity, let us do good to all people, especially to those who belong to the family of believers. (Gal. 6:7–10)

Whether the language is sowing and reaping, cause and effect, a contemporary understanding of good and bad karma, or simply understanding that what goes around comes around, wisdom begins at connecting the dots between the quality of our decisions and the quality of our lives. Before we can even begin to talk about the wisdom that comes from having the mind of Christ, we have to at least begin here. Wisdom begins by making the obvious connections that others seem to overlook.

BACK FROM THE FUTURE

I turned on Fox News last night and to my surprise and, yes, even disappointment, I saw a credible political journalist interviewing a modern-day psychic. People were calling in and getting advice. They seemed to find comfort and a sense of security when they believed he knew something about their futures that they did not know. I was struck by the desperation that accompanied their uncertainty. When facing the unknown, we have a heightened sense of instability. When everything around us seems uncertain we find ourselves destabilized. There was a time when the major concern in regard to the unknown was the after-life. That certainly isn't true today. Just thinking about tomorrow seems to create enough anxiety in the life of the average person.

One of the interesting presuppositions of turning to a psychic is that the future is static, concrete, unchanging. The Scriptures give a very different view of the future. The future is dynamic, active, inter-active. For some reason many of us would rather know the future than create it. After all if someone can simply tell us the future, we can abdicate any responsibility on our part. All we have to do is just let it happen. God gives us far more privilege and responsibility than this. He offers us confidence in relationship to the future; He prom-ises that if we will follow Him we will have both a future and a hope. He even goes as far as to assure us that no matter how badly we mess things up, when we love Him and are called according to His pur-pose, He will make everything work together for the good.

Yet while we cannot know the future, we can strangely live in the present from the future. Just because the future is filled with mystery doesn't mean that everything about the future is mysterious. Having pastored for twenty years, I have counseled men and women in almost every imaginable situation. In each crisis the individuals involved are certain their particular dilemma is unique. No one has ever gone through what they've gone through. How many times have you heard someone say, "No one can understand what I'm going through. No one can know how I feel"? Yet the truth of the matter is that we have more common experiences than we can imagine. Certainly we share common emotions. Beyond this you begin to dis-cover over time that we even share common patterns. As we grow in wisdom, these patterns of life become more clear. We don't have to face every circumstance as a blank slate. We can learn from the mistakes and failures of the past. I mean, how many times do you have to touch a hot stove before you conclude it's not a good idea?

In the same way we can develop an uncanny ability to "predict" the future. As a futurist, I have described the essence of my work as the study of human values. While many look at trends to evaluate the course of culture, I am convinced it is far more profitable to examine cultural values. When you understand what a person cares about, you get a better sense of his or her internal compass and direction. This is why counseling becomes easier over the years. Not that helping people through painful problems is ever easy, but complicated situations are more easily unraveled.

From my vantage point, counseling is never about telling a person what to do but about helping him see the path that will be paved by the choices he is about to make. Thankfully, many times the people you are striving to help are able to see through your eyes and add that to their present perspectives. Other times, the result is quite different. There have been occasions when I've sat with a couple who made poor moral choices during their dating, were ignoring huge issues while they were engaged, and then moved blindly into marriage and found themselves in severe crisis and conflict just six months later. In those cases and others like them, I recognize that my words are simply falling on deaf ears and that their hearts are not in a condition to listen. I will generally end the session reinforcing to them the likely outcome of the unwise decision being made.

Sometimes it's years later that someone will come back and ask me in all sincerity, "How did you know? Everything you said would happen happened." My favorite response is to say without hesitation, "It's because I'm from the future. I came back to the present just to warn you, but you wouldn't listen." Of course I say that only to make a point: that all of us can live in the present as if we're back from the future.

The future is the sum total of all the choices that are made in the present and in the past. Fortunately, that sum total includes the choices made by God. A significant aspect of wisdom is having a future orientation. Wisdom gives us a perspective that always looks toward the future from the present and always looks from the future to the present. It is both future-present and present-future.

RELATIONALITY

"I'm not hurting anyone but myself." Ever heard that one? A forty-two-year-old husband and father was drinking himself into a bottle. He's a functional alcoholic, able to do his job, and has had significant accomplishments. He has even worked his way to upper-level management. His wife is beautiful, his children publicly well-behaved; his portfolio is a picture of success, yet his whole world is a facade. Everyone who is dear to him is drowning in the tidal wave of his own addiction. His legacy will be abuse. His children will resemble him in ways that go far beyond genetics. All the while he convinces himself, "I'm not hurting anyone but myself."

From the vantage point of the fool, the world appears to exist in segmented, isolated units. The connection between the absentee father and the promiscuous daughter remains undetected. The relationship between bitterness toward your parents and coldness toward your children is unperceived. The repercussions of extramarital infidelity are never linked to premarital promiscuity. Debt remains unconnected to greed; violence remains unconnected to hate; the loss of hope remains disconnected from the loss of faith.

At its extreme the fool faces every crisis, every challenge, every circumstance for the first time every time. In the same way foolishness never factors in the relational ramifications of any action or decision. Wisdom in contrast sees everything in life as interconnected. Wisdom does not allow us to stand apart from the rest of the world. Maybe this is why in the Scriptures wisdom is personified in the feminine—Sophia. Certainly women have a greater intuition to the interconnectedness of all things than most of us men. Just the experience of childbirth would make this probable. As much as I love my children, they have never spent one day living inside me—at least in the literal sense. We husbands are at a parental disadvantage. For nearly the first year of our children's lives, we're the outsider.

This one experience may explain why women seem to be more organic in their thinking while men often appear to be more segmented. Especially in our health-conscious era, I hear stories of women who stopped smoking or drinking alcohol while they were pregnant. It was inescapable that their personal decisions had consequences beyond themselves. Even in regard to abortion, our government has placed in the hands of women the choice and power to terminate or take to term the births of their children. As empathetic as a man may be, this is a reality outside of his experience.

Nevertheless, even science is advocating a more organic view of reality. Quantum physics speaks of the interconnectedness of all creation. While science has tended to move at light speed away from a belief in God, there has at the same time been an underlying advocacy for the worship of Gaia. If nature is not seen as God, it is certainly perceived as a solitary living essence. This move from theism to pantheism is an attempt to explain an ever-clearer understanding of the universe as uniquely interconnected. Yet thousands of years before these radical advancements in science, the Scriptures described the organic nature of the universe. While the Scriptures are clear that nature is not God, it is equally clear that nature is reflective of His character. It shouldn't surprise us that our relational God would create all things in relationship to each other.

Strange how from our vantage point our actions affect no one but ourselves, but from God's vantage point, one human action has cosmic repercussions.

Romans 8 gives us the extraordinary picture of creation groaning as a result of the separation between God and man. If quantum physics describes an avalanche in Antarctica as the result of a butterfly flapping its wings in the Amazon, so God describes the chaos and decay of all creation as a result of one fruit plucked from a forbidden tree. Not only this, but the Scriptures tell us that creation itself will be liberated from its bondage when we are brought into our freedom. Strange how from our vantage point our actions affect no one but ourselves, but from God's vantage point, one human action has cosmic repercussions.

As you move from foolishness to wisdom, you recognize the implications of your decisions on the quality of life of those around you. The choices you and I make directly affect the conditions of others. In fact, our demand for freedom may actually result in tyranny over others. Our pursuit of personal pleasure may result in the suffering and pain of others. Evil is consumptive in nature. When evil eats, others are starved. Evil moves like a plague, leaving nothing behind for others to enjoy. This is why in the end a life of self and a life of wisdom exist as adversaries. The world of self is consumed by *I*. The world of wisdom is filled with *we*. Wisdom is not a shift from *me* to *you*, but a shift from *me* to *us*.

Wisdom sees all life through relationships—our relationship to God, our relationship to others, our relationship to nature. It is not about self-depravation, but a recognition that our best selves can only be discovered when we consider others above ourselves. When we walk in wisdom, we cannot even think of ourselves outside of the context of relationships. Isn't this in fact the essence of true character? What does it mean to have character outside of the context of relationships? How in the world have we come to the place where we can see ourselves as spiritually mature without it affecting our relationships? Can integrity be measured outside of relationship? Can humility? Or gratitude? Or any other virtue we admire?

Over the generations, wisdom has become more ideas than living. Philosophy is literally the love of wisdom. Having traveled the philosophical road, I can assure you that there's little of wisdom's original essence left in the discipline. It so much easier to escape to Thoreau's Walden Pond and contemplate life than it is to return from it and really live.

When we are children, we are naive to the interconnectedness of life. A part of good parenting is helping our children make the right connections. It's so much fun to watch a baby discover his or her feet for the first time. We can spend endless hours playing peek-a-boo because the infant cannot figure out how you keep disappearing behind the blanket. His or her journey of discovery is almost magical, yet for us there is only the obvious in the places where a child finds mystery. Eventually we know it is not only inevitable, but essential that the child begins to make the connections. As we grow, more and more things begin to connect. When we grow in the wisdom of God, we begin to recognize that everything connects. Wisdom frees us from living disconnected lives. Wisdom frees us from superstitions that constrain us and broken relationships that cripple us.

When we grow in the wisdom of God, we begin to recognize that everything connects.

STANDING IN THE EPICENTER

Wisdom is endless in its applications. The transformation we go through is so multifaceted that it becomes increasingly difficult to get a simple description of how wisdom affects or changes us. No matter how long we live or how much we go through, we can avoid becoming wise if we're really committed to it. How many of us haven't looked back on at least one life experience and thought to ourselves, *If I only knew then what I know now?*

Wisdom is like a time machine that allows us to see the end result long before the action begins. Wisdom does more than change our perspective. It transforms the way we see reality. Wisdom blurs the distinction between the visible and the invisible. It sees no distinction between the physical and the spiritual. Einstein discerned that mass and energy were in the end of the same essence. Our experience tells us that this isn't possible, yet science has proved our experience wrong and shown us that our personal observations are limited.

There is no real distinction between secular and spirit. They do not exist in different categories. The material world is not a world we should be trying to escape. It is the only world God has given us. It should not only comfort us, but exhilarate us that God, who is spirit, created everything that is material. And after He created the material universe, He declared it good. Even in a fallen world, wisdom sees the good, not just the good that is or that must be done, but the good that will come through choices made. This distinct view of reality known as wisdom is nothing less than seeing life from God's vantage point. The epicenter of all wisdom is God Himself.

The Scriptures remind us that the fear of the Lord is the beginning of all wisdom. I've often reflected, with some discomfort, on the phrase "the fear of the Lord." We live in a time when only familiar language about God is acceptable. We tend to think of God more as our peer than our judge. We are comfortable thinking of God as our buddy and our copilot. The idea of fearing God seems even inappropriate in our time. Yet to overlook the implications of fearing the Lord is to miss the starting point of true wisdom.

It is here that our quest for enlightenment both begins and ends. We will never know the wisdom of God if we do not know the fear of God. Then what exactly does this mean? After all, the same Bible tells us that perfect love casts out all fear. Isn't God the source of perfect love? Isn't His promise then that in His presence all fear fades away? Strangely, both these realities are dramatically true. In fact they work in combination to create for us a place of freedom. When we fear God, we fear nothing else. It is only in fear of God that we find ourselves free from the fear of death, of failure, and all the other fears that bind us.

When the fear of God is absent from our lives, we become slaves to lesser fears. How many times have you found yourself a captive to the fear of rejection or the fear of failure? We have become a people bound and controlled by fear. We have become more sophisticated in our language of fear and have created endless categories describing our phobias. Only the fear of God frees us from fear born out of superstition. What you fear is what you are subject to. Your fears define the boundaries of your lives. When you fear God, you are subject only to Him. You align yourself to love and truth. You are never afraid to love or forgive when you fear God. You are never afraid to do the good when you fear God. You are never afraid to face the truth or speak the truth when you fear God. You live with a calm assurance that in all these things God finds great pleasure.

The fear of God is the beginning of wisdom, for only in this place are we forced to face ourselves and see ourselves for who we really are. When you are a follower of Jesus Christ, you are committed to follow the truth wherever it leads you. You have embraced a life, for all that is false is stripped away and you relinquish the right to live in any self-delusion. Beyond this, the fear of God frees you to risk, to fail, to dream and attempt great things. When you fear God and nothing else, you discover the freedom to pursue great adventure.

Oddly enough, when you fear God, you do not live even in the fear of sin. You would think that fearing God would cause you to live in terror that you might sin at any time. The exact opposite is true. When you fear God, you understand that you have come to Him in a condition of sinfulness. You know God as not only a God of holiness, but also a God of infinite compassion. You live with the knowledge of His grace. You accept that He has separated you from your sin as far as the east is from the west. You bask in the promise that if you confess your sin, He is faithful and just to forgive you of all your sin and to cleanse you from all unrighteousness.

It is only in the fear of God that we are truly free. We see God for who He really is. We see ourselves for who we really are. We understand the condition of the world in which we live. And we are enlightened to see a world—or should I say kingdom—that waits to come. Wisdom frees us to live passionately for the good and, yes, wisdom makes it clear to us that God is an enemy to evil. God opposes us when we are proud. He stands against us when we are greedy. He is at war against all who would choose to oppress the poor. Wisdom understands the heart of God. The woman of wisdom, the man who is wise, embraces that heart and lives by it.

Of Jesus, Isaiah wrote, "The Spirit of the LORD will rest on him—the Spirit of wisdom and of understanding, the Spirit of counsel and of power, the Spirit of knowledge and of the fear of the LORD—and he will delight in the fear of the LORD. He will not judge by what he sees with his eyes, or decide by what he hears with his ears; but with righteousness he will judge the needy, with justice he will give decisions for the poor of the earth" (Isa. 11:2–4a).

When we walk in wisdom, we not only fear God, but *delight* in the fear of God. It is only in this unusual place that we become free from all the constraints of the world around us. It is only here that we are truly free. The quest for enlightenment is a journey of moving from darkness to light. Like the blind man who came to see in phases, we at first see men as trees. We should not become discouraged when it appears we are walking through a fog and find our feet struggling through the marshland. Wisdom is a gift from God, but it does not come in a void. Like an odyssey, this quest is filled with danger and difficult challenges. Like the mariners who were lured to their destruction by the seductive songs of the sirens of Greek mythology, you will find yourself pulled in many directions that always invite you to leave the path of wisdom. In those moments you must push yourself free from all the distractions that call you to another way and hear the voice that calls you to live far beyond where the echoes stop.

My son, if you accept my words and store up my commands within you, turning your ear to wisdom and applying your heart to understanding, and if you call out for insight and cry aloud for understanding, and if you look for it as for silver and search for it as for hidden treasure, then you will understand the fear of the LORD and find the knowledge of God. For the LORD gives wisdom, and from his mouth come knowledge and understanding. He holds victory in store for the upright, he is a shield to those whose walk is blameless, for he guards the course of the just and protects the way of his faithful ones. Then you will understand what is right and just and fair—every good path. For wisdom will enter your heart, and knowledge will be pleasant to your soul. Discretion will protect you, and understanding will guard you. Wisdom will save you from the ways of wicked men, from men whose words are perverse, who leave the straight paths to walk in dark ways, who delight in doing wrong and rejoice in the perverseness of evil, whose paths are crooked and who are devious in their ways. (Prov. 2:1–15)

DESTINATION

12

The Greatness of Servanthood

Our longing, though we may not be able to explain or define it, is to travel and live free from the constraints of conformity and compromise. If we listen carefully enough, we begin to realize that we are trapped inside an echo chamber. Words we thought were ours were someone else's. Our thoughts and ideas, which appeared so original, natural, and distinct, were nothing more than summaries of what we heard when others insisted on speaking the loudest. I've been amazed over the years how many people were certain that their unique philosophy was theirs and theirs alone. At first I was surprised that all the unique questions and answers were the same. It didn't take long for this experience to take on the quality of tragedy.

How is it possible that so many people could be so convinced that their thinking was uniquely theirs when they were only mimicking the common beliefs of the world in which they live? There is nothing wrong with believing something someone else has passed on to you. If there is truth, certainly it existed before it formed in my mind. If I am the first to speak it, to think it, or to know it, is there any real value in my thought at all?

To run free is not to be disconnected or isolated. It is a commitment to live a life of reflection and self-awareness. God's voice is so easy to miss, even though He is the only one speaking from heaven and the only one who speaks into the deepest caverns of the human soul. There's just so much noise, so many sounds to drown out the one sound we most desperately need to hear. Especially when it comes to Jesus, it seems this is most true. Most everyone seems to like Jesus. Some other religions even embrace Him. He has become the addendum of every world religion and every pseudophilosophy. We have attempted to silence Jesus by speaking for Him rather than letting Him speak for Himself. We've twisted His words and changed His meaning because what He was saying didn't settle well in our souls.

The teachings of Jesus go against the cravings of our broken humanity. His way is not our way. His path does not parallel our path. God has not shrewdly created many paths that lead to the same destination. Every path but His is not a dead end; it is just a cul-de-sac that circles us back, taking us no further than where we started.

There is a reason why the way of Jesus is different from all the rest. It is because *He* is different from all the rest. Jesus is without ambiguity when He tells us that He is the way, the truth, and the life, and that no one comes to the Father except by Him (John 14:6).

His invitation is to join an uprising. If we choose to follow Him, there will be within us a revolution of the soul. He will do nothing less than translate us from a kingdom of emptiness into His kingdom where we will begin to live in a new reality. His way is not near to ours. Where He leads is diametrically opposed to every other path. If every other path leads to the same destination, Jesus' path will take us far from it. It should not surprise us that His ways are different than our ways, that His thoughts are different than our thoughts.

The way of God is the path of servanthood. This is not a test to see if we deserve better. It is God offering us the best of Himself and the best of life. God calls us to the servant way because God is a servant. Sounds like heresy doesn't it, to call God a servant? It seems demeaning to call the Creator of the universe something so common and so low. Jesus continuously reminded His disciples that this wasn't some kind of cosmic trick or bait and switch about Himself. He would need to clarify that the Son of man did not come to be served, but to serve. Just this reality sent everyone reeling in confusion. How in the world could this be possible? To the one who kept looking back while saying he desired to follow Him, Jesus responded, "No one who puts his hand to the plow and looks back is fit for service in the kingdom of God" (Luke 9:62).

It was all about service. The invitation was to be like the Son who only came to serve. To the disciples who argued about which of them would be the greatest, Jesus reminded them, "He who is least among you all—he is the greatest" (Luke 9:48).

When John and James asked for the privilege to sit to His left and right when Jesus returned to His glory, and the other disciples became indignant by their request, Jesus again summarized, "Whoever wants to become great among you must be your servant, and whoever wants to be first must be slave of all. For even the Son of Man did not come to be served, but to serve, and to give his life as a ransom for many" (Mark 10:43–45). He repeated the same when the mother of the sons of Zebedee came and made the same request.

It's almost as if no one would believe Him. Everyone kept hoping that if they served long enough they would find a different outcome in the end. Servanthood is not God's way to get us to the place where we will only be served; it is both the way and the life of the kingdom of God.

Is it possible that the reason the servant will have the primary place, that the least will share in God's greatness, is that here is where God has been all along? If we push ourselves to the top, we are pushing ourselves away from the presence of God. When we move ourselves to the place of servanthood, we join God in His eternal purpose. When we serve others, we look strangely like God.

God stands alone as Creator and Redeemer. This doesn't seem difficult for many of us to grasp. He stands there also as servant. He created us to be creative. He invites us to reconcile men to Himself. He also calls us to choose the path of servanthood. This is not about religion; it is about revolution. Paul reminds us, "For in Christ Jesus neither circumcision nor uncircumcision has any value. The only thing that counts is faith expressing itself through love" (Gal. 5:6).

This is the way of God. There is healing in service. It resonates with the human soul. This path is not only a promise of adventure; it is a promise of wholeness. When we choose this journey, from the first step forward, we grow in the image of God. Each step shapes us to look more like Him.

On this journey we discover that not only does humility lead to integrity and integrity lead to courage, that gratitude leads to wholeness, which results in generosity, but we will also discover that faithfulness develops perseverance, which grows us in wisdom.

If this were not enough, there are other gifts laced in this journey. As we grow in humility, gratitude, and faithfulness, we find ourselves with the strength of character to endure the greatest hardships and overcome our greatest challenges. Our capacity to be resilient will increase as we journey deeper into these virtues. When we are resilient, we have an unexplainable capacity to recover from illness, adversity, and even depression. We will find within ourselves the ability to not only flex and adapt to our environment, but also to be replenished and renewed. The resilient spring back—or should I say forward. The best description for what happens within the spirit of a person who walks in humility, gratitude, and faithfulness is that he or she becomes resilient. Resilience makes you unstoppable. It gives you the strength for the quest.

You will also find that as you grow in integrity, wholeness, and perseverance, you will find integration in your life. While we may never become perfect in this life, we can live in the promise of becoming mature and complete, not lacking anything. In a world filled with brokenness, the capacity to integrate all the pieces is critical for health. This is a part of God's promise in the work of transformation.

Finally, as we live a life committed to these basic principles—not stages we pass through, but virtues we embrace for a lifetime—we will find ourselves surprised at the strength of courage, the depth of wisdom, and the extent of generosity that we will express. The ultimate expression of the life in God as we pass through the gauntlet of this character matrix is not only a life of sacrifice but of unimaginable creativity.

The ultimate end of character transformation is not freedom from sin, but freedom to once again be all that God designed for us to be. The Creator of the universe built you to be a creative expression of Himself. Every human being was born to be creative. Not all of us are artistic, but each of us has a unique contribution to make to the tapestry of human history.

When we live lives of generosity, we become generative and creative in our contributions to the good of others. When we walk in the wisdom of God, we see the hidden possibilities and opportunities missed by so many others. What is lost for others is found by those who see through the eyes of God. Wisdom always finds a way. It is the fountain of intellectual creativity and innovation.

When we fear God, we find the freedom and the courage to pursue dreams far too big for ourselves, yet courage is the only hope for great dreams. To see the creative possibilities but to lack the courage to pursue them would be too great a sorrow to bear. It is here where the synergistic interplay of courage, wisdom, and generosity make us most creative. This is God's gift to us. His gift to us once again is Himself.

The character of God, the beauty of His personhood, the expression of His goodness, He longs to share with us. What would the world look like, what would we look like, if we became like Him? The One who wrapped a towel around His waist and washed His disciples' feet invites us to become like Him in His servanthood.

This is the ultimate destination, to become the person God dreams of and to share those dreams with others.

"You, my brothers (and sisters), were called to be free. But do not use your freedom to indulge the sinful nature; rather, serve one another in love. The entire law is summed up in a single command: 'Love your neighbor as yourself'" (Gal. 5:13–14).

START

POINT OF ORIGIN
2 - The Drowning Pool | 1 - Running Free

RESILIENCE
3 - Rising Out of The Ashes | 6 - Creating Out of the Pieces | 9 - Coming Out of Nowhere

THE GAUNTLET

INTEGRATION
4 - The Unifying Power of Believing | 7 - The Healing Power of Belonging | 10 - The Sustaining Power of Becoming

CREATIVITY
11 - The Divine Imagination | 8 - The Generative Spirit | 5 - The Warrior's Heart

DESTINATION
12 - The Greatness of Servanthood

FINISH

The transformation of our character is more revolution than reformation. It is forged from battles fought far more than by beliefs held. It emerges out of crisis, not out of classroom. It doesn't just come to you; you must run to it. It is like a gauntlet waiting to be conquered. Character is like a hero asleep within you waiting to be awakened. Its power sweeps through you in waves of transformation. In pursuing a life that is not about yourself you find yourself living the life you've always longed for. And with each challenge faced, with each victory won, you suddenly come to the realization that you are a different person than the one who began the journey. Simply attempting the gauntlet has changed you forever.

ABOUT THE AUTHOR

Erwin Raphael McManus serves as lead pastor and cultural architect of Mosaic in Los Angeles and founder of Awaken, a personal and organizational creativity development group. As a national and international consultant, his expertise focuses on culture, change, leadership, and creativity. He partners with Bethel Theological Seminary as distinguished professor and futurist and is also a contributing editor for *Leadership Journal*. He is the author of *An Unstoppable Force* (a 2002 ECPA Gold Medallion Award finalist), *Chasing Daylight, Uprising,* and *The Barbarian Way.* He and his wife, Kim, have two children, Aaron and Mariah, and a daughter in the Lord, Paty.

For more information visit
www.mosaic.org and/or erwinmcmanus.com.

ACKNOWLEDGMENTS

Character is formed in community—as is anything of great worth and lasting meaning. So, too, is this work an expression of community, collaboration, and synergy.

Even a fool can become a source of wisdom if he is willing to become a human sponge. The contents of these pages are just my attempt to squeeze out some of what I have had the privilege to absorb on this subject. There are so many that need to be thanked. I would like to name a few that represent the whole.

There are always artisans in my world who translate the ideas into images. Without them so much beauty would be lost. Thank you, Noemi Martinez Bary, Joby Harris, and Jeremy Yates for your amazing talent, your sacrificial spirit, your passionate creativity, and most of all your love for Christ. With them come others whose contribution has been invaluable. Thank you, Eric Bryant, Shelly Martin, Robbie Sortino, Lucas King, Neil Nakamoto, Rick Yamamoto, and Greg Bourgond. Each of you has shaped what is expressed on the pages of this manuscript and have been a gift to my own life and transformation.

As with each of my books, words would never become text without Holly Rapp. How someone can move 240 words in a minute I will never understand. It is nothing short of a miracle that someone can listen as fast as I talk, much less write it down. Also, thank you, John Torres, for joining our team and filling the gaps with such humility and excellence.

To the elders, the lead team, staff, and community of Mosaic: Thank you for embracing tribe McManus with the calling and mission God placed on our hearts.

I am amazed by and indebted to the wonderful team at Nelson Books. Thank you, Mike Hyatt, for inviting me on the team. Thank you, Brian Hampton and Kyle Olund, for your contribution to the quality of the message. Thank you, Jonathan Merkh, for your commitment to get the message in the hearts of those who long for a revolution of the soul. And to my good friend, Sealy Yates—I'm still not sure if you're an agent or an angel. In either case I'm glad you're here.

To my life partner, Kim, to my son, Aaron, and to my daughter, Mariah: Thank you for your love and support. You not only make for a great family, but a great team! The world is both our playground and burden.

And most of all to Him who calls us to become what we cannot be without Him. To the One who is most lovely, most noble, most virtuous. To Him who is most admirable. To Him and Him alone. I long to be like You, O Jesus!

You call me to come. I run.

Create in us an uprising—a revolution of the soul.

—ERM

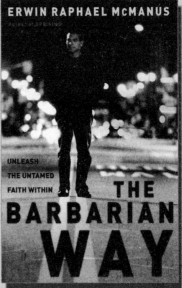

NELSON BOOKS
A Division of Thomas Nelson Publishers
Since 1798

www.thomasnelson.com